ALSO BY JOEL OSTEEN

I Declare
Every Day a Friday
Every Day a Friday Journal
Daily Readings from Every Day a Friday
Your Best Life Now
Daily Readings from Your Best Life Now
Starting Your Best Life Now
Your Best Life Now Study Guide
Your Best Life Now for Moms
Your Best Life Begins Each Morning
Your Best Life Now Journal

BREAK OUT!

5 KEYS TO GO BEYOND YOUR BARRIERS AND LIVE AN EXTRAORDINARY LIFE

JOEL OSTEEN

Faith
Words

LARGE PRINT

FaithWords

Hachette Book Group

237 Park Avenue

New York, NY 10017

www.faithwords.com

Printed in the United States of America

RRD-C (split)

First Large Print Edition: October 2013

10 9 8 7 6 5 4 3 2 1

FaithWords is a division of Hachette Book Group, Inc.
The FaithWords name and logo are trademarks of Hachette Book Group, Inc.

The Hachette Speakers Bureau provides a wide range of authors for speaking events. To find out more, go to www.hachettespeakersbureau.com or call (866) 376-6591.

The publisher is not responsible for websites (or their content) that are not owned by the publisher.

Library of Congress Cataloging-in-Publication Data

Osteen, Joel.
    Break out! : 5 keys to go beyond your barriers and live an extraordinary life / Joel Osteen.
        pages cm
    ISBN 978-0-89296-974-6 (hardcover) — ISBN 978-1-60941-826-7 (audiobook) — ISBN 978-1-4789-2459-3 (audio download) — ISBN 978-1-4555-7602-9 (large-print hardcover) 1. Christian life. I. Title.
    BV4501.3.O85 2013
    248.4—dc23
                                    2013022026

CONTENTS

PART III
Pray God-Sized Prayers

PART IV
Keep the Right Perspective

PART V
Don't Settle for Good Enough

BREAK OUT!

PART
I

Believe Bigger

CHAPTER ONE

Get Ready for a Shift

I was in a long line for a popular ride at an amusement park with our two children, Jonathan and Alexandra, years ago. At first everyone was in a single file, but as we moved closer to the ride we entered this small room about twenty feet by twenty feet. We were the first inside and we walked to the front doors. As we stood there so excited, knowing that we would get the best choice of seats, other people began crowding in behind us. I tried to politely hold our position at the front, but a few teenagers cleverly maneuvered ahead of us. Then, a few more, and more, and more.

We ended up being pushed all the way to the very back of the room right where we'd entered originally. I tried not to let it bother me. After all, we were there to have fun. A young woman worker came out and stood before the front doors. She greeted everyone and said we were just about ready to board the ride. She gave us instructions for getting on.

Then she said, "Okay, we're ready to go. Now, turn around and go back out the same doors you came in." That was right where we were standing. Suddenly, the last were made first!

In the same way, all God has to do is shift the direction, and you'll go from the back to the front. One touch of His favor can put you fifty years ahead of where you thought you'd be. You can be at a lower position at the office, you're going along, being your best, honoring God, and suddenly things can change. One good break, one idea, one person who likes you, and you look up and find yourself in a top job. You didn't see it coming. Things just fell into place.

What happened? You came into a shift. God can cause opportunity to find you. He has unexpected blessings where you suddenly meet the right person, or suddenly your health improves, or suddenly you're able to pay off your house. That's God shifting things in your favor. What used to be a struggle is not a struggle anymore. What should have taken years happened in a fraction of the time. You may feel like you're stuck right now. You could never accomplish a dream, never overcome a problem. It's just been too long. You've missed too many opportunities. But God is saying, "Get ready. I'm about to shift things." Doors will open for you that have not opened in the past. Those who were against you will suddenly change their minds and be for you. Problems that have dogged you for years will suddenly turn around. You are coming into a shift. Because you have honored God, He will put you in a position you never could have attained on your own. It's not just your education, not just your talent, or the family you come from. It's the hand of God shifting you to a new level of your destiny.

Sometimes you need faith and victory spoken over your life. Words have created power. When you receive them into your spirit, they can ignite seeds of increase on the inside. That's the reason I've written this book. You were not created to just get by with an average, unrewarding, or unfulfilling life. God created you to leave your mark on this generation. You have gifts and talents that you have not tapped into. There are new levels of your destiny still in front of you. But break out starts in your thinking. As you put these keys into \action, making room for increase, expecting shifts of God's favor, praying bold prayers, and keeping the right perspective, then God will release floods of His goodness that will thrust you beyond barriers of the past into the extraordinary life you were designed to live.

I'm not just trying to make you feel good. I'm

declaring, "A shift is coming." A shift in your health. A shift in your finances. A shift in a relationship. It may not look like it in the natural, but we serve a supernatural God. He's about to breathe in your direction in a new way.

The enemies you've seen in the past you will see no more. The addictions and bad habits holding you back are being broken. God's favor is being released in a new way. It will propel you forward. What should have taken you forty years to accomplish, God will do in a split second.

The shift is acceleration. The shift will take you where you could not have gone on your own. The shift is overcoming what a medical report said was impossible. The shift is seeing that wayward child change his mind and get back on the right course. The shift is having your best year when the circumstances say you should have a down year. The shift is seeing God not only provide but also do exceedingly, abundantly, above and beyond.

Your new attitude should be: "God, I'm ready. I'm taking the limits off of You. I'm enlarging my vision. I may not see a way but I know You have a way. I declare I'm coming into a shift."

You need to check doors that have been closed to you in the past. Things have shifted. The dream you had to start a new business, to go back to college, to take a mission trip—it may not have happened the first time, but that's okay. It's prepared you for this time. Don't give up. This is a new day. Things have shifted. Pursue your dream again.

When God breathes in your direction, people change their mind. Closed doors suddenly open. The *no*s turn into *yes*es. *Not now* turns into *It's your time*.

A construction manager I know had been out of a job for three years after twenty-five years of steady work. He'd had a very good position at a successful company, but when the recession hit and building tapered off, his company had to let him go. He went to one job interview after another, month after month, with no success. He finally took a much lower-level position in a small city, to which he had to travel a couple of hours every day. It was taking a toll on his health, his marriage, and his savings. It looked like his job situation would never change. But about six months later, his former boss called and said, "Hey, are you ready to go back to work?"

His old company had landed the largest contract in its history. He not only got his job back but also all of his benefits. He used to have to travel around the country. Now he gets to work in town. Plus, they increased his salary significantly. He said, "This is exceedingly, abundantly, above and beyond."

What happened? He came into a shift. Suddenly,

things changed in his favor. One phone call. One contract. One good break. He went from barely getting by to having more than enough.

Now *you* need to get ready. These shifts are in your future.

The Israelites were enslaved for many years and mistreated by their captors. They were forced to work long hours and not given the proper rest or food. When they didn't meet their quotas they were beaten with rods. It was very unfair. But one day, through a series of events, God supernaturally brought them out. The Scripture says that as they were leaving, "God caused them to have favor with their enemies."

Notice, God *caused them* to have favor. The same people who had oppressed them for years, the same foes who had pushed them down and mistreated them, suddenly changed their minds. They said in effect, "We've decided that we like you now. We want to be good to you."

Before they left, the captors gave the Israelites their gold, silver, and jewels. What happened? The Israelites came into a shift. God changed the mind of their enemy. Proverbs says God can turn the heart of a king. We may not be able to change people's minds, but God can. He controls the whole universe.

You may have people in your life like this, some who don't like you, a boss who is hard to get along with, or a family member who is disrespectful. It's easy to become discouraged and to think, "This will always be this way. They will always be against me."

No, stay in faith. God has a shift coming. God knows how to cause them to like you. God can cause them to see you in a new light. They may have been against you year after year, but when God shifts things they'll go out of their way to be good to you. Instead of hindering you, they'll help you.

Bottom line: God will not allow any person to keep you from your destiny. They may be bigger, stronger, or more powerful, but God knows how to shift things around and get you to where you're supposed to be.

I have a friend who worked for someone he never liked. Nobody at the company liked this young supervisor, who was condescending and a source of frustration year after year. At first, it looked like this young man could be supervising at this company for another twenty or thirty years. My friend has a good attitude, but deep down he thought, "Putting up with this guy for a long time will be a real pain. I don't know if I can take it."

Then, one morning he arrived at work, and management called a staff meeting. They explained that the young supervisor's wife had been transferred to another state for her job. The unpopular supervisor had resigned that morning.

Half the staff fell on their knees and offered a prayer of thanks to God! What happened? A divine shift. Suddenly, God changed things.

Quit worrying about those trying to hold you back. God knows how to move the wrong people out of your life and bring the right people in. And even if God doesn't move them, it says in Psalms, "You can run through a troop and leap over a wall."

God can cause you to go over them, or around them, or even through them, but God will get you to where you're supposed to be. The truth is, you are one shift from seeing a dream come to pass. One shift from paying your house off. One shift from seeing your health improve. One shift from meeting the right person.

It says in Isaiah: "This is God's year to act." Not next year. Not five years. Not in the Sweet By and By. This is the year God will shift things in your favor. He is lining it all up. What you could not make happen on your own, God will cause you to accomplish. It will be bigger than you thought. It will happen quicker than you imagined, and it will be more rewarding than you ever dreamed possible.

In Genesis 48, there is a story of Jacob when he was an old man very close to death. His son Joseph came to visit him and say his good-byes. He and his father were very close. Joseph was Jacob's favorite child. He was the youngest son. You may remember him as the child to whom Jacob gave the coat of many colors.

At one point Jacob thought Joseph was dead. The father was very sad until he found out Joseph was alive and living in Egypt. They reunited just as Jacob was about to pass. Joseph was standing before him with his two sons, Manasseh and Ephraim, Jacob's grandsons.

Jacob said, "Joseph, I will bless your sons as if they were my own children."

The right hand in those days always gave the greatest blessing. It belonged to the firstborn son. That was the tradition. So Joseph put his oldest son, Manasseh, in front of Jacob's right hand and his younger son, Ephraim, on his left.

Jacob was nearly blind. When he went to give the blessing Jacob crossed his hands and put his right on the younger son, Ephraim, and his left on Manasseh, the older son.

Joseph said, "No, Dad. You can't see. I had them lined up. I put Manasseh in front of your right hand. He deserves it. Give him the greater blessing."

Then Jacob said something very interesting. It gives us insight into our God. He said, "No, Joseph. I've crossed my hands on purpose. Ephraim may have come second, he may have been in the back, he may not deserve it. He didn't qualify for it. He is not next in line, but I'm shifting him to a new position. I'm taking him from the back up to the front. I will give him what he doesn't deserve."

That's the way our God is. He has shifts in your future that will put you in positions you didn't earn, you didn't qualify for, or weren't next in line to receive. Maybe you didn't have seniority, but God, just like He did with Ephraim, will cross His hands and say, "I will move them up from the back to the front, from not being qualified to suddenly being qualified, from being looked down on or disrespected to being honored and seen with influence and credibility."

When you move up some people will be bothered by it. They'll think: "That's not fair. I worked harder. I have more seniority." But the fact is, it's just the goodness of God. He said because you honor Him, He would give you houses that you didn't have to build. You would reap from vineyards you did not plant.

That's God crossing His hands, giving you what should have taken years to earn. God is saying to you what Jacob said to Ephraim, "I will bless you on purpose. I will move you up. I will accelerate your dreams. I will give you what you didn't deserve. I'll shift you into a position you could never have reached on your own."

We can all make excuses: "Joel, this is not for me

today. I'm not qualified. I've made too many mistakes. I don't have the talent, the size, the personality, the confidence."

God says: "I know all that. I created you, but I'm about to cross My hands and bless you in such a way that everyone will know it's Me and not you." Now don't talk yourself out of it.

Moses said, "God, not me. I stutter. I can't go speak to Pharaoh."

God said, "Moses, don't worry about it. I'm crossing My hands. I'm giving you what you need."

Gideon said, "God, I come from the poorest family. I'm the least one around here. I can't lead this army."

God said, "Gideon, don't worry. I'm crossing My hands. You're coming into a shift. I will move you from the back to the front."

David could have said, "God, I'm too small, too young, too inexperienced. There's a whole army of talented, successful, confident warriors who can face Goliath."

And God would have said, "David, I know that. I could have chosen them, but I'm crossing My hands. I'm moving you up from the background to the foreground, from the shepherd field to the battlefield, all the way to the throne."

Esther could have said, "God, I can't go in there

and speak to the king. He will not listen to me. I'm an orphan. I don't have any influence."

And God would have said, "Esther, don't worry. I've got you covered. I'm crossing My hands. I will give you respect, credibility, honor that you didn't deserve, you didn't work for."

A shift is coming! Whatever level you are at now, God is about to cross His hands and put you in a position you never could have reached on your own. He will give you what you weren't in line to receive.

Why don't you start expecting unprecedented favor, believing for God to do something new in your life? I know you can say like me that God has been good to you. You're blessed and healthy and you have a good family and a great job, and that's all perfect. But I can tell you that you haven't seen anything yet!

God has shifts in your future that if He showed you now you wouldn't believe. It's exceedingly, abundantly, above and beyond. You think you're hitting on all cylinders, but if you only knew what God has in store. It's like you're in second gear. You're making progress. You're healthy. You're moving forward. But God is about to shift you out of second, past third, past fourth, into overdrive. You will see the surpassing greatness of God's favor.

Because you've honored God and lived with excellence and integrity, God will take you beyond your training, beyond your education, beyond your income, beyond where anyone in your family has gone before you. This shift will put you at a place where you look back and say, "Wow, God. You have amazed me with Your goodness."

When the Israelites were in the desert headed toward the Promised Land they had manna to eat each day. It was similar to bread. After a while they grew tired of it. They complained to Moses that they didn't have any meat to eat. Moses told God about their concerns. God said, "Moses, I will give you meat not for one day or five days or twenty days, but for a whole month."

Moses said, "God, that's impossible. There are two million people out here. Even if we butchered all of our flocks, all of our herds, we wouldn't have that much meat."

God replied, "Moses, is there any limit to My power?"

He was saying, "Just because you don't see a way, Moses, doesn't mean *I* don't have a way. All I have to do is shift a few things around and I can bring it to pass."

That's what God did. Numbers 11:31 says, "God shifted the wind and brought quail in from the sea and caused it to fall into their camp."

Notice how good God is to His children. They didn't even have to go out and hunt or fish. The quail came to them. They just went out of their tent and picked up as many as they wanted.

What am I saying? God knows how to shift things so that blessings come to you. The right people search you out. Good breaks find you.

I have a friend who works for a professional sports team. He wasn't raised in church. He started watching our program and he gave his life to Christ. He decided to get into a good Bible-based church. All he owned were very casual clothes, T-shirts and jeans, tennis shoes. He went to a church and they were very accepting, like ours. It doesn't matter what you wear, but he had a desire to dress up to go to church. He had never owned a suit before. He went to the mall and looked at some different suits, but they were more than he wanted to spend. He could certainly afford them. He was just very frugal.

One day he was running an errand and he randomly met this man. They struck up a conversation. This man found out how my friend worked for the professional sports team. The man told my friend that he loved going to the team's games, but so many of them were sold out he rarely had the chance to buy tickets.

My friend is very generous. He said, "A lot of times I have extra tickets. I'll call you and you can come to a game."

The man attended a game, and afterward he

thanked my friend. "You've been so good to me I want to do something good for you," he said. "I own a clothing store. I want to make you a custom-made suit."

The last time I talked to my friend he said, "Joel, I have sixteen custom-made suits. He's given them all to me. Eight sport coats, a tuxedo. My whole closet is filled with dress clothes."

When you honor God, when you're good to people, kind, compassionate, and merciful, the blessings will come looking for you. Like the quail, you don't have to go after them. God will shift things to cause the right people to come across your path. God will put you at the right place at the right time so provision, opportunity, comes to you.

Zechariah said it this way: "It's not by might, nor by power, but by the Spirit of God." That word *spirit* in the Hebrew means "breath." It's saying it will not happen just by your talent, just by your connections, just by those you know. It will happen because God breathes in our direction. God shifts the winds and blows healing and promotion, restoration, our way.

How will you get well? The medical report says it's impossible? No, God is breathing healing your way. Health, wholeness, and restoration are headed toward you.

How will you accomplish your dreams? You may not know the right people or have the money or feel like you have the talent. But God is breathing ideas, resources, and the right people.

If you will stay faithful and just keep honoring God, like my friend discovered, suddenly things will change, suddenly you come into abundance, suddenly your child straightens up, suddenly you get well.

A few years ago, one of our faithful church members suffered a major stroke. He was only in his midfifties, but he was paralyzed on the left-hand side of his body. He couldn't walk or talk. The prognosis wasn't good. He was told that with intense therapy he might regain his speech, but he would never walk again.

For two years he had no feeling on the left side of his body. He was in a wheelchair and had to have constant care. It didn't look good, but this man kept coming to Lakewood. He knew all God had to do was shift the winds and blow healing and restoration his way.

One morning he woke up, and suddenly he began to have feeling on the left side of his body. The doctors, the therapists, the nurses—they were amazed. They couldn't understand it. Long story short: a few weeks later, he walked into Lakewood with no help for the first time since he had that stroke.

He spoke clearly. He didn't stumble when he walked. He didn't limp. He walked like nothing had ever been wrong. What happened? He came into a shift. God breathed in his direction. What he could not do in his own power, in his own strength, suddenly became possible.

You may have struggled in an area, your health, your finances, with a relationship, for a long time and you keep wondering, "Will this ever change?" God is saying, "Yes. A shift is coming. I will shift you out of sickness into health. I will shift you out of lack into abundance. I will shift you out of struggle into ease. I'm about to cross My hands and give you what you do not deserve."

Now you need to get ready. You are coming into a shift. Because you have been faithful and honored God, I believe and declare, God will put you in a position you could have never gotten to on your own. Doors will open that have never opened before for you. What should have taken you forty years to accomplish God will do in a split second. You're coming into acceleration.

Suddenly, a dream comes to pass. Suddenly, a promise is fulfilled. Suddenly, the negative turns around. You need to get ready for the surpassing greatness of God's favor!

CHAPTER TWO

A Flood Is Coming

I was watching the television news when the weatherperson announced that we were under a "Flash Flood Warning." That means conditions are ripe for possible flooding. Water could escape its normal boundaries and increase in such a way that drainage ditches and bayous are overwhelmed.

Just like that weatherperson, I'm here to announce to you that you're under a Flash Flood Warning. Conditions are just right. You've honored God. You've been faithful. You've passed the test. Now God is saying: "There's about to be a flood, but not with water. You will see a flood of My goodness, a flood of opportunity, a flood of healing, a flood of good breaks, to where you are overwhelmed with God's favor. It's beyond your expectations. It puts you into overflow."

Now you may have experienced a lot of negative things in the past: bad breaks, disappointments, and heartache. It's easy to become discouraged and let that overwhelm you. The negative thoughts will tell you: "You'll never get well. You saw the medical report," or "You'll never rise any higher and accomplish your dreams. You've gone as far as you can go."

Instead you need to get ready. Things have shifted. You're about to come into this flash flood where suddenly you meet the right person, you qualify for that new home, you are accepted to a college, you're chosen to play the lead role in a new television series, your song hits the radio, and your career takes off.

You will see the surpassing greatness of God's favor. It will take you beyond your normal boundaries. It will supersede what the medical report says. It will supersede your talent, your education, and your experience. It will thrust you to a level that you could have never reached on your own. It won't be a little drizzle or a little sprinkle. It will be a flood of favor, a flood of talent, a flood of ideas, a flood of opportunity.

Why don't you get this down in your spirit? A flood of God's goodness.

One time the Bible's King David needed a breakthrough. He faced an impossible situation. He and his men were up against this huge army—the Philistines. They were greatly outnumbered and had little or no chance of winning. David asked God for help and God gave David the promise that He would go with them and they would defeat the opposing army. So David and his men went out, and that was exactly what happened. God gave them a great victory. David was so overwhelmed by it, he said in 1 Chronicles 14:11: "God has broken through to my enemies like the bursting forth of water."

David named the place of his great victory Baal-Perazim, which means, "the God of the breakthrough." Notice, David likened God's power to "the bursting forth of water." In other words, he described it as a flood. He was saying when the God of the breakthrough shows up and releases His power it will be like a flood of His goodness, a flood of His favor, a flood of healing, a flood of new opportunity.

Think about how powerful water can be. Three or four feet of rushing water can pick up a huge car weighing thousands of pounds and move it all around. I've seen on the news, in these big floods, whole houses floating down a flooded river. Nothing can stop the force of that water. Anything in its way is moved out of its path. You may have difficulties that look extremely large, obstacles that look impassable, or dreams that look unattainable.

But know this: when God releases a flood of His power nothing will be able to stop you. That sickness may look big but when God releases a flood of healing it doesn't stand a chance. Your opposition may be stronger, better financed, better equipped, but when God opens up the floodgates they'll be no match for you.

You may not have the connections to accomplish your dreams. You don't know the right people. You don't have the funding. But when God releases a flood of favor, people will come out of the woodwork to help you out. You won't have to look for them. Good breaks, opportunity, the right people, will all search you out.

You need to get ready, not for a trickle, not a stream, not a river, but a flood of God's favor, a tidal wave of God's goodness, a tsunami of His increase. God is going to take you to a level that you've never been before. It will be unprecedented. You will go farther, quicker, than you ever dreamed of.

God said in Exodus 34:10: "I'm going to do great things that I have never done before anywhere on Earth. People will see what great things I can do because I'm going to do something awesome for you." Now when God uses the word *awesome*, He is not talking about a trickle, a stream, a river. He is talking about a flood of favor, a flood of ideas, a flood of healing. It may not look like it in the natural right now, but remember you're under a Flash Flood

Warning. Any moment the heavens could open up. Any moment you could meet the right person. Any moment God could do something awesome, something that you've never seen before in your life.

The real question is this: will you let this seed take root? Every voice will tell you why this is not for you. "I just happened to be reading this book." No, God has you here at the right place, at the right time, because He wants to do something amazing in your life. Get in agreement and say, "God, this is for me today. I'm raising my expectations. I'm shaking off doubt, negativity, disappointments, self-pity, little dreams, and little goals, and God, I will make room for a flood of Your goodness."

I met a lady a couple of years ago after a Lakewood Church service. She was in town for treatment at MD Anderson, our local cancer hospital. She was scheduled to have a tumor removed, and then she was to be treated with chemotherapy. All of her medical records, blood work, and X-rays were shipped from her hospital in her hometown. Her doctors in Houston wanted her to retake all the tests and redo all the X-rays just to double-check and verify everything. She was already scheduled for surgery when the doctor called her in. After reviewing the new tests, he couldn't find the tumor. It was very clear on one of her hometown hospital's X-rays, but on the new one done at MD Anderson, the doctors could not see it at all.

"I've been doing this for twenty-six years," her Houston doctor said. "I have never seen anything like this before."

What was that? A flood of healing. A flood of restoration. Friends, God can do what medicine cannot do. God made your body. He has you in the palm of His hand. The good news is, God has the final say. He said, "The number of your days I will fulfill." That means sickness doesn't determine how long you will live; God does. Nothing can snatch you out of His hand. If it's not your time to go, then you won't go. You may be facing a major illness. It doesn't look good in the natural, but you're under a Flash Flood Warning. Any moment you could see a flood of healing. Any moment God could turn that around.

Isaiah said: "When the enemy comes in like a flood, the Spirit of God will raise up a barrier." Several commentators believe that the comma was misplaced during translation. Instead of placing the comma after the word *flood*, they believe the comma should have been placed after the word *in*. It would say, "When the enemy comes in, like a flood God's Spirit will raise up a barrier." In other words, the flood imagery emphasizes God's power and not the enemy's.

I've learned when the enemy attacks, God reacts. God doesn't just sit back and think, "Well, I wonder what's about to happen. I wonder what they will do." God goes to work. You are His most prized possession. It says in Psalms: "God is close to those that are hurting. He is close to the brokenhearted."

God knows when you've got a bad medical report. He knows when you're struggling with your finances. He knows when you're being mistreated. You may not see anything happening, but you can be assured Almighty God not only is aware but He also is at work. He already has the solution. If you will stay in faith, at the right time, He will release a flood of His power, a flood of healing, a flood of restoration. He will not only bring you out, He will bring you out better off than you were before.

That was what happened to David when he defeated this great army. After he named the place of his victory "Baal-Perazim—the God of the breakthrough," anytime David and his men passed that city they would say, "Remember that? That's where the God of the breakthrough showed up. That's where God released His favor like a flood."

No doubt, even generations later, when David's grandchildren and great-grandchildren passed through that city, they would say, "Oh, yeah. Granddaddy told us about this place. This is where the God of the breakthrough gave them a great victory. This is where God helped them defeat an enemy almost twice their size."

Every one of us should have some Baal-Perazims. We should have places where we can look back and say, "That was where the God of the breakthrough did something amazing in my life. That was where God healed me. That was where God promoted me. That was where God protected me. That was where the God of the breakthrough visited my house." When I drive up to our beautiful Lakewood Church each day I know it is our Baal-Perazim. I can say, "This is where the God of the breakthrough released His favor like a flood and gave us a beautiful facility, even though all the experts said we didn't have a chance."

Every time I see my mother I know her surviving cancer is another Baal-Perazim. I can say, "That's where the God of the breakthrough released His healing like a flood."

There is a popular country song that says, "Let's give them something to talk about." God wants to give *you* something to talk about. He wants to overwhelm you in such a way that everywhere you go you can tell your friends, your neighbors, your children, and your grandchildren about the great things God has done for you.

We are not supposed to drag through life defeated and discouraged, saying, "I never get any good breaks. I never get promoted. My back has been hurting for three years." No, get over into faith. If you'll start living breakthrough minded, God promises He will show up and give you something to talk about.

Not long ago this lady came up to me so excited. Her family member needed a series of surgeries. It was vital for this family member to continue living a productive life. But the problem was the surgeries were expected to cost $400,000, and they were not covered by insurance. She didn't have the funds. But month after month, this lady just kept praying, kept believing, kept trusting that the God of the breakthrough would make a way. She didn't need a trickle. She didn't need a stream. She didn't need a river. She needed a flood of God's favor.

Then, one day out of the blue her employer called her in. She had worked for this company for nearly thirty years. She didn't even know they were aware of her relative's health situation. But they said, "You've been so good to our company. We've decided to underwrite the surgeries that your family member needs."

Four hundred thousand dollars! What was that? It was the God of the breakthrough releasing a tidal wave of His favor. Like a flood, God's goodness came over her. Now everywhere she goes, she can't keep quiet. She tells everyone what God has done for her family. God gave her something to talk about. He wants to do the same thing for you.

What are you expecting? What are you believing for? Would you ever release your faith for something that big? Or would you think, "Joel, that would never happen for me. Four hundred thousand dollars? I never get any good breaks. Besides, my boss doesn't even like me."

It doesn't matter who likes you or who doesn't like you. All that matters is God likes you. He accepts you. He approves of you. His favor surrounds you like a shield. Promotion doesn't come from people. It comes from God. If you'll be bold enough to believe big, then the God of the breakthrough can release a tidal wave of his goodness, a tsunami of His favor in your life.

In Psalm 112, David said: "When darkness overtakes the righteous, light will come bursting in." At times in life it may seem dark. You may not see how it could ever work out. Maybe you don't have the funds to pay your bills. Maybe other problems seem insurmountable. But if you will stay, breakthrough-minded God promises the light will come bursting in.

Notice, it won't just trickle in. It won't barely get there. No, like a flood, like the breaking forth of waters, it will come bursting in. That means, suddenly, it will change in your favor. Suddenly, you will catch the break you need. Suddenly, your health turns around. Suddenly, your problems are resolved. Suddenly, a new door opens.

God likes to do things suddenly. When it's dark, don't start complaining. Don't turn negative. Keep reminding yourself that the light is about to come bursting in. It may be today, may be tomorrow, next week, next month, next year. But know this: suddenly, things will change in your favor.

My friends Craig and Samantha have a son named Connor. He's a very handsome, fun little boy. Connor has autism. At five years old, he didn't speak in complete sentences. He would speak phrases here and there, maybe three or four words together, but nothing much more than that.

Day after day, Craig and Samantha just kept speaking faith into Connor, telling him that he was more than a conqueror, that he could do all things through Christ. Every night at bedtime either Craig or Samantha would sit down and read two or three books with little Connor. Then they'd pray together before they went to bed.

Then one night, just as Samantha was about to turn off the light in Connor's room she heard him speaking. He went on and on, so clearly, and so fluently. She ran and found the video camera and captured the first real complete sentences her son ever put together. Here's what he was saying:

"This is my Bible. I am what it says I am. I have what it says I have. I can do what it says I can do...."

What happened? Like a flood, God's favor came on little Connor—a flood of healing, a flood of restoration, a flood of wisdom. Now, Craig and Samantha have another Baal-Perazim. That's a night that they will never forget. Even though little Connor still doesn't speak perfectly clearly, they know he is well on his way. What God started He will finish.

This happened because Craig and Samantha take the DVDs from my messages home and little Connor watches them. They said that normally when he's looking at cartoons, he'll only watch for five or ten minutes. But he'll sit there all through the day and watch my whole thirty-minute messages one after the other.

I once told Craig: "When a five-year-old chooses me over Barney, I know I have favor!"

But I love the fact that God gave them something to talk about. They were so excited about it, they tell everybody what God has done for little Connor. It was dark but the light came bursting in. Whenever they're tempted to be discouraged, all they have to do is put that video in. They can see the favor of God like a flood.

When I'm tempted to think that something will not work out, or looks impossible, all I have to do is drive down to our beautiful church in Houston. And I'll think, "God, You did it for us once. I know You can do it for us again."

God wants to release a flood of His power, not a trickle. Not a stream. Not a river. Get ready for a flood of favor, a flood of restoration, a flood of healing, a flood of promotion. You may be thinking too small. Maybe you've settled because you think you've reached your limits. You think your sick child will never get well, or that you'll never accomplish your dreams.

No, I can see something in your future. Through my eyes of faith I can see a tidal wave coming your way. It is not a wave of defeat, a wave of discouragement, a wave of more of the same. It's a wave of God's favor, a wave of promotion, a wave of deliverance, a wave of restoration. It's the God of the breakthrough releasing His favor like a flood, causing you to overcome obstacles that you thought were insurmountable, causing you to accomplish dreams that you never thought possible.

Dare to believe. If you think "trickle," you will receive a trickle. If you think "barely get by," then you will barely get by. If you think that your problem is too big, it will keep you defeated. But if you will learn to think "flood," you will experience a flood. If you think "overflow," you'll experience an overflow. If you dare think "tidal wave," then God can release a tidal wave of His goodness in your life. This is what Jesus said: "According to your faith it will be done unto you."

We were out to dinner several years ago with our son Jonathan. He is college age now, but then he was just fourteen years old. When he went to order Jonathan said to the waiter, "I would like a steak." The waiter asked him, "Do you want a six-ounce, a ten-ounce, or a fourteen-ounce?"

Jonathan didn't think about it twice. He didn't ask me if it was okay. He didn't look at the menu to check the price. He immediately said, "I want the fourteen-ounce."

When it comes to food, Jonathan was not expecting a trickle or a stream. He was expecting a flood. He not only has a big appetite, but he knows who his father is. He knows I want to be good to him.

That's the way we need to be when it comes to our Heavenly Father. Don't have a small-minded mentality. Don't have a narrow, limited vision. Some people act like they're inconveniencing God. They don't think they can expect their dreams to come to pass. If they can just barely get through life, that's good enough.

"I don't expect to get out of this problem," they'll say. "God, if You'll just help me to endure it."

"I don't expect to ever meet someone and really fall in love. God, if You'll just help me to not be so lonely."

No, you are thinking "trickle" when God has a flood. You are thinking "survive" when God has abundance. You are thinking six-ounce steak when God has a fourteen-ounce steak. When you think bigger, God will act bigger.

If you will dare to be bold and step up to the plate like Jonathan and say, "God, I know You control the whole universe. I know You're longing to be good to me. So I want to thank You for releasing a flood of Your favor in my life."

In other words:

"God, I want to thank You that my little Connor one day will speak fluently."

"God, I want to thank You that I'll be totally free from this addiction."

"Thank You, God, that I'll be totally healthy and whole."

"God, thank You for letting all the dreams and desires You've put in me come to pass."

When you release your faith in a big way like that, in a fourteen-ounce serving, God doesn't say, "Who do they think they are? The nerve of those people—don't they know they don't deserve it?"

No, when you talk like that it brings a smile to God's face. He says to the angels, "Listen to what they're saying. They believe I can do great things. They believe I can turn any situation around. They've got their trust and confidence in me, so I won't disappoint them. Let me open up the windows of Heaven and pour out a flood of favor, a flood of healing, a flood of promotion, a flood of vindication."

When my father first started ministering, he would travel from town to town speaking in small auditoriums and small churches. Back then, in the 1950s, he carried all of his sound equipment in the back of his car. When he went into an auditorium he would set it up and be ready to go in no time at all. One night, there were a couple hundred people expected. It was a big deal for him. He was this up-and-coming young minister, and so he arrived a couple of hours early to make sure he had plenty of time to set up.

But in the midst of all the excitement he accidentally locked his keys in the trunk of the car. He knew he couldn't have his big service without that sound equipment. So he tried to pry open the trunk of the car with no success. Some bystanders came up and helped him. They shook it and they wiggled it and got some coat hangers and some tools. They couldn't open the trunk, either.

Time was running out. They were way out in the

country and didn't have time to bring in a locksmith or to tow the car to a repair shop. It looked like my father's big evening was about to be ruined. Just when he was preparing to give up, it dawned on him that he had not prayed about it yet.

He announced to the people that he was going to pray and ask God to open up the trunk. They looked at him like he had lost his mind. They began to snicker and laugh. "You've got to be kidding. You can't pray that God will help you open up a trunk."

The doubters did not bother my father. "Sure I can," he said. "You have not because you ask not."

He went over, put his hands on the trunk and said, "Father, I know there is nothing too difficult for You. You know I need this sound equipment to have this meeting tonight. So I'm asking You to somehow, some way, help me to open this trunk."

He began to shake it and rattle it more vigorously than ever, but it still would not open. As he turned and walked away, the laughter and the snickering grew a little bit louder. But all of a sudden they heard this *pop*.

They all turned around, and the trunk had popped open. Just like slow motion the trunk lid began to rise up toward the heavens, just as if God was saying, "I told you I would do it. I'm the God of the breakthrough."

The people helping him nearly passed out. From then on they did anything my father asked. It was, "Yes, sir." "No, sir." "Whatever you say, sir."

That was a Baal-Perazim in my father's life. Here I am fifty years later still telling the story. But I don't believe it would have happened if my father had not been living breakthrough minded. You may not need a trunk to open, but maybe the doctors have told you there is nothing more they can do. Maybe it's a sickness trying to pull you down. Get ready for the God of the breakthrough to show up. Maybe it's a relationship that needs to be restored, a family member whose life is off course. Start declaring, "The God of the breakthrough is turning it around."

Or maybe your dreams just look so big, like it's not possible. Don't ever rule out the God of the breakthrough. Like a flood, His favor can overtake you. Like a flood, God can cause your employer to pay for the surgeries your family member needs. Like a flood, God can cause your little boy to start speaking clearly. Like a flood, God can cause a trunk to supernaturally pop open. I'm asking you to live breakthrough minded.

You may be accepting things in your life that are far less than God's best. It's been so long you don't see how it could change. But this is a new day. New seeds have taken root in your heart. And the good news is the God of the breakthrough is about to visit your house, not with a trickle, not with a stream. No, get ready for a flood of God's favor, a tidal wave of God's goodness.

Release your faith in a greater way. If you don't pray for the trunk to open, then it won't. Dare to believe. God wants to give you something to talk about. He wants to give you some new Baal-Perazims; new landmarks where you can look back and say, "I know that was the God of the breakthrough."

Isaiah said: "The Spirit of the Lord is upon me to announce a day when the free favor of God profusely abounds." Notice the word he used to describe God's favor, *profusely*. That means, "overwhelming, out of the norm, exceeding."

Like Isaiah, I've announced that a flood of God's power is coming. Favor like you've never seen before. Instead of being overwhelmed by burdens, you will be overwhelmed by God's blessings. But the real question is this: can you receive this into your spirit?

It's easy to think, "This is not for me, Joel. I don't see anything different happening. I tried before and it didn't work out. I've been through too much." That kind of negative thinking will stop the flood. God works where there is an attitude of faith. When you believe, all things are possible. The enemy cannot stop this flood. He doesn't have that much power.

Other people cannot stop it. The only one that can stop it is you. You control your own destiny. God is for you. The enemy is against you. You get to cast the deciding vote. I'm asking you to take the limits off of God. He wants to do something new, something amazing in your life.

But the real battle is taking place in our thought life, those thoughts that say, "It will not happen. You're too old. You've made too many mistakes. You'll never get well. You'll never accomplish your dreams."

No, this is the day you will see the free favor of God profusely abound. God has floods of blessings in your future. He has tidal waves of increase and joy and healing and mercy. Make room for this flood. Get in agreement with God.

Paul prayed in Ephesians that the eyes of our understanding would be flooded with light so that we would know the amazing future God has in store. It's interesting that Paul used that phrase: "flooded with light." Paul had experienced a portion of this flood, but we're living in a better time than his.

This is the day where Paul declared we would see the surpassing greatness of God's favor. Paul was saying in effect, "I've seen one level of God's goodness, but the day we're in, we will see God's goodness like no generation has seen it before."

I can tell you firsthand, Victoria and I have

experienced this flood of God's favor. God has over-whelmed us with His goodness. I'm not bragging on us. I'm bragging on God. God has taken us beyond our education, beyond our talent, beyond our train-ing, and He has unleashed His abundance, His wis-dom, and His favor in our lives.

For this to happen, you have to keep God in first place in your life. Honor God. Then, learn to take the limits off of Him.

Like Jonathan, we should ask for the fourteen-ounce. Believe big. Pray bold prayers and live with this expectancy that God has floods of favor, floods of wisdom, and floods of goodness in our future.

My prayer for you is that the eyes of your under-standing would be flooded with light, that you would know how much God loves you, how much He is for you, and what an amazing future He has in store. My prayer is that faith will fill your hearts, that you will raise your level of expectancy, and that you will see God's goodness like never before. Like Isa-iah, I've announced to you that you're under a Flash Flood Warning. You need to get ready. You're about to see the favor of God profusely abound in your life. Because you've honored God, because you have been faithful, things have shifted in your favor.

My encouragement for you is for you to wake up every morning and say: "Father, thank You for this flood of favor in my life." Then go out expecting it. If you do that, I believe and declare you will see God's goodness overwhelm you. You are coming into floods of favor, floods of healing, floods of wisdom, floods of good breaks, floods of mercy. Get ready for it. It's headed your way.

CHAPTER THREE

Further Faster

In December 2003, we signed a sixty-year lease with the City of Houston for our Lakewood Church facility. We always wanted to own it, but the lease was the best thing to make it happen at the time. Deep down I knew sometime during that sixty-year period God would give us the ability to purchase the building. In 2003, I was forty years old. I would be one hundred years old at the end of the lease.

I prayed, "God, I want to purchase this building in my lifetime. I don't want to leave it up in the air for the next generation."

Seven years into our sixty-year lease, the city was running low on funds. The tax revenues were not what they projected. They decided to sell off some of their excess properties to make up for the shortfall in the budget. The mayor's office called and asked if we would be interested in purchasing the facility, buying out the lease. A building like ours would cost $400 million to construct. Of course, we were interested, but we had to see what the sale price would be. The city did an appraisal. They had to take into account that any new buyer would still have to honor our sixty-year lease. The appraisal came back not at $100 million, not at $50 million, but at $7.5 million!

Today, we own our beautiful facility free and clear. No lease involved.

Here's my point: What could have taken sixty years, God did fifty-three years sooner. He took us further faster. We're living in a day where God is speeding things up. Because you honor God, He will do in a fraction of the time what should have taken you a lifetime to accomplish.

In your career, maybe it should take you twenty years to work your way up to that position, twenty years to build up your business. No, things have shifted. God will give you breaks that you didn't deserve. He will bring the right people across your path. You will see opportunity like you've never seen before. It will take you further faster. Get those two words down in your spirit. It may look like in the natural it will take you years to get out of debt, years to get well, years to overcome that problem. No, you need to get ready. You've come into this shift.

Think of it as a car. When you shift from second gear up to fourth gear the engine is still running at the same speed. It's not working any harder, but you're going faster. You're covering more ground. The higher gears have greater capacity. They're designed to go faster. In the same way, because you've kept God in first place, He is shifting you to a higher gear. You will go further faster, not because you're working harder, trying to make it all happen. No, you're putting forth the same effort, being your best every day, but all of a sudden you get a good break that thrusts you years down the road. You get a promotion that you weren't qualified for.

You will look up and think, "How did I get here? It should have taken me another twenty years but here I am."

"The medical report said it would take me five years to recover, but I did it in six months."

"It should have taken me most of my career to get into management, but here I am at the age of thirty."

What is that? God taking you further faster. Part of the shift is acceleration. It will not take as long to accomplish your goals as you think. It will not take as long to get out of that problem as it looks.

Almighty God, the Creator of the universe, is breathing in your direction. He is causing things to fall into place. The right people will be drawn to you. Good breaks, opportunities, healing, restoration, favor. It's not business as usual. You've come into a shift. It will be business as unusual.

I talked to a gentleman who'd had a stroke just a few months before we met. He was a young man in his early fifties. Because of the stroke, he'd lost control of his left side. He couldn't move his left arm. He had to drag his left leg. The left side of his face was paralyzed. I asked him about his prognosis. He told me in slurred speech that his doctors had estimated that even a partial recovery would take three to five years of therapy if he kept at it five days a week. The doctors said he'd never be able to lift his left arm.

I told this gentleman what I'm telling you. God can speed things up. He is in control. I encouraged him to keep believing. Keep hoping. I saw him six months later. The first thing he did was lift his arm way up in the air. He said, "Joel, give me a high five."

"I thought you said it would take five years to do that?" I said.

"That's what they told me, but I did it in less than two months," he replied.

His therapist told him that in thirty years he'd never seen such a speedy recovery.

What happened? God accelerated things. You may think it will take you thirty years to get out of debt, thirty years to pay your house off. You've already run the numbers, calculated it all. By the time you're 107 years old you will be debt free. Yeah, you will be in Heaven debt free! No, you don't know what God is up to. You don't know what God has already destined to come across your path. One phone call like we received, one contract, one good break, one inheritance, and you're totally debt free. You're into overflow. Now you need to get ready. God is saying, "It will happen sooner than you think. I am shifting things in your favor. You will come into acceleration." What should have taken you a lifetime to accomplish, He will do in a split second of time.

Now don't talk yourself out of it.

"Well, I don't know, Joel. I don't have the seniority."

"I have all these college loans, this debt."

"I've gone as far as I can."

Be a believer and not a doubter. You may not see a way, but God still has a way. Your attitude should be: "God, I'm in agreement with You. I believe You have shifted things in my favor. You are taking me further faster. I will accomplish my dreams sooner than I think. I will overcome these problems quicker than I thought."

When you do that, Almighty God will open doors

that no man can shut. He will connect you to the right people. His favor will thrust you years down the road. Back in 1949, a young minister named Billy Graham traveled around the country holding meetings in large auditoriums. He was having success, but he wasn't really nationally known. That summer he conducted a meeting in a big tent in Los Angeles. A gentleman by the name of William Randolph Hearst showed up to hear Billy Graham speak. Mr. Hearst owned newspapers all across the country. He was so touched that night he sent a message to all of his publishers to write favorable articles about Billy Graham. The next week the whole country was talking about this young minister. Reverend Graham came to national prominence practically overnight because of this one man.

What was that? A divine shift. God taking him further faster. It could have taken Billy Graham his whole lifetime to gain that kind of respect and credibility, but God used one man to show him favor and opened doors that took his ministry to a new level.

Now the good news is God has already lined up the right people for you. They are already in your future. It's just a matter of time before they show up. They will open doors that you could not open. They will show you favor even though you didn't ask. They will use their influence to make you look good.

They're ordained by God to accelerate His plan for your life.

What's interesting is Billy Graham didn't search out Hearst. Instead, the newspaper chain's owner searched out Billy Graham. You don't have to try to find the right people. You just honor God and the right people will find you. They'll pick you out of a crowd. They'll knock on your door. They'll show up at your office. For some reason they will want to be good to you.

That's a divine connection. God will cause them to use their expertise, even their funds, to take you further faster. Here's what will happen: You will accomplish more in less time. You will be promoted beyond your education. You will increase beyond your experience. The right people will help you go where you could not go on your own.

The Scripture tells us about the first miracle Jesus ever performed. He turned water into wine. He had just attended a wedding. Afterward, He went to a big reception, and right in the middle they ran out of wine. Jesus' mother, Mary, came up and told Him about the problem. Jesus said, "Mom, why are you telling me that? I can't do anything about it. My time has not yet come."

I can imagine Mary just smiled and said to the

workers, "Do me a favor. Whatever He asks you to do, just do it."

Mary knew what He was capable of.

There were six stone water pots over to the side. They held about thirty gallons each. Jesus said to the workers, "Fill those pots up with water."

They filled them up. Then Jesus said, "Now dip out some of the water"—which He had transformed into wine—"and take it to the host of the party."

When the host tasted it, he called the groom over and said, "This is amazing. Most people serve the best wine first, and then when people have had a lot to drink and don't know any better, they'll bring out the less expensive wine. But you've done just the opposite. You saved the best wine for last."

I read up on how long it takes to make wine. It's a very lengthy process. It starts with the planting of seeds in the ground. The grapevines have to grow and produce their fruit. The grapes have to develop. When they get mature and just right, workers pick the grapes and eventually the grapes are made into wine. The process from the time they plant the seed to the time they have wine is typically three to five years. And that's just average-quality wine.

The higher-quality wines take between five and seven years to make. To increase the quality and make it more valuable, often they will age the wine, put it up on a shelf, and leave it for years and years. You've seen wine that's twenty or thirty years old. That would be considered the best wine.

Here's what I want you to understand: in the first miracle Jesus ever performed, He created fine wine, a process that should have taken twenty years, but He did it in a split second. The twenty-year winemaking process was accomplished in a moment of time.

Maybe it should take you years to recover after an illness. But just like Jesus sped up the process of making wine, He can speed up the process of healing. Maybe in the natural it should take you thirty years to pay off your home mortgage. You've run the calculations but they are based on the laws of economics. The good news is, God has a faster calculator. He can give you one good break that will allow you to pay off your mortgage on His much faster schedule.

A woman visited our church while in Houston awaiting a liver transplant at the medical center. She had just been approved for the list of recipients. Doctors told her it could take between three and five years. She wasn't sure she could make it that long. I encouraged her that God could heal her without the transplant, or God could speed things up and she'd get her new liver sooner than the doctors had predicted.

We prayed and she went on her way. A few weeks

later I saw her back in the Lakewood Church lobby again. She smiled real big and said, "Joel, you are looking at a woman with a brand-new liver."

She received a call from the hospital just two weeks after she was put on the transplant list. It just so happened a perfectly matched liver for her had become available. It wasn't suitable for anyone else on the list. Her doctors said, "If you can get here tonight, this is your liver."

She jumped on a plane, drove to the medical complex, and immediately went into surgery. The good news was there were no complications. She said, "Joel, I feel better today than I've felt since I was a teenager."

What happened? God turned her water into wine. God took what should have taken five years and did it in one month's time. If you too will take the limits off God you will see Him do amazing things. You'll look up and say, "How in the world did I get to where I am?"

"I'm not the most qualified, but I'm running the company."

"I'm not the most talented, but they all ask me for advice."

"I never went to seminary, but I've got a pretty big church."

Or, "It should have taken me till I retired, but I've already paid my house off."

One touch of God's favor can put you thirty years down the road. One good break, one promotion, one inheritance, or one divine connection can make a huge difference.

"Well" you say, "Joel, you're just getting everybody's hopes up. I don't believe God will accelerate things in my life. I don't believe this will happen for me." Then this book is not for you. This is for believers! This is for those who will rise up and say, "Yes, Lord. I know You're the God of Acceleration, and if you did it for the wedding party centuries ago, if you took a twenty-year process and did it in a split second, then I know You can accelerate things in my life. I know You can thrust me years ahead."

I have a friend who is now thirty-two years old. I've known his family for many years. His parents are good people and they love the Lord, but they've maintained the same lifestyle for thirty years. They've stayed at the same level as their parents and grandparents. There is nothing wrong with that, but I believe God wants every generation to build upon the accomplishments of the last.

Right after he graduated from college, he went to work for a major corporation. My friend, their son, had a big vision for his life. His dream was to one day lead a major corporation. He was hired to begin at the very bottom level of this big company. He started in sales. He just kept giving it his best day in and day out. After three years he was in the top 5 percent of sales. They promoted him to manager. The next year he landed a new account. It was the largest account in the company's history. That one good break immediately made him the top salesperson by far. At twenty-eight years old, he was appointed vice president. He was in charge of the company's entire southwest division.

Things continued to fall into place. His boss left and went to another company. My friend earned another promotion. The CEO of his corporation was only fifty-one years old. It looked like he had another twenty years in him. But one day, unexpectedly, he went to the board and said, "I'm resigning and I would like to nominate this young man as my successor." They voted my friend in as the top man and today, at thirty-two years old, he is the youngest CEO in that corporation's history. He is running a major company with thousands and thousands of employees.

That is God accelerating things. In the old days my friend's rapid rise in the corporate world would have taken a lifetime, but in these times God is turning water into wine faster than ever before. If you will believe, if you will put your trust in Him, if you will live to honor God, then as with my friend, God will give you good breaks. He will open the right doors. He will move people out of the way. He will cause you to stand out in a crowd. He will let His face shine down on you, and you will accomplish goals in a fraction of the time.

This is what happened to David in the Bible. God put a big dream in his heart as a teenager. David knew one day he would accomplish great things. But year after year went by, and he didn't see anything happening. He was stuck out in the lonely pastures taking care of his father's sheep. Nobody knew him. He didn't have any influence. No one paid him much attention.

I'm sure young David felt like he was falling behind, like he would never get to where God wanted him to be. One day David went into battle and faced Goliath. He didn't have any military training. All the odds were against him, but he knew the Most High God was with him. When David defeated Goliath in a split second he became a national hero. In an instant, he had this influence and credibility that could have taken him his whole lifetime to earn otherwise.

What happened? God turned his water into wine. One touch of God's favor thrust him many, many years ahead. What's interesting is God used an obstacle to promote David. When you face giant obstacles in your own life—disappointments, setbacks, things don't work out—don't become discouraged. That adversity could be the very thing God will use to promote you. That could be where you see God speed up the time and you accomplish something that should have taken your whole lifetime.

Like David, you may feel like you've fallen behind. Maybe you are not where you had hoped to be in life. You have big dreams in your heart, but you haven't caught any good breaks. Doors have closed. It's easy to get discouraged. But let me challenge you: if you will just keep being your best day in and day out, if you will live a life that honors God, He will not only make up for lost time, He also will thrust you further. He will do more than you can even ask or think.

Our friends Jerry and Jana Lackey attended Lakewood for many years and then they moved to Botswana, Africa, to do mission work. They live far out in a rural area where antelope and other wild creatures still roam. There they take care of the orphans, feed the poor, teach people, and do amazing work.

God's favor has been on their lives, but their big dream was to build a major youth center. Seventy percent of the population in Botswana is under the age of twenty-five. This youth center would be a place where the young people could come and grow and learn and make friends. But it was estimated to cost $5 million. That's a lot even here, but over there where the annual income is less than $1,000, that was unheard of. Jerry and Jana have raised substantial funds over the years, but nothing even close to this magnitude.

Then one day a German businessman was visiting Botswana with his wife, and they fell in love with the country. They decided they wanted to do something to help. They Googled the phrase "Botswana orphanages," and the Lackey's organization came up. It's called Love Botswana Outreach. The German businessman sent them a donation for $20,000. He said, "I want to do more." A few weeks went by. He sent them a $300,000 donation!

The Lackeys were so thrilled. Then their benefactor said, "I want to come see you."

That man and his wife came to Botswana, and they stayed at an exclusive safari resort about fifteen miles from the Lackey's mission complex. Jerry drove to pick him up one morning. The man who owned the resort said to Jerry, "Hey, the resort is for sale. Would you like to buy it?"

He thought Jerry was a wealthy businessman. Jerry kind of laughed and said, "I'm a missionary living down the road. I don't have that kind of money, but thank you."

The German businessman overheard the conversation. He asked Jerry to find out more about it. Jerry thought he wanted to buy it for himself, but that German man bought this big, exclusive, beautiful resort and gave it to Jerry and Jana for their outreaches. They were overwhelmed, and rightfully so!

The German man came to see their mission complex, and he noticed the plans they had drawn for a big youth center. This was the greatest thing that Jana and Jerry had ever dreamed to do, something that they prayed and believed that somehow they could accomplish in their lifetimes. The German asked them how much the youth center would cost.

"Five million dollars," they said.

"I'll write you a check," he replied.

On April 4, 2013, our friends dedicated that brand new youth center, totally paid for by their German benefactor.

What was that? God taking them further faster. They're young people in their forties. Before their German friend came around, Jerry and Jana thought they would be praying, believing, raising funds their entire lives, but they came into this shift. God brought one man across their paths, a divine connection.

You don't need everyone to help you. You just need one person God ordained, and you will accomplish in a split second what could have taken you your whole lifetime. You may say: "Well, Joel. I don't know if this will happen for me. I never get any good breaks."

It will not happen with that attitude. You cannot harbor thoughts of defeat and lack all day and expect to have abundance. You can't talk mediocrity and expect to have victory. You are prophesying your future. If you want to see this shift occur in your own life you've must get in agreement and say, "Yes, God. This is for me. I believe You have lined up the right people. I know they're already in my future. I want to thank You that I will accomplish my dreams sooner than I think."

In the natural it may not look like it, but remember, we serve a supernatural God. He is about to release floods of His favor, floods of healing, floods of good breaks. Take the limits off God. Don't think of all the reasons your plans will not work. God wouldn't have given you the dream unless He already had a way to bring it to pass.

If you will stay in faith, like the Lackeys, it will not only happen sooner than you think, it will be bigger than you imagine. That's the way our God is. He likes to do exceedingly, abundantly, above and beyond.

I read that the Chinese bamboo plant barely grows aboveground for its first four years. You hardly see anything happening. Even though you water it, fertilize it, make sure it's getting sunlight; it looks like you're wasting your time. But what you can't see is that under the ground it's developing a massive root system. The roots are spreading out in every possible direction. In the fifth year, once the roots are properly established, the plant will take off and shoot up to as high as eighty feet in the air—from zero to eighty feet, all in one year.

Many of you, like Jerry and Jana, have been faithful. You've given. You've served. You've helped others. You've sown a lot of seeds but you haven't seen a lot of progress. Yes, God has been good to you. You're grateful, but nothing really out of the ordinary has occurred. So far, you've lived the equivalent of your four years of developing roots. You were proving to God that you would be faithful. You were proving you would do the right thing when it was hard. Now you need to prepare. God is saying, "You're coming into your fifth year. You will see explosive growth that will take you to levels beyond your income, beyond your training, beyond your experience."

In this fifth year, good breaks will find you. The right people will search you out. Opportunity will come knocking on your door. The fifth year is harvest time. It's favor time. You will reap from all the seeds you've sown down through the years. Nothing you've ever given has gone unnoticed. Every sacrifice you've made, every time you stopped to help someone, God sees that.

The Scripture talks about how God will reward us in this life, not just in the Sweet By and By. Because you've been faithful, there is a harvest stored up. As with the Lackeys, God is about to release everything that belongs to you. It will happen sooner than you think. It will be bigger than you imagined. God will bring out gifts and talents you didn't even know you had. He will open up new doors of opportunity. This fifth year is when God will shoot you up higher than you ever even dreamed.

I have a good friend who had been caught in a difficult legal situation for at least a year. It had been very heavy on her heart. She was told that it could take ten years to resolve. Her opponents could drag it out just to make her life miserable. At one time she was a very upbeat, fun person to be around, but after months and months of waiting and setbacks and pressure, it was like she was a different person: no joy, no peace, no victory, very solemn, very serious. It looked like there could be years and years of this stress and frustration. But a week ago as I write this, she received the good news that the case was totally resolved in her favor. Everything was cleared up.

She said, "Joel, I can't even tell you what a load is being lifted off of me."

What happened? She came into her fifth year. What could have taken ten years, even twenty years,

God did in less than a year. Just like with her, because you've been faithful, problems you've struggled with for years will suddenly resolve. God will cause things to fall into place. The right people will show up.

You will soon see acceleration. Let me declare it. It will not take a lifetime to accomplish your dreams. It will happen in a fraction of the time. Get up every day and say "Father, thank You for taking me further faster. Thank You for turning my water into wine." If you do that, I believe and declare just like Jerry and Jana, divine connections are coming your way. Like us, with the Lakewood Church building, what should have taken you sixty years will be accelerated to a few years. Because you honor God, He will take you further faster.

CHAPTER FOUR

Explosive Blessings

I was driving through the mountains not long ago, and on one side there was a huge wall of rock where the road had been cut into the mountainside. The builders had used dynamite to blast away the rock; otherwise, the stone would have been there probably forever.

We all have things in our lives that seem permanent. Maybe it looks like you will never get out of debt, or like you will stay at the same earning level the rest of your life. But just as the builders used dynamite to blast away the rock so they could create that mountain road, God has explosive blessings that will remove obstacles, which may look permanent now.

One touch of God's favor can blast you out of debt. One good break can blast you to a new level.

God has a way of removing what looks permanent by showing us an explosion of His goodness. A friend of mine wanted to go to a certain college but he needed a scholarship. He had applied months before, and although his grades were good enough, the college informed him there were no more scholarships available. He couldn't afford a major college, so he enrolled in a junior college.

At that point, it looked like his dream of going to his favorite college was over. It looked permanent. He was told there were no available scholarships at the school he really wanted to attend. He didn't have the funds.

All the facts said it was not going to happen for him. But four weeks before school was to start, his favorite college called back and said a scholarship had opened up. Instead of offering him the two-year partial scholarship he had applied for earlier, they offered him a four-year full ride. Now when he gets out of school, instead of graduating and owing thousands of dollars, he'll be totally debt free. That is an explosive blessing.

You may think your current situation is permanent. You've been there a long time, and you can't see how you could ever move up. All the facts are telling you it's impossible that things will improve, but God has ways to increase you that you've never dreamed of. He's saying today: "You need to get ready. I have explosive blessings coming your way. Where you are is not permanent. I will take you higher. I will increase you beyond your normal income. I will bless you beyond your salary. I will suddenly change things for the better in your life."

One definition of the word *explosion* is "a sudden, widespread increase." That's what God will do for you. Suddenly, you're not expecting anything. It's out of the ordinary. It's not small. It's not mediocre. It's a widespread increase. It's so amazing you'll know it's the hand of God.

A gentleman stopped by Lakewood Church recently and brought a very large donation to the ministry. It was his tithe. He said he'd received an inheritance from a relative he'd never met. He didn't even know they were related, but this man left him a gift that thrust his family to a whole new level financially. He not only paid off his own home loan but also paid off the mortgages held by some other people.

You may feel that in the natural you could never accomplish your dreams. You don't have the connections, the resources, or the education, but God is saying: "You have not seen My explosive blessings. You haven't seen the surpassing greatness of My favor. I have blessings that will catapult you years ahead. I have increase beyond your calculations."

I've learned God doesn't always take us ahead in normal increments. There are times where God takes us little by little. We have to be faithful day in and day out, but when you hit an explosive blessing instead of moving up from seven to eight to nine you'll go from seven to eight to thirty-three, to thirty-four. That's widespread increase.

You may say, "Joel, if the economy was better, I might believe this. If business wasn't so slow I might get my hopes up, but this is not the time to talk about increase. This is not the time to talk about paying things off. I'm just hoping to survive. I'm just hoping to not go under."

The Scripture says God will make rivers in the desert. He'll make streams in the barren places. It may be dry and barren. The economy may be down. Business may be slow. The good news is the economy is not our source. God is our source. And God is not having a down year.

The economy in Heaven is doing just fine. As long as we stay connected to the vine, putting our trust in Him, then you and I are connected to a supply line that will never run dry. Our attitude should be: "God, I may not see how it could happen, but I know you have explosive blessings coming my way. I'm expecting a sudden, widespread increase. I'm expecting to rise to a new level. I'm expecting to pay off my house. I'm expecting to be a bigger blessing to others. I'm expecting to set a new standard for my family."

Release your faith for explosive blessings. Blessings beyond your normal income. Blessings beyond your salary.

I heard about a married couple who were buying a home in another state and were looking at this very prestigious neighborhood. They found a house they really liked. But every time they tried to move forward, they just didn't feel good about it. After several months, they found a larger piece of property right on the outskirts of that subdivision.

In the natural, being in the neighborhood would have been a better investment. The property values were higher. Even though they could have afforded the lot in the prestigious neighborhood, they didn't feel at peace with doing that. Instead, they purchased the other property outside the neighborhood.

About six months after the couple moved in, two men showed up at their door. They were geologists working for an oil company.

"We've been studying this area for several years, and we've discovered there is a massive amount of oil under this whole subdivision," the geologists said. "But the property over there is too densely populated. There's nowhere we can drill. If you'll let us lease part of your property we will not only give you the commission from your property, but also we will give you a portion of the commissions from all the homes in the subdivision next door."

There were 1,200 homes in that neighborhood. So instead of getting a commission for one home if they would have bought in the subdivision, they were getting a commission off 1,200 homes.

God knows where the good deals are!

In the Scripture, God says, "I will give you hidden riches found in secret places." That property just outside the subdivision was a hidden treasure. God knows where all the oil, the minerals, the gold, and the silver are buried. He put them there. When Jesus needed money to pay His taxes, He sent Peter to the lake, and the first fish Peter caught had enough money in its mouth for both Jesus' and Peter's taxes.

Jesus knew right where the treasure was. God knows the inventions that have not yet been created. He knows the ideas that will be successful. He knows the properties and the real estate that will be valuable. He may not cause you to strike oil, but He can give you one idea that will catapult you to a new level.

This is what happened to Truett Cathy. In 1946, he and his brother opened a little restaurant, the Dwarf Grill, south of downtown Atlanta. He noticed that hamburgers were the rage. But one day God gave him an idea. He thought if people like hamburgers, maybe they'd like chicken sandwiches, too.

So instead of just making sandwiches with beef patties, he offered boneless chicken breast sandwiches to his customers, too. They were so popular, he opened his first shopping mall fast food restaurant in 1967, and called it Chick-fil-A. Today, there are more than 1,700 Chick-fil-As in thirty-nine states. The Cathys give millions of dollars to help people around the world—an explosive blessing.

God has all kinds of inventions just waiting to be released. He knows everything that will ever be created. He has new businesses He is just waiting to trust people with; new books just waiting to be written, new technology, new medicine, new procedures. Get out of a rut, enlarge your vision, and start thanking God for the explosive blessings coming your way.

If you will be faithful with what you have and prove to God that you can be trusted, then God will show you the hidden riches found in secret places. God will give you ideas, dreams, visions, good breaks, and the right connections to take you to a level you never thought possible. It's time to rise up and be the head and not the tail. It's time for us to lend and not borrow. In these coming days there will be a transfer of wealth. There will be a major shifting in finances and resources. God will do unusual things.

Lakewood Church is a $400 million facility that we bought for about $20 million. After we renovated it, our investment in the church was still less than a fourth of what it would have cost new. That's a shifting of wealth.

For many years we were on the other side of Houston, in wood buildings, then metal buildings. The roads weren't big enough. The parking lots were not adequate. At times we were looked down on, seen as second-class, but one day we came in to an explosive blessing that blasted us to a new level.

We saw the exceeding greatness of God's favor. God has given us the premier facility in the fourth largest city in America. That's what God is doing today. He's stepping it up a notch. We were never created to be second class and just barely get by. The Scripture says we are supposed to reign in life as kings.

You may not be there yet, but don't settle where you are. Get ready for God to do something new. He's about to release buildings, contracts, ideas, favor, influence that will catapult His people to new levels. He is about to open up doors wider than you thought possible, just as He did for our church. You need to make room for explosive blessings in your thinking.

Get ready for them. God is about to release hidden treasure for you.

A friend of mine who attends Lakewood started his business with just one employee—himself. Within a few years he had a whole floor in a downtown high-rise for his business. Recently he was awarded a contract to build one of the largest refineries in all of China, a multi-billion-dollar project.

"Joel, I was the least likely one to get it," he said.

He explained that there were much larger competitors with much more influence. The competition included well-established companies that had been in business for decades, but somehow God caused his company to stand out. Now my friend is seen as one of the leaders in the field. His company is part of the shift of wealth to God's people, who will further the kingdom.

God will cause you to stand out just like my friend. He can cause contracts to come your way. You may seem the least likely for a promotion in the natural, but with the blessing of God on your life the odds dramatically change. You and God are a majority. You need to get ready for this shift. It will be an explosion of God's goodness, a sudden, widespread increase.

That means something that goes far and beyond anything you've ever seen. What is that? It's the immeasurable, limitless, surpassing greatness of God's favor.

Proverbs 13:22 talks about this shift. It says: "The wealth of the ungodly will eventually find its way into the hands of the righteous for whom it has been laid up."

God has already stored up businesses, contracts, buildings, increase, promotions, and ideas. They already have your name on them, and if you'll just keep being your best, blessing others, honoring God, and dreaming big, then eventually they will find their way into your hands, the hands of the righteous.

Something is looking for you right now—not bad breaks, not lack, not depression, not defeat. You are the righteous. Increase is looking for you. Favor is looking for you. Promotion is looking for you. Contracts are looking for you. Good ideas are looking for you. God says the wealth of the ungodly will eventually find its way into the hands of the godly.

The building where our church is located was used for sports purposes and concerts for thirty years. It was called the Summit at first, and then later the Compaq Center. But I believe if you peeled those names back thirty years ago when it was first built, you would have seen the name Lakewood Church already there. The stadium eventually found its way into our hands. You don't know the amazing things that God has already put your name on. They're already laid up for you.

Somebody else may have started them. Maybe somebody else did the hard work, but God says eventually they will find the way into your hands. You have some "eventually"s in your future. You know what an "eventually" is? It's an explosive blessing: Unexpectedly a business falls into your hands. Maybe it's a real estate deal that could only be God's doing, or an extraordinary contract comes to you even though you weren't the most qualified.

Your "eventually" may be an inheritance from someone you didn't know or a restructuring at the office, or you suddenly rise from working for a company to running it. God is saying: "I'm shifting things from the hands of those who are not concerned about Me, from those who don't walk in integrity or those who don't care for others to the hands of people I can trust with furthering My kingdom."

I believe that's you and me. Get ready for the surpassing greatness of God's favor. It will be favor like you've never seen before: Favor that takes you beyond previous limitation. Favor that blasts you to a new level.

The psalmist David said, "What would have happened to me if I would not have believed I would see the goodness of God?" I'm asking you to believe that

God has amazing things in store. Believe that you can break out of what's holding you back and become everything God created you to be. Incredible power is released when we believe.

One day after a Lakewood service I talked to a young couple who said they had been trying to have a baby for six years. The mother had been through a couple of miscarriages and for some reason just couldn't carry a baby full term. They went to specialists and tried everything medically, with no success. Finally they just turned it over to God and said, "Our hopes and dreams are in your hands. We trust you. We know you're in complete control."

Years earlier the young lady's sister had a dream and she saw the couple from our church with the most beautiful blond-haired, blue-eyed little boy you can imagine. They believed that was a sign from God.

On Mother's Day, 2009, the couple came to a service celebrating Lakewood's fiftieth anniversary. I talked that day about the year of jubilee and how everything that has our name on it is coming back in. I made the statement, "The business that has your name on it is coming in, the good health that has your name on it is coming in," and then I said specifically, "The baby who has your name is coming in."

They couple looked at each other in amazement. They knew I'd said that exactly for them. I went on to talk about how God is accelerating things and it will happen faster than we think. The whole time they were letting the seed take root.

That's the key: The only promises that will come alive in your life and end up becoming realities are the promises where you rise up and say, "Yes, that's for me." You have to get in agreement with God and let it take root.

I can speak faith and victory over your future for a lifetime, but it won't do any good if you just sit back and think, "Well I don't think this will happen. I've had a lot of bad breaks, and I just don't see how I'll ever rise higher."

If you make excuses and talk yourself out of it, then that promise will not take root. But when the soil of your heart is fertile, you have expectancy in your spirit. If you hear the promise that God has blessings in your future, then you'll rise up like that couple at Lakewood did and say, "That's for me. Lord, I believe. I release my faith for explosive blessings, for the immeasurable, limitless, surpassing greatness of your favor."

That's what allows God to do great things.

The couple went out after the service knowing that the baby with their name was coming in. They knew it was going to happen quicker than they thought. Four hours later, as they were celebrating Mother's

Day with their family, their office manager called and asked if they would be interested in adopting a baby boy to be born in July.

They knew that was the hand of God. Eight weeks later they were in the hospital room when the little boy was born. He was a beautiful blond-haired, blue-eyed baby, just like his new mother's sister had seen in the dream. The couple who had wanted a child so much were the first to put their arms around the baby.

The dad even cut the newborn's umbilical cord. They named their son Asher, after Jacob's son in the Old Testament. One meaning of that name is "gift from God." In Scripture, David asked what would have happened if he had not believed. I wonder what would have happened had this couple not released their faith. Maybe they wouldn't have received that phone call asking if they wanted to adopt the baby boy.

I'm convinced there are times when we don't see God's amazing hand at work, because we don't activate our faith by believing. We let our mind talk us out of it. We think of all the reasons why it won't happen. I'm asking you to be a believer and not a doubter. Let this seed take root. God has explosive blessings in your future. He is about to release another level of His favor in your life. He is going to give you the desires of your heart.

Things you've been praying about for years are about to come to pass. Situations that have been stuck for a long time are about to break loose. There is promotion and increase in your future like you've never dreamed of. It will not happen in an ordinary way, or the way you had planned. God will do it in an extraordinary way so you know it's His doing.

This is the generation for the surpassing greatness of God's favor. It will be above and beyond what you've seen before. A pastor friend of mine was planning to build a $40 million sanctuary. He was raising the funds and drawing up the plans. One day, out of the blue, the mayor in his town called and said the developers of a huge casino near his church had gone bankrupt before finishing it. The casino had more than forty acres of parking. The completed building could contain four football fields inside. It was just a few miles from his existing church.

The mayor asked my friend if he was interested in purchasing the huge casino. The pastor thought the price would be $50 million or more. The mayor said, "No, you can purchase it for under two million dollars."

The owner of a production company heard that the pastor was considering buying the casino property for his sanctuary. He told the pastor that he had a giant screen used for concerts and sporting events that would be wonderful for the new church. The screen was more than 150 feet long. It cost $3 million new. But the company owner said he would sell it to the pastor for $50,000.

Everything fell into place. Instead of building his own facility, a much bigger and better building dropped into his hands. That's a part of the shift, the transfer. Somebody else built it, somebody else paid for it, but at the right time the building found its way into the hands of the godly.

Right now, something is looking for you. Something already has your name on it. As long as you're doing your best to honor God and you have a heart to help others, an explosive blessing will find its way into your hands.

God knows where the hidden treasure is. He knows where to find the property, the contracts, the ideas, and the good breaks you need to fulfill your destiny. You may be stuck in a rut, thinking that you've gone as far as you can go. But God is saying, "Where you are is not permanent. I have explosive blessings coming your way. Blessings that will blast you to a new level. Favor that will take you beyond previous limitations."

CHAPTER FIVE

Increase Your Capacity to Receive

Even though God has amazing things in your future, He is limited by your capacity to receive. It's as if you have a one-gallon bucket, yet I have fifty gallons to give you. The problem is not with the supply. The problem is you don't have the capacity to receive. If you trade in that small container and get something bigger, then I can give you more.

It's the same way with God. If you think you've reached your limits—whether it's because of a bad economy, your health is poor, or you can't afford the house you want—God has the ability and resources to help you, but your container is too small.

You have to enlarge your vision and make room for the new things God wants to do. You attitude should be: "The economy may be down, but I know God is still on the Throne. I know He has promotion and increase already lined up for me. His favor surrounds me like a shield. Goodness and mercy are following me. This will be a great year."

When you change your thinking like that, you enlarge your capacity to receive. Then you will see the goodness of God in new ways. Some people go around with a small cup, so to speak. They're not expecting much; maybe it's because they've struggled for many years.

Others may have a bucket instead of a cup. They've done okay. They're surviving, but they're not planning on going any further. Still others have traded in the bucket. They've stretched their faith. They have a barrel. They believe they will go higher.

Yet there's one other group; this group is very unusual. They believe in far-and-beyond favor. They believe God will prosper them even in a recession. They believe their children will be mighty in the land. They're expecting explosive blessings. They know they've come into a shift and a supernatural increase is coming.

They don't have a cup. They don't have a bucket. They don't have a barrel. Their faith is so strong they have a barn. They have a whole warehouse. They're expecting God to open up the windows of Heaven and pour out unprecedented favor, supernatural opportunities, and exponential increase.

The Scripture says, "Open your mouth wide and I will fill it." My question is this: "Do you have your mouth opened wide? What are you expecting? What are you saying about your future?"

"Oh, man, it's going to be a tough year. I don't think I'll ever meet my sales goals."

"I don't think I'll ever be promoted."

"I don't think I'll ever get well."

If those are your thoughts, then your mouth is barely open. You're not expecting increase. You're not expecting good breaks. You're not expecting God to turn it around.

Jesus said, "According to your faith, it will be done unto you." He was saying in effect, "If you have a cup I'll fill you with a cupful of blessings. If you have a barrel then I'll fill you with a barrelful of blessings. But if you have a barn, then I will give you a barnful of blessings."

If you'll take the limits off God—if you'll get up every morning expecting far-and-beyond favor—then He won't disappoint you. When you have your mouth opened wide, you're not complaining about the economy. Instead, you are expecting to have a blessed year.

Your child may be off course, but you're not praying: "God, just keep him from driving me crazy." Instead you're saying: "God, You said my children would be mighty in the land, so I want to thank You that You will turn him around and use him to do great things for You."

When your mouth is open wide, you're not just believing you will make the monthly mortgage payments; you're believing you will pay off your whole house, to live totally debt free. That's barn level.

The question is this: "Do you have your mouth opened wide? Do you believe in increase? Do you go out each day knowing that favor is in your future, or are you stuck in a rut? Have you decided you've reached your limits, so you've just settled where you are?"

That's what happened to the children of Israel. They were headed toward the Promised Land. They had big dreams and big goals, but along the way they faced adversities. They had some disappointments.

They were like many modern-day people who lost money when the stock market dropped, or lost their homes when the recession hit. The children of Israel had their own adversities. They became so discouraged they gave up on their dreams and just settled where they were.

One day God said to them, "You have dwelt long

enough on this mountain." I believe God is saying that to each one of us. You have been where you are long enough. You may have been carrying that cup year after year. Maybe that is how you were raised and that's all you've ever known. You may have had your sights on the barn at one time, and dreamed big, but after some setbacks you just settled for the bucket.

God is saying to you, "This is a new day. Get your fire back. Where you are is not where you're supposed to stay."

I'm asking you to increase your capacity to receive. Stretch your faith and dream bigger. Go beyond the barriers that have held you back. Make room for God to do something new. Give Him permission to increase you. You have to give God permission to prosper you.

God brought things across my path years ago, but I turned them down. I thought they were too big. I didn't think I was qualified. It was so far beyond what I thought I could handle, I didn't release my faith for it.

I wasn't giving God permission to increase me. I missed that opportunity to go farther. God will not force us to live His abundant life. It starts in our own thinking. Jesus said, "No one pours new wine into old wineskins." He meant that you can't go to a new level with an old way of thinking. You may be ready for God to do something new. When you hear that God has more in store this excites you. Something on the inside says, "Yes this is for me."

But many times your mind will try to talk you out of it. It will come up with reasons why it's not going to happen:

"You know what the economy is like. You will not have a blessed year."

"You know the doctor said you will not recover."

"You've been single for a long time. You will never be married."

No, get rid of the old wineskins. Trade in those containers for something bigger. This is a new season. What's happened in the past is over and done. You may have been through disappointments. Maybe you tried and failed. It didn't work out. That's okay. God is still in control.

Have a bigger vision for your life. Our attitudes should be: "This is my year to go to a new level. This is my year to see a supernatural increase. This is my year to become totally healthy. This is my year to meet the person of my dreams."

God promises that if you'll open your mouth wide, then He will fill it. But it all starts with your capacity to receive. You can't go around thinking thoughts of mediocrity and expect to excel. You can't think thoughts of lack and expect to have abundance. The two don't go together. Take the limitations off God. Trade in that cup. Throw away that bucket. Get rid of that barrel and come over to the barn-sized level. God is a God of abundance.

In 2 Kings there's a story of a widow whose husband died. She doesn't have money to pay her bills. The creditors are coming to take her sons as payment. All she has of any value is a small pot of oil. Elisha the Prophet stops by her house and tells her to do something strange—to go to her neighbors and borrow as many big empty pots as you can find. These pots normally hold very expensive cooking oil.

He told her specifically, "Borrow not a few." He was saying, "Don't short-change yourself. Make room for abundance." She went out and gathered up five or six empty pots. When she returned Elisha told her to pour the little oil that she had into one of those empty containers. It looked as if she was just transferring it from one to another, but the Scripture says the oil never ran out. She kept pouring and pouring. God supernaturally multiplied that oil until every one of those containers was completely full.

Here's my point: She determined how much oil she would have. If she had borrowed only one container, then just one container would have been filled. If she had borrowed ten, she would have had ten full.

If she'd borrowed fifty, then fifty would have been full.

The amount of increase she received wasn't up to God. He has unlimited supplies. It was up to her. That was why the Prophet said, "Borrow not a few." My question is this: How many containers are you borrowing? What kind of vision do you have for your life? If you think, "The economy is so bad and my business is slow, and I'm just hoping to make it through this year," God says, "All right, I'll fill that barely-get-by container."

Or maybe you have five or six containers. You believe you can pay your bills, feed your family, and have a little left over. That's good. God will fill those containers. But I believe you are different. You have radical faith. You are dangerous. You don't have one. You don't have five. Instead, you're calling Home Depot to say: "I need a couple thousand empty containers."

You know God can do exceedingly abundantly above and beyond. You know He is El Shaddai, the God Who is more than enough. You're making room for this far-and-beyond favor. You're positioned under the open windows of Heaven.

God is saying, "You need to get ready. I'm going to fill your containers." It may not have happened yet, but God has favor in your future. He has good breaks, opportunities, and blessings that will chase you down. You may not see how it can happen, but God has ways to increase you that you've never thought of.

He has explosive blessings that can thrust you to a new level. Like the widow woman and the pots of cooking oil, God wants to bless you beyond your normal income, beyond your salary, and beyond your retirement. God can give you one good break; one promotion, one inheritance, and all those containers will be filled to overflowing.

Make sure you don't shortchange yourself. God is saying to you what He said to this lady: "Borrow not a few." Don't limit your vision. You may not see how it could happen. That's okay; that's not your job. Your job is to believe. God has a thousand ways to fill your containers that you've never thought of.

Don't go around year after year expecting the same thing the same way. God is a God of increase. He has greater levels. Where you are is not where you're supposed to stay. You're supposed to rise higher. Have a bigger vision. Not, "God if you'll just give me this small raise, then I'll be happy. God, if you'll just help my car to not break down. God, if you'll just help me to scrape by, you know how bad the economy is."

Don't borrow tiny little containers. They limit

what God can do. A fisherman was on a riverbank one day when he saw another man fishing nearby. Every time the other man caught a big fish, he threw it back, but he kept every small fish he hooked.

This went on all day, and the more the first fisherman watched the more curious he became. Finally he went over and said, "Sir I've watched you all day and I just can't understand. Why do you throw the big fish back, but you keep the small fish?"

"Oh, that's simple," said the other man. "All I have is a ten-inch frying pan."

It's sad to say, but there are a lot of people like that. Instead of making room for increase, instead of believing for great things, they go around with that ten-inch frying-pan mentality. It's been in their family for generations. Mama used it. Granddaddy used it. It's an attitude that says, "I could never live in that neighborhood. I could never afford that college. I'll never be that successful. Our family always struggles. We've always been this way. We're just ten-inch frying-pan people."

That's the way my father was raised. He was exposed to poverty, lack, and defeat. In high school, he was given the Christmas basket donated for the poorest family. All they could afford to drink was something called "Blue John" milk. It was milk with the cream drained off, which gave it a blue tint. On farms it was usually fed only to the hogs. It wasn't meant for people to drink. My father couldn't stand it.

To make matters worse, my father's name was John. He thought: "Why did they have to call it Blue John? Why couldn't they call it Blue Mark, Blue Bill, or Blue Leroy?"

My father was tempted to think: "This is just my lot in life." Every circumstance said, "You've got a ten-inch frying pan." But at seventeen years old he gave his life to Christ and something rose up inside of him—a faith, a boldness, that said, "My children will never be raised in the poverty and defeat I was raised in."

He rejected the ten-inch frying-pan mentality. He took the limits off God and went on to live a blessed, abundant life.

No matter how you were raised or what has pushed you down or held you back, God is saying, "I created you as the head and not the tail. I made you to lend and not borrow."

God has some big fish in your future. Do yourself a favor and get rid of that ten-inch frying-pan mentality. Who says you can't rise out of poverty? Who says you'll never own a nice home? Who says you'll never take a mission trip? Who says you'll never start a charity? Who says you'll never send your children to college? Who says you'll never meet the right person?

All it takes is one touch of God's favor. Get in agreement with Him. God has explosive blessings in your future, blessings that can thrust you years ahead. Second Peter 3:8 says, "To the Lord a thousand years is like one day and one day is like a thousand years."

If you'll stay in faith, God can take a thousand years of blessings and release them in one day. Dare to say, "God, I'm asking You to give me the blessings that my ancestors missed out on."

That may seem far out, but we serve a far-out God. What He has planned for your future is more than you can imagine.

I read about a twenty-nine-year-old baseball player who was on a minor league team but dreamed of making it to the Major League. Several years ago he bought a fifty-acre plot of land from his great-aunt so she could afford to move into a senior's home. He paid $1,000 an acre—$50,000 for the land.

The land really wasn't worth that much. It was out in the country, in a small town. He did it just to help out his family member. He thought about building a home there, but discovered that the ground was too hard. But that turned out to be a very good thing. A surveyor discovered that right under the surface of the property was solid stone, a type of rock called Goshen stone.

It's some of the most beautiful and sought-after

landscaping stone around. Geologists estimated there were twenty-four million tons of this stone on his property. It sells for about $100 a ton, which means the stone on his land was worth more than $2 billion!

If you open your mouth wide God will fill it. I'm asking you to get rid of the cup, get rid of the bucket, and get rid of the barrel. God has a barnload of blessings stored up for you. Don't let a limited mind-set hold you back. You may not see how it can happen, but God has a way. If you'll take off the limits and make room for Him to do something new, you'll go beyond the barriers of the past and step into the abundance God has in store.

PART
II

Consider God,
Not Circumstances

CHAPTER SIX

Unshakable Faith

When God puts a promise in your heart, you have to come to the place where you believe in that promise so strongly no one can talk you out of it. It may seem impossible. Your medical report may say there's no way you will get well. It may look like you'll never get out of debt. All the circumstances may indicate you'll never accomplish your dreams, never meet the right person, or never see your family restored. But deep down you've got to have this confidence—a knowing that God is still on the Throne.

He is bigger than any obstacle. He already has a way. He is working behind the scenes. What He promised will come to pass at the right time. You don't get discouraged if it takes a long time. You don't complain if there is a setback. You have this unshakable confidence.

This is what the Apostle Paul did. He had a made-up mind. He said in Acts 20:24: "None of these things moves me." What were these things? Circumstances that looked impossible, or people saying it will never happen, or negative or discouraging thoughts. His attitude was: "It doesn't change my mind. I'm not moved by what I see. I am moved by what I know. And I know if God is for me who dares be against me? I know all of God's promises are *yes* and *amen*. I know God has the final say."

Your attitude should be: "I'm not moved by what the medical report says. I respect and honor those trying to help me get well, but I know God can do what medical science cannot do. I know God made my body. Doctors can treat me, but only God can heal."

Or: "I'm not moved by the economy being up and down, by the stock market, or by my job situation, because I know God supplies all my needs. He's promised to prosper me even in a recession."

A parent's unshakable attitude might be: "I'm not moved by how my children are acting. I'm not stressed out because they're off course, or making poor choices. I know it's just a matter of time. As for my house and me, we will serve the Lord."

A single person might think: "I'm not moved by the fact that I'm single and I haven't met anyone. I know

God has already picked out the perfect person for me. God has already ordained someone to come across my path. I am fully persuaded this person is in my future."

That's an unshakable faith. You're not moved by the circumstances. You are not up when something good happens and down when you don't see anything happening. You know everything God promised you is in your future. So you live in peace. You are not upset, frustrated, or discouraged. You are content.

You know God is on the Throne working on your behalf, so you go out each day with passion, with expectancy, and looking for the great things God has in store. Abraham did just that. God gave him a promise that his wife would have a child. In the natural, childbirth was impossible for them. Abraham and his wife Sarah were each nearly a hundred years old. But it says in Romans 4:20–21: "Abraham never wavered in believing God's promise. In fact, his faith grew stronger, and in this he brought glory to God." How could Abraham have this unwavering faith when in the natural all the odds were against him? I could see how he could have had at least a glimmer of hope, but it says he was fully persuaded.

What was his secret? Romans 4:19 says, "He considered not the weakness of his own body nor the deadness of Sarah's womb." The key to having unshakable faith is to not consider your circumstances, but consider your God. Your circumstances, like Sarah's womb, may look barren. Your financial situation may look impossible. The medical report may look hopeless. All the experts may say you will never accomplish your dreams. If you consider only the negatives, you will be discouraged and doubt will creep in, keeping you from God's best.

You must be like Abraham instead and say, "I will not focus on the negative things in my mind or what the experts are telling me. I will not focus on how big my problems are. Instead, I will focus on how big my God is. He spoke the world into existence. He flung the stars into space. He's not limited by the natural. He has supernatural power."

When you focus on God instead of on your circumstances, amazing things can happen. We were headed to one of our events recently when we hit a traffic jam. The event was set to start at 7:30 p.m. We left our hotel with time to spare, but a car was stalled on the freeway. Traffic was barely moving. It should have taken us no more than thirty minutes to reach the arena, but after more than an hour on the road we were still a long way from our destination. It looked like we weren't going to make it on time.

One member of our group called ahead and

informed those waiting for us that we were running late. They sent a police escort to meet us and bring us in. When the officers found us, one of them got in our car to drive. He steered out of traffic and onto on the shoulder so he could drive around the other cars. After passing the stalled car causing the traffic jam, our driver steered back onto the clear freeway. He drove fifteen miles over the limit, even speeding past other patrol cars.

Our driver just waved to his fellow officers. We could break the law because the law was riding with us. Without that officer in the driver's seat, we would have been pulled over and ticketed for speeding. But because the law was in our car, we could exceed the speed limit. You can benefit in the same way. In the natural it may be impossible for you to get well. The laws of medical science may say, "no way." But the good news is Someone who is riding with you supersedes those laws. God's law supersedes the laws of medicine, the laws of science, and the laws of finance.

Too often we consider only what we can see and only where we are right now. You will limit yourself by thinking: "This is what I make and if I get a cost of living raise the next twenty years here's where I'll be." We analyze and do projections based only upon the cold hard facts. We look at charts and dissect data.

It's good to have a plan, but there are times when every circumstance and every report will say, "It's impossible. It will never happen. Might as well settle where you are." But you've got to dig down deep and say, "Wait a minute. I've come too far to stop now. I will not focus on just what my medical report says. I will not focus only on what my bank account looks like. I will focus on my God and His power to supersede all things in the natural."

Business may be slow. The economy may be down. But God says He will prosper you even in the desert. Your checkbook may say you will not make the mortgage payment, but God says He will supply all of your needs. It may seem like you will never get out of debt, but God says, "You will lend and not borrow."

Your medical report may say your only option is to live with that sickness, but when you consider God, He says, "I will restore health unto you."

When you focus only on feelings of discouragement and loneliness, you may not be able to foresee anything good happening in your life. But when you consider God, you realize your best days are ahead. Your future will be brighter than your past. The greatest victories are not behind you; they are in front of you.

Are you considering your circumstances? Or are you considering your God? He is called "the Great I

Am." He's saying, "I am everything you need. If you're sick, I'm your healer. If you're struggling, I'm your provider. If you're worried, I'm your peace. If you're lonely, I'm your friend. If you're in trouble, I'm your deliverer. If you need a break, I'm your favor."

When you consider God and not your circumstances, God will show up and do amazing things. My friend Courtney applied for a scholarship at a major university. She wanted to study acting and theatre. Twenty-six hundred students applied for only twelve scholarships. She could have thought, "What's the use? Those are terrible odds. Less than half of one percent." But instead of focusing on the odds, she considered her God.

Her attitude was: "God, You control the whole universe, and if You want me in this college, then I believe You will cause me to stand out. I'm not moved by what I see; I'm moved by what I know. I know Your plans for me are for good. I know You have far-and-beyond favor. I know You reward those who honor You."

A few months ago, Courtney was notified that out of twenty-six hundred applicants, she was one of the twelve chosen for a full scholarship, a very prestigious position.

In the Scripture, God asks Abraham, "Is anything too hard for the Lord?" You may be spending too much time analyzing your situation. You have so many facts and figures that you've talked yourself out of what God can do. If you spent more time considering your God and thinking about His greatness and the times He's made a way in the past—dwelling on His promises, declaring victory and favor—then like Abraham, and like Courtney, you will see God show up and do supernatural things.

When we acquired the Compaq Center for Lakewood Church, our architects said the renovations would cost about $100 million. We had to put in a whole new power plant and do many other major renovations. I thought: "How in the world will we pay for all that?"

Our financial team ran the numbers and projected how much the church would take in from donations in coming years. We considered selling a piece of property owned by the church. After running the numbers, we realized that even if everything went just right, we still would be significantly short of the funds we needed for renovations.

We couldn't make it work on paper. I studied those numbers so much that I woke up in the middle of the night dreaming about them. I analyzed them a hundred different ways, and no matter how I looked at the calculations we always came up short.

One day I did what I'm asking you to do: I said, "God I've considered the numbers. I've considered the facts. I've had very intelligent people give me charts, projections, and analyses. It doesn't look good. But now, God I'm changing my focus and considering you. I know you parted the Red Sea for Moses. You stopped the sun for Joshua. You protected Daniel from hungry lions. You took five loaves and fed five thousand. You turned water into wine. I know You did all of those great things back in biblical times, but in my life I've seen you heal my mother when she was diagnosed with terminal cancer. You brought my father out of poverty and defeat, leading him into a life of abundance and purpose. You spared my life on the freeway when my car was spinning around and an eighteen-wheeler was a few feet in front of me. You caused Victoria and me to stumble on a house that doubled in value overnight. Now You gave us this beautiful building when all the odds were against us.

"God, You said You would finish what You started in my life. You said we'd see the surpassing greatness of Your power. You said You would supply our needs according to Your riches."

When I changed my focus and considered my God instead of my circumstances, then my doubt, fear, anxiety, and negativity didn't have a chance.

Faith rose up. Expectancy rose up. Hope rose up. I became fully persuaded. I knew God would make a way, even though I didn't see a way.

That's exactly what happened. Today, all of us at Lakewood Church are not just believing for the promise, we're also enjoying the promise. We're not just dreaming the dream; we also are living the dream in our beautiful facility.

What you focus on is so important. What are you dwelling on right now? Is it the size of the obstacle, or the size of your God? If you go around all day thinking about your problems, worried, anxious, and playing all the negative scenarios in your mind, you will draw in the negative.

You're using your faith, but you're using it in reverse. It takes the same amount of energy to be negative as it does to be positive. It takes the same amount of energy to worry as it does to believe. I'm asking you to use your energy for the right purposes.

Most people have considered their difficult circumstances long enough. They've considered the medical report, the bank statement, and the odds against them over and over. Now it's time to make a switch and start considering God.

Why don't you spend that same time you would normally be worrying on thanking God instead? Thank Him for working. Thank Him for the answer that's on its way. Thank Him for being in complete control.

Instead of overanalyzing a bad situation, spend your time meditating on the Scripture: "God always causes me to triumph. I can do all things through Christ. I am strong in the Lord."

Instead of reading the bad medical report for the twelve hundredth time, overanalyzing every word, instead of spending four hours Googling that disease, reading about every person who has died from it, take the same time and go walk in the park and with every step say: "Lord, thank You for the healing flowing into me. Thank You that I'm getting better, stronger, healthier."

With every breath, pray: "Lord, thank You that You're still on the Throne. You have me in the palm of Your hand, and nothing can snatch me away."

Here's a key: When you make God bigger, your problems become smaller. When you magnify God instead of magnifying your difficulties, faith rises in your heart. That faith will keep you fully persuaded. Pay attention to what you focus on. Be aware of what's playing in your mind all day. Are you considering your circumstances, or are you considering your God?

One time Jesus was on His way to pray for a sick girl in a nearby town. Along the way He was stopped time and again, one delay after another. At one point these people came up and said to those with Jesus, "Tell Jesus He doesn't need to come any more. It's too late. She has died."

The Scripture says Jesus overheard it but ignored it. Sometimes in order to stay in faith you have to ignore a negative report. It doesn't mean you deny the facts and act like they are not there. Instead, just like Jesus, you may hear the negative report, but you choose not to dwell on it.

You don't go around defeated, thinking, "Just my luck. I knew I wouldn't get well. Look at this doctor's report." You may have one negative report, but the good news is, God has another report. The medical report may say as far as medical science is concerned you won't get well, but God's report says, "I am restoring health unto you and healing you of your wounds."

Whose report will you believe? The financial report may say you will never get out of debt, or that you could never afford the house you want, or you will never take a mission trip. You see the numbers. You've run all the projections. That's one negative report. Don't deny it, but choose to believe the report of the Lord instead.

God says, "Whatever you touch will prosper and succeed. You will lend and not borrow." Get in agreement with God. Other reports may say, "You'll never accomplish your dreams. You'll never meet the right person. You'll never get that promotion." God's report says, "Because you delight yourself in me, I will give you the desires of your heart."

If you are to have unshakable faith and become everything God created you to be, then learn to ignore the negative report and choose to believe the report of the Lord. One time Jesus saw some men on the beach folding up their fishing nets, putting their equipment away. They had been out fishing all night. Jesus asked them if He could borrow their boat so he could push away from the shore and teach the gathered crowds. They didn't know each other, but the men agreed and He borrowed the boat.

When Jesus was finished teaching, he thanked the fishermen by telling them to launch into the deep where they would catch a great number of fish. These men began to reason in their minds, and doubts rose up. They thought: "This man is a teacher. We're professional fishermen. This is how we make a living. We know when the fish bite and when they don't. We've been doing this for years. We are experts and this is not the time to fish. Nothing is biting."

The problem with some people is they know too much. They know all the reasons why they can't get well and why they can't get out of debt and why they won't be successful. Sometimes our intellects get in the way of what God wants to do.

A lady once told me after a Lakewood service that she had a rare form of cancer and a very short life expectancy. Even though I'd just talked about someone beating cancer three times, she had no hope. She told me all the details of why she couldn't get well. She gave me story after story of people who didn't make it. She went on and on about how the medicines that worked for other forms of cancer didn't really affect her type.

By the time she finished, she had convinced me. I was depressed, too. I wasn't even sick, but I was ready to plan my funeral! Do you know what her problem was? She knew too much. She analyzed it and reanalyzed it and studied it and thought about it and researched it. No wonder she didn't have faith.

It's good to have information. I'm not saying you should live with your head in the sand, but at some point you have to say, "I will not fill my mind with any more doubt and disbelief. Yes, I want to know the facts, but I don't need to know all the details of why I will not get well or why I'll never be debt free or why I'll never accomplish my dreams."

Sometimes you have to turn off your mind. If you listen to the experts long enough, they can talk you into the ground. With all the facts and statistics and details, they can make you feel defeated. It's like this guy I heard about who was standing on a bridge about to jump. He was so depressed, so discouraged. A man ran up and said, "Please, please don't jump. Just tell me what the problem is." For the next three hours, in great detail he told the man all of his problems. When he finished, they both jumped!

That's why I want to know the facts, but I don't want to know too much. If you don't cut off negative information it will depress you. Step out of the natural and say, "This may be impossible with men, but I know with God all things are possible."

The fishermen said to Jesus, "We've fished all night. We didn't catch anything. We're very experienced. We're very knowledgeable. This is not our first time out here. We appreciate your advice but we're the experts, we know the facts. The latest fishing report was e-mailed to us this morning, and nothing is biting."

Jesus told them in effect, "What I've promised you may not make sense in the natural, but I have supernatural power. Your report may say there are no fish out there, but you have to understand, I control the fish. They may not have been there last night, yesterday, or last week. But I can assure you the fish are out there right now."

Jesus finally convinced them. Even though it

seemed like they were wasting their time, one of the fishermen said, "Nevertheless at your word I will let down the net."

They had to turn off their doubt-filled minds. They had to ignore what their reasoning and logic and experience told them. I've learned God is not always logical. His ways are not our ways. They went out and caught so many fish that their boat began to sink. They had to call other fishermen to bring another boat.

Make sure you don't talk yourself out of what God wants to do in your life. It may not seem logical. All your reasoning may say it will never happen. You may feel you're too old, or you don't have the experience. It may seem that the report is too bad and all the odds are against you. But dare to do what the doubt-filled fishermen did and say, "God, this promise You've given me doesn't make sense. It doesn't seem like it will ever come to pass. I don't know why I should even get my hopes up. Nevertheless, if You say so, I believe so."

Mary, the mother of Jesus, did just that. She was a teenage girl living in Nazareth. One day an angel appeared to her and said, "Mary, you are a highly favored child of God. You will give birth to a baby without knowing a man, and He will be the Son of God."

God spoke an incredible promise to her. You can imagine the doubts that bombarded her: "You can't have a child without a man. That's impossible. That defies the laws of nature."

If Mary had just looked at what was possible in the natural she would have given up. But Mary understood this principle: She didn't consider her circumstances. She considered her God.

I love the way she replied to the angel. Mary didn't say, "This sounds really far out. It's not logical, I don't see how it could happen."

Instead, she was bold. She said, "Be it unto me according to your word."

Mary was saying, "I'm in agreement. Let it happen. If God says I'm highly favored, then I will not talk myself out of it. I believe I'm highly favored. If God says the impossible can happen, then I believe the impossible will happen."

That's the way we need to be when God puts a promise in our hearts. We may not understand how something can happen, but we don't reason it out. We don't come up with excuses. We do as Abraham did and become fully persuaded.

You may be sick, but God puts the promise in your heart that He will restore health unto you. You can say, "The doctor's report doesn't look good. My great-grandmother died of this same thing. It's been in our family for five generations." You can talk yourself out of believing the best, or you can do as Mary did and say, "God, if You say I will be well, then I believe I will be well."

Mary said something interesting when the angel told her she would have a child. She asked how that could be possible, since she had never been with a man. She was talking about the physical, but I believe there's a deeper meaning to her question. God was saying, "My promises are not dependent on man." You don't have to have a certain person to fulfill your destiny. You don't need your boss to give you a promotion. You don't need someone with power to help you catch a break. God's promises are not dependent on who you know or who you don't know. The main thing is for you to know Him. God controls it all.

The Scripture says promotion doesn't come from people, it comes from God. When it's your time to be promoted or healed or restored, God doesn't check with your friends, your boss, or your family. As the angel told Mary, God will make it happen without a man.

If God can do it without a man, then He can do it without a bank. He can do it without medicine. You may have spent long enough considering your circumstances. It's time to start considering your God. He is the all-powerful Creator of the universe. What

He has spoken over your life may seem impossible. It may look too big. When you run the numbers, it may not seem logical. But don't do as the fishermen did and overanalyze. Don't try to reason it out, because you'll talk yourself out of it.

Do as Mary did and say, "God, I don't see a way, but I know You have a way. Let it happen." When negative thoughts come, learn to ignore them. That's one report, but God has another report. He's saying, "What I have spoken over your life I will bring to pass. What I have promised I will do."

Because you have this unshakable faith, because you are fully persuaded then, like Abraham, God will do supernatural things in your life. He is bringing you out of debt into abundance. You will live healthy and whole. You will break every addiction. You will see your family restored. You will meet the right people. You will accomplish dreams greater than you ever imagined.

CHAPTER SEVEN

Be Confident in What You Have

It's easy to focus on what we don't have. People tell me often that they don't have the talent, the education, or the personality they'd like to have, but as long as you think you're lacking it will keep you from God's best. It's not enough to just have faith in God. That's important, but you should take it one step further and have faith in what God has given you. You have to believe you are equipped. You are empowered. You have the talent, the resources, the personality, everything you need to fulfill your destiny.

Here's the key: you don't need a lot of talent. You have exactly what you need. If you will use what God has given you, He will get you to where you're supposed to be. I've learned it's not necessarily the amount of talent, the amount of education, or the amount of money. What makes the difference is God's anointing on your life. You can have average talent, but when God breathes in your direction, you'll go further than someone with exceptional talent.

You can have an extraordinary problem, but with the favor of God, He can provide an ordinary solution and make you victorious. That's what happened with Samson when a huge army surrounded him. He had no weapons, no protection. All the odds were against him. He began to look around to try to find something to defend himself. All he could find was the jawbone of a donkey. He could have thought, "Oh, great, just my luck. I need a sword. I need a shield and all I have is this jawbone."

It was small. It was ordinary. But Samson didn't dismiss it. He was smart enough to realize that this jawbone was part of his divine destiny. He picked it up and used it to defeat the entire army. Even though that jawbone was ordinary, it became extraordinary when God breathed on it.

You don't have to be bigger, stronger, or tougher to overcome your obstacles. You don't have to have great talent in order to do something great. When you honor God with your life, you have the most powerful force in the universe breathing in your direction.

God knows how to take something ordinary and make it extraordinary.

Get in agreement with Him and be confident that you have exactly what you need. Don't ever say, "I don't have the strength. I don't have the looks. I'm too tall. Too short. I'm too young. Too old."

Zip that up and declare, "I am anointed. I am equipped. I am empowered. I am the right size, the right nationality. I know the right people. I have the right amount of talent."

The Bible tells us about a day when Jesus had been teaching thousands of people. It started to get late and the people were hungry. Jesus turned to his disciples and said, "I want you to give them something to eat." They were out in the middle of nowhere. There were no grocery stores and no other source of food. It seemed Jesus was asking the impossible. But here's a key: God will never ask you to do something and then not give you the ability to do it. I hear people say, "I know I need to forgive, but I just can't do it. It's too hard." Or "I know I should take that management position, but I don't feel qualified." The truth is they have exactly what they need.

The disciples weren't confident that Jesus could provide food for all those people. They said, "It's impossible. We don't see a way."

When Jesus heard all their excuses, He finally said,

"You've told me all about what you don't have. All I want to know is what you *do* have."

They said, "Jesus, we just have five loaves of bread and two fish. But what is that among so many?" They looked at what they had and dismissed it as not enough.

They were like those who say to me: "I'd believe if I had more talent, more education, and just more going for me..."

I tell them God says to you what Jesus said to his disciples: "Give Me what you have. Don't make excuses. Don't sit on the sidelines of life intimidated, thinking that you're unqualified. Put your life, your dreams, your goals, and your talent into God's hands."

You know the story: Jesus took the five loaves and two fish and prayed over them. It all was multiplied. And somehow it fed more than four thousand people. That's what happens when you give God what you have. He will multiply it.

Now what you have may seem small compared to what you're facing, compared to the financial difficulty, the medical problem, or the size of your dreams. You could easily be intimidated. But God is saying, "Just give Me what you have."

If you'll be the best you can be right where you are, living with confidence, believing that God is breathing in your direction, then God will do for you what He did for the hungry crowd. He will take the little and He will turn it into much.

Still, people say, "I've got a big problem, but I don't have big resources." That's okay. God does. He owns it all. He's got you in the palm of His hand. Your obstacle may be high but our God is the Most High. That enemy may be powerful, but God is all-powerful. He has the final say.

Here's what I've learned: God is not looking for supertalented people. He is looking for ordinary people who will take the limits off Him so He can show His goodness in extraordinary ways. Be confident in what you have. When David went to face Goliath, all he had was a slingshot and five smooth stones. It didn't look like much.

Goliath was nearly twice his size. Goliath had been trained in the military. He was wearing a full set of armor, had a lot of experience, and was extremely powerful. David was a teenager. He had no formal training, no equipment, and no battlefield experience. He was a shepherd. When Goliath saw David and how small he was, the giant warrior laughed. Goliath said in effect, "David, have you looked in the mirror lately? You are no match for me. I am bigger, stronger, tougher."

But David understood this principle: even though

his slingshot was small, he realized it was given to him by God as part of his divine destiny. The Scripture says David ran toward Goliath. You would think if you're half your opponent's size, you would sneak up. You would try to surprise him. But it's different when you know you are equipped and empowered. When you realize God has given you what you need, you will not shrink back in fear. You will run toward your enemies.

God used a simple slingshot to thrust David to a new level of his destiny. My question for you is this: Are you overlooking something small, something ordinary, that God has given you? Are you sitting back thinking, "I don't have the talent, the education. I don't know the right people."?

You have exactly what you need. It may seem small, but when you take these steps of faith God will do for you what he did for David. He'll breathe on your life and what was ordinary will become extraordinary. When my father went to be with the Lord in 1999, I knew I was supposed to step up and pastor the church, but I had never ministered before. I thought of all the reasons I couldn't do it. I don't have the experience. I don't have the training. I don't have the booming voice. I don't have the dynamic personality. On and on, I came up with all these excuses.

One day I heard God say something to me, not out

loud, but just inside my heart. He said, "Joel, you've told Me all about what you don't have. I'm not interested in that. All I'm asking you to do is use what you do have." I stepped out with a little talent, a little ability, a little experience, and a little confidence. I didn't have much to give, but I realize now I had exactly what I needed. It looked small. It seemed ordinary.

When you give God what you have, He will take the little and He will turn it into much. Now quit telling God what you don't have and what you can't do. Be confident. You have exactly what you need. It may not be as much as others have, and that's okay. You're not running their race. Don't envy their talent. Don't covet what they have. Don't wish you had their looks, their personality, or their opportunities.

If God gave that to you it wouldn't help you; it would hinder you. You're not anointed to be them; you're anointed to be you. When God breathed His life into you, He equipped you with everything you need to fulfill your destiny. You have the talent, the confidence, the strength, and the creativity to fulfill your purpose.

Now it may seem small at first. When I started, I felt unqualified and intimidated. But as you take steps of faith, believing that you are equipped, and confident in what God has given you, God will take the small and He will multiply it. One day you will look up and say, just as I did, "How in the world did I get to where I am?"

That's the goodness, and favor of God.

Here's how the Scripture puts it: "It's not by might, not by power, but by His spirit." It's not just talent. Not just education. Not just what family we come from. We excel and go places we've never dreamed of when the Most High God breathes on our lives. Sometimes, we feel like David must have felt: "All I have is a slingshot and he's five times my size."

You're up against a huge giant. But you can stay in faith. You don't have to lose any sleep. Your slingshot, with God's anointing, is more powerful than a giant warrior with no anointing.

You may be up against a major challenge in your health, your finances, or a relationship. You may feel that you have a big problem but little faith. Let me encourage you. It isn't necessary to have great faith. Just use what you have. Jesus told us that if we have faith as small as a mustard seed we can say to a mountain, "Be removed." Nothing is impossible.

When you use even small faith, God can move mountains. It is okay to say, "God, I don't know how this is going to work out. I don't know how my dreams could come to pass. I don't know how I could get over this medical situation. But God, I trust You. My life is in Your hands."

Even if it's small faith, that's what allows the Creator of the universe to go to work. The Scripture tells us that one time there were four lepers sitting outside the city gates. They were contagious, so they had to stay away from people. To make matters worse, an army surrounded their city. They cut off the water supply and they were waiting for the people to get so weak they could walk in and attack them. These lepers had nothing going for them and no future to speak of. But one of the lepers said to his three friends, "If we just sit here we're going to die for sure. Why don't we take a chance and march toward the enemy's camp and see what happens?"

Notice they didn't have great faith. They didn't say, "We know God will protect us, deliver us, and save us." Their attitude was, "We are 99 percent sure we're going to die. What do we have to lose?" They had small faith. They marched toward the enemy's camp.

Don't you know God saw them take that journey of faith? They could have been sitting outside the city gates depressed, bitter, and complaining, blaming God. Instead, they were using what they had—not much, just a little faith, a little effort, and a little strength.

The Scripture says, "As they marched toward the enemy, God multiplied the sound of their footsteps and caused them to sound like a vast army." When the enemy heard it, they thought they were under attack by thousands of troops. They panicked and ran for their lives, scared to death. They left in such a hurry they didn't even gather up their belongings. They left behind all their treasures, their livestock, and their food.

When these lepers arrived in the camp and nobody was there, they were amazed. They went back home and told their families. They all returned and gathered up the spoils. God not only saved their lives, He also used them to spare the entire city. That's what happens when you use what you have. It doesn't have to be great faith. Even little faith, just doing something small, just showing God that you're trusting Him, that's when supernatural things can begin to happen. God can cause people to hear what He wants them to hear.

Years ago when I worked in the television department at Lakewood Church, I was meeting with this salesman about buying television equipment. He had flown in from another state because this was a big order. We had a good meeting. He called back in a few days and mentioned that he could give us the discount we had requested. He said it was the largest discount he had ever given. He had been with the company over thirty years.

I said, "That's great. What is the discount?"

He seemed kind of confused. He said, "What do you mean, Joel? You told me the exact price. You gave me the amount that you could afford."

I thought, "I never told him that. That's not even my personality."

That was God causing him to hear what He wanted him to hear.

Here's what I've found: God can cause you to be seen the way He wants you to be seen. You may not feel very powerful or very influential. The good news is it's not how you feel that matters; it's how God causes you to be seen.

Get in agreement with God. You may not feel it, but part of faith is acting like it. Act like you're strong, anointed, confident, secure, empowered, and blessed. You've probably heard the saying, "You've got to fake it till you make it."

Don't ever say, "I don't have the strength. I don't have enough money. My company could never compete with this other business. They've been going for years."

You don't know how God is causing you to be seen. You may feel weak, but because of God's favor on your life, everyone you encounter thinks you're as strong, as confident, and as successful as can be.

What is that? It's God causing you to be seen the way He wants you to be seen.

Do yourself a favor. Don't tell everyone how you feel. Just put your shoulders back. Stand up tall; don't act weak or intimidated, but like a child of the Most High God. When you stay in faith like that, God will multiply what you have. He will multiply your talent, multiply your resources, and multiply your influence.

God is a God of multiplication. What you have may be small right now, but you need to get ready. It won't stay small. You will come into increase, to good breaks, to the right people, to healing, to restoration, to new opportunities, and to favor like you've not seen before.

When Moses was leading more than a million people through the desert trying to get to the Promised Land, they had just come out of Egypt, and it didn't look like they had any way to protect themselves. They appeared vulnerable to their enemies. Moses was down and discouraged. People were complaining. He was just about to give up, thinking that he didn't have what it took, but God said to him, "Moses, what do you have in your hand?"

He was holding a rod. He looked at it and said, "It's nothing, God. Just a stick. Something I picked up along the way."

God said, "Throw it down."

He threw it down and it turned into a snake.

God said, "Pick it up."

He picked it up and it turned back into a rod.

God was showing him he had what he needed. It looked ordinary. It looked insignificant, just a rod. But if it needed to be a key to open a door, God could turn it into a key. If it needed to be a shield to protect him, God could turn it into a shield. God was saying, "I can become what you need. I can turn a rod into a snake. I can take four footsteps and cause them to sound like a vast army. I can use a simple slingshot to defeat a skilled warrior."

Quit talking about what you lack and start using what you do have. You may have small faith today. That's okay. Use it, and God can move mountains. You may have average talent. That's all right. Use it, and God can do something exceptional. You may feel weak but don't you dare act weak. Put your shoulders back. Hold your head up high, and God will cause you to be seen the way He wants you to be seen. It's not by your might, not by your power.

Right now God is breathing on your dreams. He is breathing on your finances. He is breathing on your health. He is breathing on your children. His favor will cause you to go further than you ever thought possible. God is going to multiply what you have. He will multiply your talent, your resources, and your creativity.

This is not the time to shrink back in fear. This is the time to move forward in faith. Get up every morning knowing you are anointed. You are equipped. You are empowered. You have everything you need to fulfill your destiny.

CHAPTER EIGHT

Yes Is in Your Future

When God laid out the plan for your life He lined up the right people, the right breaks, and the right opportunities. He already has your *yes*es planned out. Yes, to that promotion. Yes, to a clean bill of health. Yes, you will get married. Yes, you will be accepted into college. You may have been told *no* a thousand times, but God has the final say and He says, "*Yes* is coming your way."

Yes, you will accomplish your dreams. Yes, you will overcome that addiction. Yes, your children will fulfill their destinies. *Yes*es are in your future.

Now here's the key: On the way to *yes* there will be *no*s. You have to go through the *no*s to get to your *yes*es. The mistake many people make is that they become discouraged by the *no*s and they quit trying. They worked hard but didn't get promoted. They prayed and believed but didn't qualify for the new home. They put time and energy into a relationship, but it didn't work out. Now they think it will never happen.

You have to go through your closed doors before you reach your open doors. When you come to a *no*, instead of being discouraged the correct attitude is "I'm one step closer to my *yes*."

What if you could see into your future and discovered you would receive twenty *no*s before you came to your *yes*? Then you'd be prepared to handle it when you faced a disappointment or a setback. If you knew your *yes* was only twenty *no*s away, you wouldn't give up if a loan didn't go through, or you didn't get a big sales contract you'd hoped to land. You would just check it off and say, "All right. That's one *no* out of the way. Now I'm only nineteen away from my *yes*." Rather than being discouraged, you would be encouraged every time you heard a *no*.

But too many people, because they've hit several *no*s in a row, they lose their passion. You've got to get this down in your spirit. *Yes* is in your future. You may have been turned down, delayed, overlooked. That was all a part of God's plan. The *no* is simply a test. Will you become discouraged and settle where you are? Or will you keep moving forward knowing that *yes*es are coming your way?

A church member told me that his supervisor at work was about to retire, and he was in line for the job along with two coworkers. He had the most seniority. He had worked for the company faithfully for many years. But he was passed over for the promotion. They chose a younger, less experienced person. He felt cheated.

The situation did not seem fair but he understood this principle. He knew there were already *yes*es in his future put there by the Creator of the universe. He didn't grow bitter. He didn't quit being his best. He shook it off and kept working unto God. About two years later, the vice president of the company retired, and they offered him that top job. His position now is many levels higher than that supervisor position he'd been denied.

God knows what He is doing. You may be in a *no* right now. Maybe a relationship ended, or you were passed over for a promotion, or you lost a loved one. Don't be discouraged. Instead, say, "I may be in a *no*, but I'll never give up on my dream. I know a *yes* is coming. Favor is coming. Healing is coming. Promotion is coming. I will not become stuck in a *no*. I know *yes*es are in my future."

The Scripture says, "All of God's promises are yes and amen." We should get up every morning and say, "Father, thank You for some *yes*es today. Yes, I'm healed. Yes, I'm free. Yes, I'm surrounded by Your favor."

I read that 90 percent of all first-time businesses fail. Ninety percent of all second-time businesses succeed. But 80 percent of those who start one business and fail never try a second time. What happened? They get stuck on a *no*. They become discouraged and think, "It didn't happen last time. It will never happen." They fail to realize they were just one *no* away from seeing it succeed.

Have you ever given up a few *no*s away from seeing a dream come to pass? What if you knew you had to go through only three more *no*s and then you would meet the right person? You would probably go out and find people to meet just to tell them *no*, and get them out of the way!

I have a friend who wanted to start a new business, so he went to his longtime bank for a loan. He had tried the business concept on a small scale and succeeded. He needed his bank to loan him the money to buy some major equipment so he could take the business to another level. He went to the bank he'd used for many years. Everyone on the staff knew him. They loved his business plan. He had proven that the concept worked on a smaller scale. But lending money was very tight. They turned him down.

It was his first *no*. He could have become discouraged and given up, but he went to another bank. The second bank told him the same thing: "It's a great idea. It's just not for us."

Ten banks turned him down. He kept trying: Twenty banks said *no*. Thirty banks said *no*.

You'd think he would get the message and turn negative, thinking, "This will never work. I'm wasting my time."

But when God puts a dream in your heart, when He gives a promise on the inside, deep down you know that you will succeed. You know your family relationships will be restored. You know your health will return. You know your business dreams will come true.

Like my friend, you realize that every *no* simply means you are one step closer to your *yes*. Thirty-one banks said *no*. Thirty-one banks said, "You're not for us." But bank number thirty-two came along and said, "We really like it. We'll take a chance. Yes, we will do it."

God had my friend's *yes*, but he had to go through thirty-one *nos* to get to it.

You don't know when your *yes* will come. You may only be five *nos* away. Or, who knows, maybe the next person you meet will be your *yes*. The next college you apply to will be your *yes*. The next time you resist the temptation, you'll break the bad habit. It will be your *yes*.

You may have seen the beautiful actress Janine Turner on television shows like *Dallas*, *Northern Exposure*, and *Friday Night Lights*, as well as many movies. This very nice lady has been to our services at Lakewood Church. Janine told me that from the time she was a little girl she had a dream of becoming an actress. She loved singing, performing, and entertaining. As a teen, she became a model and then played some small television and movie roles, but she wanted to be a more serious actress.

Between the ages of fifteen and twenty-seven, she went to as many as four auditions a day, every week, month after month, even year after year, with no success at finding a substantial role. She calculated during those twelve years she had been told *no* over one thousand times.

Time and again she heard: "You're not what we're looking for. There's not a role for you. This is not your strength." She went through a great deal of disappointment and rejection. Many actresses might have given up after one or two of those *no*s, but not Janine. Her attitude was: "That's just another *no* out of the way. Now I'm closer to my *yes*."

Janine kept pursuing what God placed in her heart. And one day when she had just a few dollars to her name and didn't know how she could pay her bills, the top producer from a major network called her about a starring role that would change her life.

"We are starting a new prime-time drama. We think you would be the perfect lead actress. We're calling it *Northern Exposure*." The show became a huge hit for five seasons, winning many awards. Janine Turner became a star thanks to that big break. But she had to go through a thousand *no*s to get to that one *yes*.

You may struggle with your own challenges; maybe it's a bad habit or an addiction. You think, "I have tried a thousand times to break this." I'm asking you to try one more time. The next time may be your *yes*.

Most likely we won't have to go through a thousand *no*s like Janine Turner. My question is, "Are you willing to go through a dozen?" Will you keep trying if five banks turn you down? Will you stay in faith if three medical reports in a row are not good? Will you take a chance on meeting somebody new if your last two relationships didn't work out? If you're to keep moving forward, you have to keep reminding yourself: "Yes is in my future. Yes, I will get married. Yes, I will be promoted. Yes, I will fulfill my destiny."

I read about an experiment in which researchers put a predator and its prey—a barracuda and a Spanish mackerel—in the same fish tank. Normally the barracuda would immediately devour the much smaller Spanish mackerel. But in this experiment the researchers put an invisible glass partition between the two fish so when the barracuda saw the Spanish mackerel and went in for the kill, it slammed into the glass partition again and again, bruising itself every time. Eventually, the barracuda got the message that he wasn't able to eat that other fish.

When the barracuda finally gave up, the researchers quietly removed the glass partition so nothing separated the two fish. What's interesting is the barracuda never again went after the Spanish mackerel. They lived happily ever after, side by side in the same fish tank. The barracuda became conditioned to think eating the mackerel would never happen. All it heard was, "No, no, no." The barracuda didn't think there were any *yes*es in his future. It had to try only one more time and the *yes* would have been there. The barracuda would have had a nice fish dinner.

What happened to the barracuda happens to many people after they've hit the wall many times, so to speak. You may have tried to break an addiction for years, but you failed. You may have worked hard, but didn't get the promotions you sought. Maybe you pursued dreams, but you ran into closed doors time and again. Like the barracuda, we've let this stronghold convince us that it will never happen.

How do you know that God has not removed the glass partition that was holding you back? How do you know that the next time you try won't be your *yes*? The partition separating you from your dream may have been up for years, but God can remove it in a split second. You'll never know unless you keep trying, you keep dreaming, you keep pursuing what God put in your heart.

In the Scripture there is a story about the Prophet Elijah and a great drought in the land. Elijah went to the top of Mount Carmel. He prayed and asked God to end the drought. After praying, he said to the people, "I can hear the sound of an abundance of rain."

He was saying, "There's a *yes* in our future. Rain is coming."

Elijah told his assistant to look on the other side of the mountain to see if there was any sign of rain. The assistant went out, and came back to report, "No, Elijah. There's not a cloud in the sky. It's perfectly clear."

Elijah didn't get discouraged and think, "I must have heard God wrong. There's not any rain coming. What will we do?" Instead, he said: "That's one *no* out of the way. Now go back and look again."

The assistant went out and came back with the same answer, "Elijah, no rain."

Elijah must have thought, "That's fine. Two *no*s out of the way." Then he said, "Go back and look again."

Three *no*s, four *no*s, five *no*s, six *no*s. After the seventh trip, the assistant came back and said, "Elijah, this time I saw a small cloud in the sky. It wasn't much. Just the size of a man's hand."

Elijah said, "You'd better get your raincoat. Get your umbrella. Rain is coming our way."

You see, it may be a small *yes*, a faint *yes*, a barely-see-it *yes*, but when you're expecting things to change in your favor—when you know God has *yes* in your future—you will latch on to even a small sign by faith. "That's my *yes*. Other people may not see it. Other people may try to talk me out of it. Other people may say I'm just too positive, too hopeful. That's okay. I'm a believer and not a doubter. I know that's my *yes*."

It wasn't any time before the heavens opened up and they saw the abundance of rain. But had Elijah given up on the first *no*, the second *no*, the sixth *no*, it would have never happened. Think about this. When Elijah sent his assistant out to look, that was an act of his faith. Faith is what causes God to move. There are *yes*es in your future waiting for you to come looking for them.

Not once. Not twice. Not a few times. Keep looking. Keep expecting. Keep dreaming. You've got to have a made-up mind. You are in it to win it. You will not let people talk you out of it. You will not give up because it didn't happen on your timetable. You will not settle for second best because a few doors have closed.

When Thomas Edison was trying to invent the lightbulb, he failed on his first two thousand attempts. Two thousand times he tried and it didn't work out. Two thousand times he was told no. He could have given up and quit, but he just kept looking for that one *yes*. After Edison came up with a working lightbulb, a reporter asked him about all of his failed experiments. He said, "I never failed once. I just found two thousand ways that wouldn't work."

You may have had some setbacks or disappointments, or you tried something that didn't work out. These were not a waste of your time. Every challenge you've gone through has deposited something on the inside. God doesn't waste anything. You are not defined by your past. You are prepared by your past. Just because you've had some *no*s, you are not disqualified from success. *Yes* is still in your future.

When you hit your big *yes* like Edison did, all the other *no*s will become insignificant.

Do not feel badly because you're not where you want to be right this minute. Don't focus on the disappointment, the failure, or the mistakes. They were all a part of God's plan to prepare you for your *yes*. Keep moving forward, being your best, honoring God, being determined and persistent, and God promises *yes* is in your future.

CHAPTER NINE

God Is Preparing the Way for Victory

We all face situations that seem impossible. It's easy to become discouraged and think that things will never work out. But the Scripture says God is going before us making our crooked places straight. You may not have the connections right now to accomplish your dreams, but you don't have to worry. God is going before you and lining up the right people. He's arranging the right breaks, the right opportunities.

You may have lost a job or had your hours cut back. It's easy to get negative and think nothing will ever change. But you have to realize this loss is not a surprise to God. He's not up in the heavens scratching His head, thinking, "Oh, no. Now what will I do?"

God has already written every day of your life in

His book. He knew exactly when that setback would occur, and the good news is He has already arranged a comeback. Before you had the problem, God already had the solution. He is going before you right now preparing the next chapter of your life. If you will stay in faith and keep the right attitude you will enter a better chapter, a chapter with greater victories and greater fulfillment.

Coworkers may be trying to push you down, playing politics. They may have more seniority than you. They may be more powerful. But when you understand this principle you won't be upset. You won't go in there and try to play their games and prove to them who you are. Instead, you will stay in peace knowing that the Most High God, the Creator of the universe, the One who controls it all, is going before you. He promised to fight your battles. He will be your vindicator. He will make your wrongs right. If you will stay on the high road and just keep being your best, you will see the hand of God at work in amazing ways.

It may not happen overnight, but at the right time, in your due season, God will not only move the wrong people out of the way, but He also will pay you back for every injustice. He will make up for lost time and guide you to where you're supposed to be. You may be discouraged and think that your situation will never change. Maybe you can't see anything happening. But if the curtain was pulled back, you could see into the unseen realm. There, you would see God at work arranging things in your favor.

He's planning to open this door and bring a certain person across your path. He's getting you in position for the right opportunities. He's even looking years down the road and arranging solutions to problems that you haven't had yet.

I want you to get this down in your spirit like never before: "God is going before me making my crooked places straight." You may have gone through a disappointment, an unfair situation, but don't settle there. Don't sink into self-pity. In your future, God has already lined up a new beginning, new friendships, and new opportunities. It's right up ahead of you. Maybe last year was rough on your finances, or in your career. If you had some setbacks, don't make the mistake of expecting this year to be the same. Get a new vision. This is a new day.

You may have taken a couple of steps backward in recent times, but let me declare over you that God will thrust you forward. God has planned explosive growth in your future. He has already lined up new sales, new clients, new business, and new partnerships. Your attitude should be: "Yes, the economy is down, but I'm not worried. I know God is going before me, and He has promised He will make rivers in the desert. He will prosper me even in the midst of a recession."

If you have health concerns, your attitude should be: "The medical report may not look good. Some may say I just have to live with this sickness. But I have another report, and it says that God is restoring health unto me. I believe that in my future, God has already released healing, health, and victory."

If your child has strayed off course, getting that child back may seem impossible in the natural, but your report should be, "I know God can do the impossible. I may not see a way, but I know God has a way. I believe God is going before my child lining up the right people to come across his path, taking away the wrong people, breaking every force of darkness, opening his eyes to every deception, and giving him the wisdom to make good choices to fulfill his destiny."

The Scripture tells us that the people of Israel faced an impossible situation. They could have easily settled where they were. In fact, their parents, whom God brought out of Egypt, had done just that. They thought their enemies were too big and their obstacles were too great. This thinking kept them from God's best. Many years later, their children and grandchildren stood by the Jordan River, about to cross over and go into the Promised Land. But this land was occupied by incredibly strong, powerful people called the Anakites. They were actually descendants of giants. In the natural, the people of Israel didn't have a chance. You can imagine how intimidated they must have felt knowing that they had to face these huge warriors. As they stood there at the Jordan, no doubt contemplating whether or not they should go through with it, God gave them a promise that helped push them over.

He said in Deuteronomy, chapter 9: "Today you are about to face people much stronger and much more powerful. You've heard the saying, 'Who can stand up against the Anakites?' But the Lord your God will cross over ahead of you like a devouring fire to destroy them. He will subdue them so that you can quickly conquer."

You may be facing a situation that seems as impossible as theirs. Maybe the people you are up against are much more powerful, or you are facing a health issue, a financial difficulty, or a legal challenge. It may appear that you don't have a chance. But God is saying to you what He said to the people of Israel: "The Lord your God will go before you and take care of your enemies so that you can quickly conquer them."

You need to receive that in your spirit. You will

come out of trouble quicker than you think. God is fighting your battles for you. You will get well quicker than you think. Your recovery will amaze the doctors. You will accomplish your dreams much quicker than you think.

Supernatural breaks are coming your way. How could this be? The Lord your God is crossing over ahead of you.

The Scripture says: "Who can stand up against the Anakites? They're big. They're strong. They're descendants of giants." In modern-day terms your concerns would be more like: "You've heard the news. The economy is down. The stock market is low. You can't be blessed. You can't be successful this year." Or, "You've heard what the medical report said. You are very sick and might never be healthy again." Or, "You remember what that coach said about you growing up. You're not talented. You don't have what it takes."

The next time someone says something discouraging to you, or the next time your own thoughts try to convince you how impossible a situation may be, just give the same reply God gave to the people of Israel.

"Yes, it may look impossible. Yes, my challenges are big. All the odds are against me. I'm not denying the facts. But I'm not worried about them. I know God has the final say, and He has promised He will cross over ahead of me and defeat my challenges for me. So my declaration is, 'I will quickly conquer them.'"

Switch over into faith. Get in agreement with God. Those obstacles trying to hold you back don't have a chance. Nothing can stand against our God. Turn around those negative thoughts that say you will never get well, never accomplish your dreams, or never overcome an addiction. Make a declaration of faith instead:

"I will overcome this addiction quickly."

"I will get well quickly."

"I will accomplish my dreams much quicker than I think."

You won't do this by your own strength or by your own power. You will accomplish this because Almighty God, the One who holds your future in His hands, will go before you, fighting your battles, and making crooked places straight.

A few years ago, I got to be friends with a man who spent several days installing equipment in our church office. We really hit it off in that short period. He lived in another state, so I saw him only once or twice over the next couple of years, but it was always like old times with him.

Then, twelve years after I first met this man, Victoria and I came into a once-in-a-lifetime business opportunity in his field of expertise. The first thing

I did was call him. He came down, and over a period of a couple of months he negotiated a very complicated contract and put it all together. The business became a huge success.

I would not even have pursued that opportunity had I not known that man. I realize now God brought him into our lives many years earlier, not just for the friendship, but for that specific purpose, too. God knows what's in your future. He knows every opportunity ahead of you. That's why He is crossing over in front of you to make sure the right people will be there when you need them.

You may think that you met someone just by accident, or that it was just a coincidence. But one day you will look back, like I did, and see how God used that person in an instrumental way to help you move closer to your divine destiny.

My brother Paul and a group of surgeons were in Haiti right after the big earthquake. They were operating on many of the injured people. One day the main monitor they'd been using to keep an eye on patients' oxygen levels, blood pressure, and pulse rates stopped working.

Without that monitor they couldn't do any more surgeries. It was too dangerous to work without tracking patients' vital signs. Paul and the other doctors put out the word that they needed another monitor. They made phone calls and did everything they could do to make their need known, but at first they had no success.

They decided to pray and ask God to give them a monitor so they could continue helping the injured people. Not long after they began praying, the administrator of the hospital, a Haitian man, came walking up. He was beaming from ear to ear, carrying a brand-new monitor still in the box, never used. It was the exact monitor they needed.

Paul and the other professionals were so amazed.

"Where in the world did you find this monitor?" my brother asked.

"I was at a convention for hospital administrators in America two years ago, and everyone who attended was automatically eligible for a door prize. I won, and the prize was this monitor."

Two years before the problem occurred—two years before the big earthquake—God had already provided a solution. Right now, God is crossing over ahead of you. He is lining up the right people, the right supplies, and the right circumstances. He knows what you will need a week from now, a month from now, even ten years from now. And the good news is, He's already taken care of it. Quit worrying about how it will work out. God is saying to you what He said to Joshua, "Be strong and of good courage."

You have someone fighting for you. The Creator of the universe is breathing in your direction. His hand of favor is upon your life. He is crossing over ahead of you, making your crooked places straight. As long as you live a life to honor Him, God has promised nothing will be able to stand up against you.

I think about the airplane that Captain Chesley "Sully" Sullenberger safely landed on the Hudson River in New York. You remember how the plane hit those large birds and both engines lost power. Now they were several thousand feet in the air, 150 or so people on board. The plane had no power. The situation looked impossible. But Captain Sullenberger is an incredibly experienced pilot. As a young man he served in the U.S. Air Force flying fighter jets. He received the Outstanding Cadet in Airmanship Award at the U.S. Air Force Academy. He served as a safety consultant for NASA and is considered one of the leading experts in flight safety in the world.

Not only that, Captain Sully is a certified glider pilot. For thirty-six years he has been flying planes with no power. Very few, if any, pilots had more experience and more expertise in flying a plane without any engines than Captain Sully. Isn't it interesting? Of the tens of thousands of flights that take off and land safely every year without any problem, the one flight that would lose power in all the engines would be piloted by the one man you would choose to be at those controls if you had planned it ten years in advance.

God knows what He is doing. He can see the big picture. God knows what's in your future: every setback, every disappointment, and every danger.

God will make sure you are in the right place at the right time, and He also will make sure the people you need will be in the right place at the right time. He is crossing over ahead of you. If it's not your time to go, don't worry about it. You will not go. Nothing can snatch you out of God's hands.

Well, you say, "Joel, if God is in control, then why didn't He stop the birds from hitting the engines of Captain Sullenberger's plane in the first place?"

God will not stop every adversity. He will not prevent every challenge. But if we will stay in faith, God promises He will bring us through every challenge and get us wherever we're supposed to be.

I like the saying "God never promised us smooth sailing, but He did promise us a safe landing." Sometimes God will allow challenges just to display His goodness in a greater way. Do you know what a testimony that was to see an airplane safely landed in the Hudson River? More people acknowledged God and His goodness that day than just about anything I've seen in my lifetime. News reports all over the world led their newscasts with stories about the "Miracle on the Hudson." People who did not believe in God were scratching their heads and saying, "That had to be divine intervention."

I want you to have a new confidence, a new sense of trust, knowing that as a believer you have an advantage. The Creator of the universe is not only fighting your battles, He also is lining up the right people, the right breaks, and the right opportunities. Just as with Joshua, God is crossing over ahead of you. Just as with Captain Sully, God will place the right people in your path. Just as with my brother Paul and the surgery monitor, God has the solution before you had the problem.

You may be facing a situation that looks like it will never turn around. Let me declare this over you: You will see it turn around quicker than you think. You will come out of debt quicker than you think. You will accomplish your destiny much quicker than you think.

CHAPTER TEN

The Gracious Hand of God

If you've seen the popular television show *The X Factor*, you know the judges are looking for contestants who have that indefinable *something* that makes them stand out as performers. No one can define exactly what that special quality is. It's not just talent, not just looks, not just personality. There's just something about them that makes them special, something that gives them an advantage.

I've heard the judges say, "I don't know what it is but you've got it."

They call it the X Factor.

When God breathed His life into you, He put something in you to give you an advantage. There is something about you that makes you stand out, something that draws opportunity, something that causes you to overcome obstacles, to accomplish dreams. On that television show they call it the X Factor, but the Scripture calls it "the gracious hand of God."

This something special is God's favor. It's His blessing. You can't put your finger on it. But you know this is not just your talent, your education, or your hard work. It's Almighty God breathing in your direction. You could call it "the favor factor."

Like me, you may wonder sometimes, "How did I get to where I am? This was not just my own ability." My mother often asks, "How did I overcome that sickness when the medical report said no way?" You may think, "How could I be this happy, this blessed, after all I've been through?" That's not just good fortune, not just a lucky break. That's the gracious hand of God giving you His favor and His blessing on your life.

Psalm 44 says, "It was not their own strength that gave them the victory. It was because You favored them and smiled down on them." Just like these people, the victories you've seen in the past weren't just your own doing. God favored you. You wouldn't be where you are if the gracious hand of God was not on your life. Every accomplishment, every good break, every obstacle you've overcome, was God opening the door, God bringing the right people, God turning it around. The Creator of the universe was smiling down on you. His gracious hand is at work in your life.

Now you may not have as much education as somebody else. But that's okay. You have an advantage. You have this favor factor. Maybe you don't come from the most influential family. That's all right. God's favor can take you where you cannot go on your own.

Deep down you have to know there is something about you that is indefinable. It can't be measured, can't be put on paper, and can't be explained. Other people won't be able to figure it out. All they know is you've got it. There is something about you they like, something that causes you to succeed. That's the gracious hand of God.

When you realize you have this advantage, an edge, you'll go out each day not intimidated by your dreams, not discouraged or thinking that the problem is too big. No, you'll put your shoulders back. You'll hold your head up high and go out with a spring in your step, confident, secure, knowing that you have what it takes. You have the favor of God.

Recently a friend told me that he wanted to start a business, but ran into a problem. He had done all this great research. He put together a fantastic presentation. But then he realized he didn't have enough experience in this type of business. When he looked at it all on paper, he wasn't qualified. His heart told him, "Yes, I can do this," but his mind kept coming up with reasons why it would not work out.

You have to remind yourself that because you keep God in first place, because you honor Him with your life, there is something about you that can't be put on paper, something that's indefinable. It's Almighty God breathing in your direction. It's God causing good breaks to come. It's the right people being attracted to you. It's the Still Small Voice giving you inside information, letting you know things that are critical to your success and can't be measured.

You can have less talent, but with God's favor you'll go further than people who have more talent. You can have less experience and less training, but because Almighty God is smiling down on you, you will go farther than people who have more training and more experience.

If you own a small business, you may not have all the equipment, all the marketing, all the money backing you up that your competition has, but because you honor God, His favor can cause you to defy the odds and outperform companies that should be running circles around you.

One of our Lakewood members had this happen to his small computer company. Even though he has only three employees, a new client came to him from a competitor that was more than a hundred times his size. This other company had a huge staff, offices all over the world, and practically unlimited resources, but this client said, "We like your work. We're going to move our account to your firm."

Now his company is outperforming a competitor many, many times his size. That other company's executives are scratching their heads, thinking, "What is it with this man?" I'll tell you what it is. It's the gracious hand of God. It's God's favor causing him to stand out. God's favor is causing people to be drawn to him.

It's not how influential or educated someone is; when you have the favor factor, you have an advantage. God's favor opens the right doors. His favor will bring good breaks. The favor of God will cause you to accomplish what you could not accomplish on your own. It gives you an edge.

Now, if you're to see the gracious hand of God at work, you can't go through the day intimidated, thinking that you're average or just hoping for some good breaks. You have to carry yourself as if you have God's hand on you. You have to think like you have favor, talk like you have favor, walk like you have favor, and dress like you have favor. Not arrogantly, thinking that you're better than somebody else, but just living with this quiet confidence, knowing that you have an advantage. You have an edge. The gracious hand of God is on your life.

That was what Nehemiah did. According to the Scripture, he heard that the walls of Jerusalem had been torn down. People were living in the city unprotected. God put a dream in his heart to rebuild those walls. In the natural it was impossible. He was living more than a thousand miles away, working as a cupbearer to the king. He didn't have the money, the manpower, or the influence. On paper he didn't have a chance. The dream was much bigger than he could accomplish on his own. But Nehemiah understood this principle; he knew he had the favor factor.

One day he asked the king for permission to take a leave of absence to go back to Jerusalem and build those walls. Notice his confidence, his boldness. He wasn't high up in the king's staff. He wasn't a cabinet member, an advisor. He was working in the kitchen, cleaning the tables. But when he asked for the time off, the king didn't hesitate.

"No problem, Nehemiah," the king said. "Go ahead and go back and rebuild those walls."

God caused him to have favor. But Nehemiah didn't stop there. He said: "Your Majesty, I need your help. I need you to write letters to all the leaders of the regions telling them I will be traveling through their realms, telling them who I am and what I'm doing. Your letter will assure that I'll have protection, so they won't harm me."

The king agreed. Nehemiah wasn't finished.

"One more thing," he said. "I don't have any money. I don't have any resources. I need you to write a letter asking the people who own the timber mills and the supply houses to give me materials to rebuild the walls of Jerusalem."

Once again the king said, "No problem, Nehemiah. I'll do it for you."

Nehemiah left that day not only with the letters of protection, but also with the materials he needed to complete the task. Nehemiah 2:8 tells us why this happened. Nehemiah said, "The king granted me these requests because the gracious hand of God was upon me."

Nehemiah recognized he had the favor factor. He knew God had put something on him. Even though on paper he wasn't qualified—he didn't have the experience or the resources—he said in effect, "I have something better than that: the gracious hand of God is on my life."

When you understand you have this same favor, then like Nehemiah you'll rise up with a boldness, with a confidence, and you'll pursue what God has placed in your heart. Nehemiah arrived in Jerusalem and he saw the city was in total disarray, much worse than he expected. He found some people and shared his vision to rebuild the walls. Trying to convince them to help, he said in verse 18, "I told them how the gracious hand of God was on my life."

Notice how Nehemiah was always bragging on God's favor. No doubt some of them said, "Nehemiah, you can't do this. You're not a builder. You're not qualified. You don't have the experience. This is impossible."

But Nehemiah's reply was: "No, there's something about me you can't see, something that can't be put on paper. The gracious hand of God is on my life."

They started rebuilding these walls and had all kinds of opposition. The city leaders tried to shut them down. The critics tried to stop them. Bandits came and started fighting. Nehemiah faced one challenge after another, but the favor of God helped him to overcome them. It should have taken them at least a year to complete the walls, but they did it in just fifty-two days.

When you realize God's hand of favor is upon you, you will accomplish your dreams faster than you ever thought possible. You may be facing a situation like Nehemiah that seems impossible. Don't go around talking about how big the problem is, or how you're never going to make it.

Zip that up and do as Nehemiah did. Declare: "The gracious hand of God is upon my life."

How will you get out of debt?

"The gracious hand of God."

How will you get well?

"The gracious hand of God."

How will you break that addiction?

"The gracious hand of God."

How will you accomplish your dreams?

"The gracious hand of God."

The more you brag on God's favor, the more of His favor you will see.

We wouldn't be reading about Nehemiah today if he had thought, "I'm just average. I'd love to rebuild the walls but I don't have the money. My boss will never let me off. I live too far away."

Don't disqualify yourself. God's gracious hand is on you.

You have the favor factor, so don't keep dwelling on everything you lack, the mistakes you've made, or the greater talents of the competition. You're just looking in the natural, at what's on paper, but there is something about you that cannot be measured, something that goes beyond your talent, your education, or your ability.

It's the favor of Almighty God.

Quit telling yourself the wall is too big, the dream is too great, or the obstacles are too high. It will not happen in your own strength. It will not happen in your own power. It will happen because Almighty God favors you.

The victory will come because God smiles down on you. Get in agreement with God. Don't go around thinking negative, self-defeating thoughts. Instead, say: "Father, thank You that Your gracious hand is upon me. I know I have an advantage. I have an edge. Other people may not see it. They may try to push me down and disqualify me. But that's okay. I know the truth. I have the favor factor. I'm well able to fulfill my destiny."

That is what Nehemiah did and he is one of the heroes of faith. When you are in difficult times, you need to declare God's favor more than ever. David said in Psalm 41, "The favor of God keeps my enemies from defeating me."

In your finances: Business may be slow. You can't see how you will ever get ahead. You need to look at that debt, that lack, and say, "You will not defeat me. I have the favor of God. Whatever I touch will prosper and succeed." Speak favor over your finances.

In your health: Maybe you're facing a sickness. The odds are against you. The medical report says, "No way." Look at that sickness and say, "You will not defeat me. The gracious hand of God is on my life. Healing is flowing through me. I'm getting stronger, healthier, better, every day."

That is what Job did. He went through a nine-month period in which everything that could go wrong did. He lost his business. He lost his health. He had big boils all over his body. I'm sure they were very painful. His wife said, "Job, just curse God and die. It's never going to work out. This is the end of us."

Job had plenty of opportunities to be negative, bitter, and to blame God. Instead, Job understood this principle: he knew the favor of God would keep his enemies from defeating him. In the midst of the adversity it didn't look good. He felt bad. All the odds were against him. But he said in Job chapter 10, "God, I know You have granted me favor."

Job was basically saying what Nehemiah said: "The gracious hand of God is upon me." Now, in the natural it didn't look like Job had any favor. It looked like every bad break that could have come did. But this is what faith is all about. You can't wait until you see it before you decide to believe it. You have to believe it first and then you'll see it.

You may be thinking, "Joel, I don't have any of this favor. God's gracious hand is not on me. If you knew my situation, or if you could only see my problem, you would understand."

You are right where Job was. You're right where Nehemiah was. Your attitude will determine the outcome. In Job 10, Job said, "God, You have granted me favor." He didn't get restored and healed and see things turn around until chapter 42. Right at the beginning of the trouble, when it hit him the hardest, when he was the most tempted to get down, that was when he dug his heels in, lifted his face toward the heavens, and said, "Father, I want to thank You that I have Your favor."

No wonder Job came out with twice what he had before. No wonder his enemies couldn't keep him defeated. Many times we tend to put things off.

"God, as soon as it turns around, then I'll know I have Your favor. Then I'll thank You."

"God, as soon as I rebuild the walls, then I'll tell people Your gracious hand is upon me."

"As soon as I accomplish my dreams, then I'll brag on Your goodness."

Yet, what causes God to defeat our enemies, what causes Him to give us breakthroughs and supernatural abilities, is our offering of thanks to God for His favor, even though we don't see any sign of favor. He steps in when you say, "Father, thank You that Your gracious hand is upon me," even though nothing is going your way. Or when you say, "Lord, I know I've got what it takes," even though you feel unqualified, inferior.

That's what allows God to do amazing things. Job would have remained defeated if he had just sat back and thought, "Well, I'm a good person. I love the Lord. I hope God will do something about this trouble." Instead, Job came out with the victory because he kicked his faith into gear and spoke favor in the midst of the adversity.

You may be up against big challenges. This is not the time to be passive. More than ever, like Job, like Nehemiah, you need to declare God's favor. All through the day say, "Lord, thank You that Your gracious hand is upon me. Lord, thank You that Your favor keeps my enemies from defeating me. Lord, thank You that Your favor will make a way even though I don't see any way."

I was reading about this small fish called a Moses sole. It's a little flounder found in the Red Sea where there also are large sharks. Sharks would typically eat this kind of fish. But back in the early 1970s, a group of researchers noticed something amazing about the little Moses sole. All the other fish that were the same size and same weight were eaten by sharks, but for some reason sharks would not eat the Moses sole.

The scientists discovered that the Moses sole has a very unique defense system. Whenever it senses any kind of danger, this fish naturally secretes poisonous toxins from its glands. The toxins literally cause the shark's jaws to freeze. One report showed a picture of this little Moses sole inside the shark's mouth. The shark had obviously come in for the kill. All the predator had to do was bite down. Dinner would have been served.

But the shark couldn't do it. God put something on this little fish to protect him, and the shark's jaw was paralyzed. He had to swim away from the Moses sole for a few seconds before his jaw would return to normal.

That's what the Scripture means when it says, "The favor of God will keep my enemies from defeating me." God has put something on you that will cause you to be victorious.

The way you release these poisonous toxins, so to speak, to keep the shark's jaws frozen is by thanking God for His favor. Every time you say, "Lord, thank You that Your gracious hand is upon me," toxins are released that paralyze the enemy.

"Lord, thank You that I'm surrounded by Your favor." More toxins, more protection is released. But just the opposite happens if you go around talking about how big the problem is, how you will never make it. That negative attitude acts like bait and attracts the enemy, making it more difficult.

When you're in tough times, remember the Moses sole. If you are negative, worried, or start complaining, you will attract more difficulty, but if you'll dare to just declare God's favor, it will release a power to keep your enemies from defeating you.

When you really understand that you have God's favor, you won't become bent out of shape when trouble comes your way. Think about this little Moses sole. When it's in the shark's mouth, the little fish's blood pressure doesn't go up. He doesn't call 911. He doesn't become depressed and say, "Oh, this is not my day."

Instead, he goes about his business. He knows there is something special about him. Before the foundation of the world God ordained that he would be protected from that enemy, so he just rests in who God made him to be. When you have a revelation that you are a child of the Most High God, crowned with favor, then when adversity comes—when you face difficulties—you won't get worried or all bent out of shape. Like this little fish, you'll declare God's favor and you'll know that those enemies cannot keep you defeated.

I saw a report on the news a few years ago about a teenage girl who had driven her car into some high water on a flooded street. She was stranded in her car. The water was rising rapidly. In just two or three minutes, the floodwaters were over her hood. She couldn't open the car doors because the water pressure was too strong. She couldn't roll down her windows because they were electric and her car's engine had stalled.

The news report showed all of this as it was happening. My heart was beating so fast. She was in there just praying and praying. Then, a man jumped in the water and swam over to her car. He beat on the window trying to break it open but couldn't. The whole time the car was floating down the road. I'll never forget seeing this. It was like the news footage was in slow motion. At one point the car tilted forward and sank underwater.

My heart sank with it. About that time another man jumped into the floodwater and swam to the teenager's car like he was Superman. Somehow he found the submerged car. He dove underwater and disappeared for about thirty seconds. It seemed like an eternity. But in a few more seconds I saw the young girl's arm come up out of the water.

I thought, "How did he get a window open or a door open under there?"

Then, the rescuer pulled her out of the water and onto dry land. She was perfectly fine and walked off on her own two feet. If that wasn't amazing enough, when the wrecker pulled the car out of the water they noticed that no windows had been broken. No windows were down. There was no evidence that any doors had been opened.

The newscaster was dumbfounded. He said, "I don't know. You figure that one out."

When you walk in God's favor, no weapon formed against you will prosper. No matter how big the obstacle appears to be, the favor of God will keep those enemies from defeating you. Just like that little fish, God has put something in you. Start declaring His favor over your life. Speak favor over your finances, over your health, and over your family. All through the day pray, "Lord, thank You that Your gracious hand is upon me."

You, too, have this favor factor. It can't be measured. There is something about you that can't be put on paper. The bottom line is, you've got what it takes. Now do your part and activate this favor. In the tough times don't complain. Be like Job and say, "Lord, thank You. I know I have Your favor."

When the dream looks too big, don't give up. Be like Nehemiah and say, "Lord, thank You that Your gracious hand is upon me." If you'll do that, then like Job you will overcome every obstacle. Like Nehemiah, you will accomplish every God-given dream. I believe and declare you will become everything God has created you to be, and you will have everything God intended for you to have.

PART
III

Pray God-Sized Prayers

CHAPTER ELEVEN

Pray God-Sized Prayers

How you pray determines what kind of life you live. If you only pray small, ordinary, get-by prayers, then you'll live a small, ordinary, get-by life. But when you have the boldness to ask God for big things, you ask Him to open doors that might otherwise never open. You ask Him to take you further than anyone in your family. You ask Him to restore a relationship that looks over and done.

When you pray God-sized prayers, you will see the greatness of God's power. All through the Scripture we see this principle. Elijah prayed that it wouldn't rain, and for three and a half years there was no rain. Joshua prayed for more daylight, and God stopped the sun. Elisha prayed for protection, and his enemies standing right in front of him didn't recognize him. God made him invisible.

The common denominator is that they asked God to do the unthinkable. If you're to reach your highest potential you have to have this same boldness. When was the last time you asked God to do something impossible, or something out of the ordinary? One reason we don't see God do great things is that we ask only for small things. Most people pray over their food. They pray for protection. They ask God for wisdom. That's all good, but it's limiting what God can do. There should be something you're praying about and asking for that seems impossible, far out, something that you cannot achieve on your own.

The phrase I hear in my spirit is *Dare to ask.* Your dream may seem impossible. You may feel you don't have the connections, or the funding, but God is saying, "Dare to ask Me to bring it to pass. Dare to ask Me to connect you to the right people. Dare to ask Me to pour out a flood of My favor."

A lot of times we pray for small things: "God, my child is making poor choices. Could you just turn him around?" That's good, but that's an ordinary prayer. Ordinary prayer gets ordinary results. God meets us at the level of our faith. If you ask small, you'll receive small.

A God-sized prayer is "God, I'm asking You to not only turn my child around but God, use him in a great way. Let him touch people all over the world."

An ordinary prayer is "God, just help me to make it by this month. Just help me to pay my rent." There's nothing wrong with that. But a God-sized prayer is "God, I'm asking You to increase me in such a way that I can not only pay off my house but I can also pay off someone else's home."

An ordinary prayer is "God, just help me to go as far as my parents. Help me not to lose any ground." But a God-sized prayer is "God, help me to take our family to a new level. Let me set a new standard. When people look back two hundred years from now let them say it was that man, or that woman, who thrust our family higher than we have ever been before." That's a God-sized prayer.

I wonder how many of your prayers are not being answered simply because you're not asking.

You may tell yourself: "God is God. If He wants to bless me He'll bless me." But the Scripture says in James 4:2, "You have not because you ask not." If you're not asking big then you're shortchanging yourself. You will never reach your highest potential if you pray only small prayers.

I'm not suggesting that you can make a wish list and pray for every whim. I'm encouraging you to ask God for what He's promised you. There are dreams and desires God has placed in your heart. They didn't just randomly show up. The Creator of the universe put them in you. They're a part of your divine destiny.

You can tell a desire or dream is from God if it involves something bigger or grander than you could ever accomplish or acquire on your own. God does that on purpose so that it will take faith. Faith is what pleases God. Faith is what allows Him to do the impossible.

God will put something big where you don't have all the talent, the connections, or the confidence. He'll also allow an obstacle to come across your path, one that you cannot overcome under your own strength. When this happens, you can do one of two things. You can turn negative and say things such as:

"Too bad it's not going to work out."

"I don't have the connections."

"The medical report is not good."

"I can't get the financing."

You can talk yourself out of your dreams and desires. Or you can say, "God, I can't do this on my own, but I know You are all-powerful. You have no limitations. There is nothing too difficult for You, so God, I'm asking for Your favor to shine down on me. I'm asking You to make a way, even though I don't see a way. God, I'm asking You to open doors that no man can shut."

You need that sort of boldness to ask big. This is what David did: In 1 Chronicles 17, God promised him that one of his descendants would always be on the throne. He would have a lasting dynasty. David could have said, "God, I'm just a shepherd boy. I was tending my father's sheep. I don't have any formal training. I'm not as big, strong, or talented as others."

Instead, David understood this promise. Even though this seemed far out, David didn't dismiss it. He said in 1 Chronicles 17:23–27:

"Lord, God, do as you have promised. May the dynasty of your servant be established forever."

Imagine the nerve David had. Verse 25 gives the key. He said, "God, I have been bold enough to pray this prayer because you have spoken it over me." In other words, "God, I'm asking You for something big, not because I have all the talent, education, and connections, but simply because You promised it."

The dreams God has placed in your heart may seem impossible. But you have to do as David did and say, "God, You promised it, now I'm bold enough to ask You for it."

When you are that bold, don't be surprised if you have doubts such as:

"You could never do that."

"You don't have the talent."

"You've made too many mistakes."

"You come from the wrong family."

The enemy gets stirred up when you start asking God for big things. He'll leave you alone if you settle and pray only small ordinary prayers, but doubts will bombard your mind when you start praying these God-sized prayers and asking Him to take you places that you've never been, to touch a family member who has been off course, or to give you the hidden dreams of your heart.

Negative thoughts will come: "Who do you think you are?" Just smile and reply, "I am a child of the most high God."

A minister I know had a four-year-old son who was very sad when all but one of his pet goldfish died. Then, one morning, they found that last goldfish floating on the top of the water, totally stiff. The little boy said with great disappointment, "Daddy, he died, too."

The father just shook his head. Before he could respond, his son said, "Dad, can we pray and ask God to heal my fish?"

The minister wanted his son to know that he could pray about anything. But as a father, he also wanted to make it clear that sometimes our prayers aren't answered in the way we want. This debate was going on in his mind. Finally he quit reasoning with himself and said, "Yes son, let's pray."

Early the next morning, the father heard his son

shout, "Yes!" He ran over to see what the excitement was about and the little boy said, "Dad, it worked. The fish is just fine."

The goldfish was swimming around as healthy as can be. That dad nearly passed out. Before seeing the fish come alive, the father had his speech prepared: "Let me tell you, son, what happened." He threw his speech away and said, "God, You can do anything."

God didn't say when you pray you should make sure it's logical and reasonable and that you've got it all figured out. Instead, He encourages us to just believe and stay in faith. That's what allows God to do the extraordinary.

Have you talked yourself out of dreams? Have you convinced yourself that you will never overcome certain challenges? Why don't you follow the example of the minister's son and take the limits off God? What if your dreams aren't happening because you're not being bold enough to ask?

The Scripture says, in Luke 12:32, "It is your Father's good pleasure to give you the kingdom." God wants to give you the desires of your heart, but you have to have the faith of a child and be willing to ask.

As a father, I would rather bless my own children than anyone else. Who would any father most enjoy seeing excel and fulfill their dreams? Nobody more than his own children. That's the way it is with our

Heavenly Father, too. It is His pleasure to give you the kingdom. That brings a smile to His face. But what if my children never asked for anything? What if they were afraid they'd be bothering me or make me feel bad?

I would say, "Come on step up to the plate. I'm your father, I want to be good to you."

You may need to step up to the plate. Quit asking small. Quit acting like you're bothering God. Quit praying weak, get-by prayers. Your Father owns it all. He created the universe. If you want to see the fullness of what He has in store you should learn to ask big.

I pray every day: "God take this ministry where no ministry has ever gone before." I pray: "God let my children supersede anything Victoria or I have done."

There are things I pray in privacy that I've never told another person. These are my secret petitions. If I shared them, you'd think: "Are you serious? You really think that could happen?"

The fact is they may not all come to pass, but if I don't reach my highest potential, it shouldn't be because I failed to ask God's help. I don't want to get to Heaven and have God say: "Joel I had all this for you—abundance, good breaks, wisdom, favor, healing, and restoration—but you never asked. You never released your faith. You stayed in the safe zone.

I wanted you over in the faith zone. You prayed ordinary prayers. I wanted you to pray God-sized prayers."

I believe one reason I've seen God's favor in my life is that I've learned to ask big. When my father died and I had never ministered before, I prayed a bold prayer asking God to help me not only to maintain what my parents had built, but also for God to let me go further. It was a bold prayer when I walked in that jewelry store, met Victoria for the first time, and prayed: "God, please let her see how good-looking I am!" It was a bold prayer to ask God to help us build our church in the arena where the Rockets used to play basketball.

I look back over my life and wonder what would not have happened if I had not prayed bold prayers. Maybe I wouldn't have met Victoria. Maybe I wouldn't be ministering at Lakewood Church. Maybe I wouldn't have written books that have sold around the world.

It's good to ask God for your needs, but I'm challenging you to ask for your dreams. Ask for your goals. Ask for big things.

A friend told me about a young mother who moved her family from Puerto Rico to New York in search of a better life back in the 1960s. They were very poor, living in a rough neighborhood. There were all kinds of drugs and violence. Her son Victor was only twelve when a gang recruited him. Everyone he knew was in a gang. That was where he found camaraderie.

By the time Victor was fourteen he was hooked on heroin. He'd already been arrested, involved in stealing, robbing, and mugging. His mother was heartbroken. She couldn't control her son. She was a very small woman, and she spoke no English, but she was feisty.

One thing this mother knew how to do was pray. Every day, seven days a week and twice on Sundays, she would go early in the morning to a little storefront church in the projects with her sister. They would pray for her son. She didn't just pray that God would protect him, keep him out of trouble, and set him free from the drugs. This mother knew how to pray God-sized prayers.

She asked God to make him a minister and use him to bring other young men to God. While he was still doing drugs, Victor would come home at three in the morning, as high as can be. His mother waited for him in the kitchen. She would hug him and say, "Victor, God's hand is on you. He has a calling on your life. He's not just saving you; He is making you a minister."

She spoke faith into her son. At first, the more she prayed, the worse Victor acted. His teacher at school told Victor's mother, "Your son is going to end up in the electric chair. I've never seen anyone so out of control."

This mother didn't let that faze her. She kept praying, month after month, even though it didn't look like Victor was improving. What she didn't know was this: while she was praying, God was moving on a young man by the name of David Wilkerson, who lived in another state. God was calling this minister to come to the roughest streets of New York and share the good news.

One day, Victor came across David Wilkerson preaching on a New York City street corner. Victor responded to David Wilkerson's message and his life was transformed. In that moment, God touched his life. Victor knelt down and gave his life to Christ. God set him free from the heroin, brought him out of the gang, and removed him from a life of violence. Today, Victor Torres is not only free from drugs; he is the pastor of a great church, New Life Outreach in Richmond, Virginia.

Victor's church has huge outreaches to drug addicts and gang members who are going through the same challenges he went through. He goes all over the world telling his story, speaking to gang members and the troubled kids many have written off as hopeless. I wonder where Victor would be if this mother had not dared to pray a God-sized prayer. Maybe David

Wilkerson would never have shown up. Maybe Victor would be in the penitentiary or even dead.

But when it looked impossible, when all the odds were against her, every voice told this mother: "You're wasting your time. Your son is too far gone; he'll never amount to anything." She dug her heels in and said, "God, You promised that my house and I would serve the Lord. God, You made the promise, and like David, I'm bold enough to ask You for it."

Most people would have prayed a normal prayer: "God protect my son, don't let him get hurt, God keep him out of trouble." That's good. But when you know how to pray God-sized prayers, He will move Heaven and earth to bring that promise to pass.

You may have a family member you're just about to write off. Like Victor, your family member may be making poor choices. It may seem like this relative will never get better. I encourage you to keep on asking God to not only bring this person back, but also to help your relative do something great.

I've found when God touches somebody who has been living a radically wrong kind of life, the person begins living a radically right kind of life. God will use them to do amazing things. Just like this mother, you have the promise: "As for me and my house we will serve the Lord." It says in Psalms that the seed of the righteous will be mighty in the land. Not ordinary, average, normal, but exceptional, powerful, amazing.

Now, don't pray an average prayer over your children. It doesn't matter what they're doing or not doing. Pray a bold prayer: "God, I'm asking that my children will be mighty in the land. I'm asking You to use them in amazing ways. Let them leave a legacy of faith that will be seen for generations to come."

Dare to ask big. During a recent Lakewood service I prayed with a college student who had just completed her master's degree program. She's in medical research, a scientist. I don't even know why I said it, but I prayed, "God, let her find the cure for cancer. Let her make an astounding difference."

She started weeping. She said, "That's what my parents have prayed over me ever since I was a little child."

Someone might ask: "What if it doesn't happen?"

I prefer to think, "What if it does?"

You have not because you ask not. God is saying, "Ask Me for big things. I created the universe. I spoke the world into existence. I flung the stars into space. Don't ask Me for a two-dollar raise. Don't ask Me to just keep your child out of trouble. Don't ask Me to just survive through life.

"No, ask Me for Compaq Centers. Ask Me to turn drug addicts around. Ask Me for children who will make history. Ask Me to part Red Seas. Ask Me to bring water out of a rock. Ask Me to open the windows of Heaven and pour out floods of favor, floods of mercy, and floods of my goodness."

God is saying: "I dare you to ask. I dare you to take the limits off Me. I dare you to think bigger. I dare you to stretch your faith, I dare you to pray God-sized prayers."

In Matthew 20, Jesus was walking through a village near two blind men sitting on the side of the road. They heard all the commotion and excitement about Jesus coming and they began to holler out, "Jesus, have mercy on us."

People around them said, "Be quiet, you'll disturb Him. You'll upset Him."

They shouted out even louder: "Jesus, please have mercy on us."

Jesus went over to them and said something interesting. He asked, "What is it that you want Me to do?"

It was obvious what they wanted. They were blind. Why would Jesus ask what they wanted? He wanted to know what they believed. They could have said, "We just need somebody to take care of us. It's hard because we're blind. We just need a better place to live. We need shelter."

These two men did not disappoint Jesus. They

were bold. They said, "Lord, we want our eyes to be open."

When Jesus heard their request, He touched their eyes and for the first time they could see. Imagine Jesus standing before you right now, and He says to you what He said to these blind men: "What is it you want Me to do?"

Your answer will determine what God does. Don't say, "God, I just want to make it through this year. Times are tough, God, I just want my family to survive. We're so dysfunctional. God, I don't like my job but just help me to endure it."

Dare to say, "Lord, I want to be free from this pain. I want to break this addiction. I want to get married. I want to see my whole family serving you. I want to pay off my house. I want to start this business."

It's not enough to just think it. It's not enough to just hope something supernatural happens. When you ask, God releases favor. When you ask, angels go to work. When you ask, strongholds are broken. When you ask, the Most High God begins to breathe in your direction.

God said in the Psalms, "Open your mouth wide and I will fill it." My question is this: How wide open is your mouth? What are you asking for? Are you praying bold prayers, or are you praying get-by prayers?

God has put seeds of greatness on the inside. He wants you to leave your mark on our generation. You're not supposed to come and go and nobody miss you. Break out of your box. Ask God for the secret petitions He's placed on the inside. If you can accomplish it on your own, then it's not a God-sized dream. Enlarge your vision.

My family and some of our staff members were at the airport parking lot late one Friday night. We had just done a Night of Hope event in another state. It was two o'clock in the morning. We got to our cars and discovered that my mother's car battery was dead. The lights must have been left on. My brother Paul and I went to work with my friend Johnny. We found some jumper cables. I pulled my car next to my mother's and put the cables on both cars. The lights in her car came on, but we couldn't get it to start. The engine wouldn't turn over at all. It didn't make a sound.

I revved my car and we waited, trying to charge up the battery. Ten minutes later, we tried to start it again, but not a sound. The engine wouldn't budge. A mechanic from the airport came out to help us. He worked and worked, but he couldn't make it happen.

Johnny got out the car's manual. He tried to see if there was something we were missing. It was freezing that night. After about thirty minutes of trying everything we could think of, Paul told my mother, "It won't start; just ride with me and we'll come get the car tomorrow."

My mother was not about to leave that car. She said, "No, Paul, I have two funerals to officiate tomorrow. I need my car."

It was now 2:30. Finally, I said, "Mother I'll give you my car tomorrow. You can drive it home tonight. Paul will take me home."

But our mother said, "I don't want your car, I want my car. Let's try it again."

We tried again. We worked at it another fifteen minutes, but still nothing happened. I said, "Mother we can stay here all night, the car is not going to start. We might as well go home."

"Give me the keys," she said.

She had that "don't mess with me" look in her eyes. I don't know if she was mad at me or at the devil. Probably both. She got in that car and started praying. When my mother really means business she prays loud. She makes sure God can hear her. I looked over there and my mother was praying over the steering wheel, praying over the radio, praying over the glove compartment.

She knows no shame. Growing up she would pray over the dishwasher, pray over the lawn mower. We're over there smiling, getting a kick out of her praying.

All of a sudden, we heard the car crank right up. The engine didn't turn over and over like it was struggling. It cranked up the first time.

My mother revved that engine so loud, she must have pressed the pedal to the floorboard. She held it there like she was running a race at Daytona. It sounded like the engine was about to explode. When she took off, we were running for cover. She drove around in circles in the parking lot—an eighty-year-old woman doing donuts at three o'clock in the morning.

I thought, "Dear God, she'll get us all arrested."

I wanted to tell her, "You're grounded."

When our mother finally drove off she didn't wave good-bye. She didn't say, "Thank you for trying." She didn't blow us a kiss. She just left us there standing in her dust.

When you face situations that seem impossible in your everyday life, God says, "I dare you to pray. I dare you to ask Me for that car to start."

You may think God has bigger things to deal with than getting a car started. But you are God's biggest deal. You are the apple of His eye. So often we limit God. We have a small view of Him. We think He's over there busy running the universe.

"I can't bother God with these small things. I can only pray if I'm facing a major catastrophe."

God knows the number of hairs on your head. He knows your thoughts before you think them and your words before you speak them. You're not inconveniencing God by asking for help in your everyday life. God wants to be good to you. He wants to show you His favor in new ways. He's saying today, "I dare you to ask."

Members of a small church in the foothills of the Smoky Mountains built a new sanctuary on land donated by one of their members. A month before the new church was to open, the local building inspector informed them that their parking lot was too small. Unless they doubled the amount of spaces they would not be allowed to open.

The problem was they had used every part of their property except the land behind them and it had a huge hill, almost a mountain on it. The pastor announced the next Sunday morning they would have a special prayer meeting that night to ask God to somehow make a way for them to open their new church.

Twenty-four of the members showed up and they began to pray. After an hour, the pastor announced, "God has never let us down before and He won't let us down this time. We will open as scheduled."

The next morning there was a knock on his door. It was a rough-looking construction foreman. He said, "Excuse me, Reverend, we're building a shopping center in the next county and we need some fill dirt. If you'll sell us the dirt on that mountain behind your new church we'll not only pay you for the dirt but also we'll pave all the areas where we dig up."

They got their parking lot for free and moved into their new building as scheduled.

When you pray God-sized prayers, God will show up in a big way. You may not be seeing great things, because you're asking only for small things. God is saying, "Ask Me to open doors that look impossible. Ask Me to connect you to the right people. Ask Me for that business you've dreamed about. Ask Me for the secret petitions of your heart."

If you're to become everything God's created you to be, you need a boldness to ask big. Like David, you must say, "God, You promised it. I see it here in the Scripture. Now I will be bold enough to ask You for it."

If you'll learn to pray these God-sized prayers, then, like with Victor's mother, you'll see your children become mighty in the land. Like with this pastor, the right people will show up at the right time. Like with that minister's son, God will give you the desires of your heart.

CHAPTER TWELVE

Remind God of What He Said

One of the most powerful ways to pray is to find a promise in the Scripture and remind God what He said about you.

"God, You said I'm blessed and cannot be cursed."

"God, You said with long life You would satisfy me."

"God, You said Your favor is not for a season but for a lifetime."

When you can say, "God, You said...," all of Heaven comes to attention. God is faithful to His word.

Isaiah 62:6 says, "Put God in remembrance of His promises." It doesn't say, "Put God in remembrance of your *problems*." Sometimes we use prayer as an excuse to complain: "God, these people at work are not treating me right." Or, "God, these gas prices are so high I don't know how I'm going to make it." Or, "God, these children are getting on my nerves. I can't take it anymore."

You don't have to tell God your problems. He already knows what you are going through. He knows every need and every concern. He knows the number of hairs on our heads. And sure, it's okay to be open and honest and tell God how you feel, but don't turn that into a self-pity session. All that will do is make you more discouraged.

If you want to see things change, if you want God to turn it around, then instead of complaining find a promise you can stand on. Go to God and say, "God, You said when the enemies come against me one way You would defeat them and cause them to flee seven different ways."

"Yes, these gas prices are high, but I'm not focused on that."

"God, You said You would supply all of my needs according to Your riches. You said You are Jehovah Jireh; the Lord my provider."

"Yes, people at work are not treating me right, but I'm not here to complain. God, You said You would be my vindicator. You said You would fight my battles. You said what is meant for my harm You will turn and use to my advantage."

When you put God in remembrance of His promises, you allow God to bring them to pass. You may not feel well. The medical report may not look good. You could easily say, "God, I don't see how I'll make it. I don't see how I will ever get well. The report is so bad."

Instead of putting God in remembrance of your problems, put God in remembrance of His promises. "God, You said You would restore health unto me and heal me of my wounds. You said I would live and not die. You said what is impossible with men is possible with God."

When you pray the promises instead of praying the problems, you will feel better, and it will change your attitude from a victim's to a victor's. God's word coming out of your mouth is alive and powerful.

When God hears His promises He dispatches angels with the answers. He sets the miracle into motion. He will change things in your favor. It may not happen overnight, but just stay in faith and keep reminding God what He promised you day in and day out.

Instead of complaining, remind Him: "God, You said…" Instead of begging, remind Him: "God, You said…" Instead of describing the circumstances, bring up His promises: "God, You said…"

If you will get in a habit of saying, "God, You

said...," then eventually you will see what God said come to pass in your life. One day instead of saying, "God, You said...," you will say, "God, You did it."

"You turned it around."

"You blessed me."

"You healed me."

"You favored me."

"You restored me."

"You vindicated me."

"You are true to what You said."

When we parents promise our children something, we will do everything possible to bring that promise to pass. Our daughter Alexandra loves to go to Disneyland. We took her there when she was just three years old, and she has been hooked ever since. Now she is a teenager, and we haven't been there in some time.

I was saying good night to her recently and she said, "Daddy, I really want to go back to Disneyland. Will you take me sometime?"

I didn't think much about it. I just said in passing, "Sure. I'll take you again. We'll go sometime."

"You promise?" she said.

"Yes, I promise."

I didn't know what I was getting myself into. The next morning bright and early, "Daddy, you said we're going to Disneyland. Now when are we going?"

I thought, "Man alive. I just got out of bed."

Every other day: "Daddy, you said, you said, you said."

I must have heard that a thousand times. She was not about to let me forget that promise. Needless to say, it wasn't long before we were back at Disneyland.

If we as earthly parents are that moved when our children remind us what we've promised—if we feel such a strong obligation to respond to the *You saids*—how much more will our Heavenly Father stand behind His word? He cannot lie.

We can break promises. I could have put off my daughter and not been true to my word, but God cannot go against His word. All of His promises are yes and amen.

You need to find some *You saids*.

"Father, *You said* I will lend and not borrow."

Remind God of that again and again.

Maybe business is slow, and you don't see how your situation could work out. Don't go to God with that. Take a *You said*.

"Father, You said You would open the windows of Heaven."

"You said my cup would run over."

"You said whatever I touch will succeed."

"You said You would prosper me even in a desert."

When you're constantly reminding God of what

He said, You are releasing your faith. I talked to a lady whose seventeen-year marriage was coming to an end. She was devastated. Her husband had left her for someone else. Her whole world looked like it was falling apart. In that situation, it's easy to get depressed and fall into self-pity and not have any hope for the future.

But I told her what I am telling you: you've got to find some *You said*s. "Father, You said You would give me beauty for ashes."

"God, You said You would pay me back double for the unfair things that have happened."

"God, You said my end would be better than my beginning. You said all things are going to work together for my good."

When you're tempted to fall into self-pity, just turn it around and declare a *You said*. All through the day we should be putting God in remembrance of His promises, just like my daughter Alexandra.

Eating breakfast, out of the blue, "Daddy, you said we're going to Disneyland. When are we going?"

"I don't know, Alexandra, yet."

"But Daddy, you said."

Finally, I told her, "Alexandra I know I've said it. You've reminded me 450 times." We went to Disneyland, not because I wanted to but because of what I'd promised.

Isaiah 62:6–7 says, "Put God in remembrance of

His promises. Keep not silent. Give Him no rest till it comes to pass."

That was what Alexandra did. She's an expert. She gave me no rest. She kept not silent.

When you are standing on a promise, you can't remind God one time and think that's good enough. It says, "Keep not silent." That means you have to be persistent. You've got to show God you mean business. Not nagging God, not begging God, but in faith going to God and reminding Him over and over what He promised you.

When you wake up in the morning and those dark thoughts come ("You will never get well. You will never accomplish your dreams. You will never get out of debt"), don't listen to them. Instead, kick it into gear.

"Father, You said the moment I pray the tide of the battle turns."

Taking a shower: "God, You said I am more than a conqueror."

Driving to work, "God, You said many are the afflictions of the righteous, but You deliver me out of them all."

At the office, under your breath: "God, You said You hold victory in store for the upright."

Driving home: "God, You said You go before me and make my crooked places straight."

It's not enough to do it one time and think you're done.

"Joel, I did this thirty-seven years ago."

You've got to be persistent. The Scripture says, "Keep not silent." You have to be a pest when it comes to reminding God what He promised you. Not begging. Not demanding but relentless.

Jesus told a parable about an unfair, unjust judge. This man neither feared God nor respected people. One day this widow woman came to him and said, "Judge, I have a problem. This man is bothering me. I need you to make him leave me alone. I need protection."

She was saying, "I have a promise from the government. The law is on my side. Judge, I'm asking you to enforce the law. Make him leave me alone."

This judge didn't give her the time of day. He didn't pay any attention to her. He said, "I'm not ruling on your case. Don't bother me with that. Just leave my courtroom."

She left, but she didn't get discouraged. She knew the law was on her side. She kept going back day after day, week after week. Every time the judge walked in his courtroom that woman was there making her case.

"Judge, enforce this law. It's my right. It's on my side."

Finally she wore the judge down. The judge said, "Lady, I'm going to help you not because I want to or because I like you. I'm going to do it just so you will leave me alone."

One Scripture says, "Because of your shameless persistence."

That's the way we need to be when it comes to reminding God what He said.

The good news is, God is not like this judge. God is for us. He is on our side. But if we're to see His promises come to pass, we must have this shameless persistence. Some promises you may have to stand on for a year, or five years, or twenty years. Whatever the case, like this lady, you should have a made-up mind. You are not remaining silent. You know what belongs to you.

My sister Lisa and her husband, Kevin, had been trying to have a baby for six years with no success. Lisa wrote a contract with God. She listed on a piece of paper all of the promises she was standing on concerning having a baby. She made it like a legal contract. She even signed the bottom of it, and she had Kevin sign it, too.

Isaiah 41 says, "Present your case before God. Make your arguments. Bring forth your proof."

Lisa wrote at the top of the contract: "God, Kevin and I are presenting our case to You. Our case is based on Your word. God, You said in Genesis 1:28 to be fruitful and multiply. God, how can we do that unless You help us?

"God, You said in Psalm 112 our children would be mighty in the land. God, how can that be unless you give us children?

"God, You said in Psalm 113 that You make the barren woman a happy mother of children. How can that be, God, unless You bless us with children?

"God, we've done all we know how to do. Now we're presenting our case based on Your word, knowing that You are faithful and true to what You have said."

She took the contract, that piece of paper filled with Scriptures, and she placed it on her bathroom mirror where she could see it. Again and again, week after week, month after month, she just kept reminding God what He had promised.

About two years later, God blessed them with twins, and today they have three beautiful children. God is faithful to His word.

My questions are: "Are you presenting your case? Do you have any proof? Have you done as Lisa did and found the promise He made so you can say, 'God, You said You would make me a happy mother of children.'"?

"God, You said You would restore what the enemy has stolen."

"God, You said You would give me the desires of my heart."

If you present your case before God, the good news is that Jesus is called our "Advocate." Another word for *advocate* is "lawyer." In the courtroom of Heaven, imagine Jesus is our lawyer. God is the judge. As long as you present your case based on God's word, you cannot lose. He will be faithful and true to His word.

It would be good for all of us to do as Lisa did, and make a list of the promises we're standing on. Put it up on your bathroom mirror; somewhere where you will see it often. All through the day, week after week, just keep reminding God what He promised you.

When those thoughts come telling you that you're never rising higher, you've seen your best days, present your case. You can say, "God, You said the path of the righteous gets brighter and brighter."

"God, You said the glory of the latter house will be greater than the glory of the former house."

"God, my case is not based on what I feel. It's not based on the economy. It's not based on a medical report. It's not based on what somebody said about me. My case is based solely on Your word, and I know You cannot lie. What You say, You will do."

That's what it means to present your case before God.

But sometimes, especially when it's difficult, instead of presenting our case we plead our case:

"God, please. You've got to help me."

"God, I went to church last weekend."

"God, I'm a good person. I volunteered at the shelter."

"God, I'm begging You to do something."

The problem with that is you don't have any proof. You're not taking any evidence. You're just describing to God how you feel. You're just describing all the circumstances.

But if you're presenting your case like you would in a court of law, you've got to be prepared. You don't just walk in and say, "Judge, I need some help." Instead, you take documents. You take evidence. You've done your research. In the same way, when you go into the court of Heaven, so to speak, you've got to remind God what the contract says.

"God, You said no weapon formed against me will prosper. Here's my evidence: Isaiah 54:17."

"God, You said You are a very present help in my time of trouble. Here's my evidence: Psalm 46:1."

"God, You said the strength of the wicked is being cut off but the power of the godly is being increased. Here's my evidence: Psalm 75:10."

When you go to God with evidence, with what He said, that's a powerful case. That's an unbeatable case. You may be busy pleading your case, but if you switch over and start presenting your case, you will see God begin to change things in your favor.

I know a lady who was at odds with her teenage daughter for several years. She often came to Lakewood to pray. She was always upset and discouraged. I would do my best to cheer her up and try to convince her to keep believing, but it seemed like she wasn't coming in to pray so much as to complain that God wasn't doing enough.

I shared with her this principle: instead of complaining to God, you need to remind God what He promised you. I gave her the Scripture in Proverbs 31:28. It says, "Children will rise up and call their mother blessed."

Now, this woman's daughter was calling her every name except blessed. But still, the mother took it to heart. She stopped complaining and instead went through the day praying, "Father, You said my children will rise up and call me blessed."

Instead of complaining when the daughter was disrespectful, the mother prayed, "Father, You said my daughter will call me blessed." She found other promises: "God, You said children are a gift from God to be enjoyed."

She presented her case, made her arguments, and brought forth her proof. About three years later her daughter had a total change of heart. Today, the mother and daughter are best friends. She's as kind and respectful as can be. They do everything together, including coming to church together.

The mother told me just recently, "Joel, now when I say, 'My children will rise up and call me blessed,' I don't say it by faith anymore. It's become a reality. God has brought that promise to pass."

That's what God wants to do in all of our lives.

Are you pleading your case, or are you presenting your case by reminding God what He promised you? There is an amazing promise in Genesis 12:2 that God makes to all of us. Referring to the seed of Abraham, God says, "I will make your name great." Another translation says, "I will make your name distinguished." That's a great promise to remind God.

I have a friend who grew up in a family with a very bad reputation. Their name was anything but distinguished. They were known for crime, drugs, and other illegal activities. Many of his relatives had gone to prison. Their reputation as criminals went back for three or four generations.

As a young man he gave his life to Christ. He headed down a better path. He was doing his best to overcome all this negative baggage, but it seemed like this dark cloud followed him everywhere he went. When people learned his last name, especially in his community, they treated him differently. They didn't want to have anything to do with him. It was like he wore this badge of dishonor.

I told him to remind God of His promises. Every

day he needed to say, "God, You said You would make my name great. You said if I would honor You, You would honor me."

Instead of pleading his case and saying, "God, this is not fair. Why was I born into this family? Why do I have to deal with this bad reputation?" he presented his case: "God, You said You would make my name distinguished."

He went on to become a very successful coach. One day, he brought me a photograph in which he was accepting an award. He was chosen as the Coach of the Year in his school district. In that school lobby there is a plaque with the names of all of the winners of that award. Each year they add a new coach to it.

He pointed to the top name. It said, "Coach of the Year" and under it in big, bold letters the plaque read, "Distinguished honorees." There was his name. He smiled and said, "Joel, God has made my name distinguished."

God is a faithful God. Don't plead your case. Don't tell God why you can't be successful, why you can't get well, why you'll never get out of debt. Present your case. Remind God what He said about you. Make a list of the promises you're standing on.

When you go to the courtroom of Heaven, so to speak, take some evidence. Bring your proof. "God, You said I'm blessed and cannot be cursed." Present your case like my sister Lisa: "God, You said You would make me the happy mother of children."

"God, You said You would restore what the enemy has stolen."

Don't keep silent. Remind God again and again. Not nagging God. Not begging God. No, go to Him in faith with a *You said*.

If you put God in remembrance of His promises and do not put Him in remembrance of your problems, then He will be faithful to His word. What God promised, He will do.

CHAPTER THIRTEEN

Power of Believing

One of the greatest abilities God has given each of us is our ability to believe. If you believe, you can be successful. If you believe, you can overcome mistakes of the past. If you believe, you can fulfill your God-given destiny. There is incredible power in what we believe.

What you believe is greater than what the medical report says. We respect medical science, but God has the final say. When you get in agreement with God and believe what He says about you, then what you believe can supersede any natural law.

What you believe is greater than what is in your bank account. I have a friend who came to the country with nothing but the clothes on his back. Today, he runs a Fortune 500 company. Against all odds, he believed he could do what God put in his heart.

Paul prayed in Ephesians 1:19 that we would understand the incredible greatness of God's power for those who believe. Notice the power is activated only when we believe. That means right now the Creator of the universe is just waiting to release healing, restoration, favor, promotion, and abundance. The only catch is that we have to believe.

Sometimes, God will put a promise in your heart that seems impossible, a promise that says, "You will be healthy. You will start a business. You will meet the right person and get married."

It's easy to think, "It's never happening to me. I've been this way too long. I've made too many mistakes. The medical report is too bad. Nobody in my family has been successful."

We can always come up with excuses. But instead of talking yourself out of it, just respond with three simple words, "Lord, I believe."

God says your children will be mighty in the land. "Lord, I believe."

God says He will restore the years that were stolen. He will bring you to a flourishing finish. "Lord, I believe."

God says whatever you touch will prosper and succeed. You will lend and not borrow, be the head and never the tail. Now, don't come up with five reasons why that will not happen. Your response should be: "Lord, I believe."

When you get in agreement with God, the incredible greatness of His power is activated.

In the Scripture a man came to Jesus and said, "My little daughter is very sick. She is close to death. Will You come to my home and pray for her?"

Jesus agreed, but along the way He kept getting stopped, one interruption after another. Finally word came back to Him saying, "No need to come. You've waited too late. The little girl has died."

The people were very distraught, but Jesus said to them, "Don't be afraid. If you will only believe, the little girl will be well."

Notice the phrase "only believe." Jesus went to the home, prayed for the little girl, and she came back to life. You, too, may be facing situations that seem impossible. In the natural you can't see how you could ever be healthy, how you could overcome the addiction, or how your family could ever be restored. But God is saying to you what He said to them: "If you will only believe, I will turn the situation around. If you only believe, breakthroughs are headed your way."

It's not complicated. God didn't say, "If you will pray three hours a day," or, "If you'll quote twelve chapters in the Scripture, then I'll do it for you." No, He said, "If you will only believe." In other words, if you will just get your mind going in the right direction and believe you can rise higher. Believe you can overcome the obstacle. Believe your family can be restored. Believe you can do something great and make your mark in this generation.

When you believe, the surpassing greatness of God's power is released. You may have to develop new habits. If you've been negative for a long time, you should retrain your thinking from "I can't" to "I can." From "It won't happen" to "It will happen." From "I'll never get well" to "God is restoring health unto me."

Reprogram your computer. Load in some new software.

First Chronicles 28:20 says don't be discouraged by the size of the task, for the Lord your God is with you. He will see to it that it is finished completely.

When you believe, God will see to it that it's taken care of. When you believe, you have the Creator of the universe fighting your battles, arranging things in your favor, going before you, moving the wrong people out of the way. You couldn't have made it happen in your own strength, but because you are a believer, the surpassing greatness of God's power is at work in your life.

Now don't be intimidated by the size of the problem, or the size of your dream. "Well, Joel, I was laid off, and you just don't know my financial situation."

But I do know Jehovah Jireh; the Lord our provider. He is still on the Throne. One touch of God's favor and you'll go from barely making it to having more than enough.

"Well, you just don't know my medical situation. It doesn't look good."

But I do know Jehovah Rapha; the Lord our healer has not lost His power. He has done it in the past. He can do it in the future.

"Well, Joel. I have big dreams, but I don't know the right people. I don't have the connections."

That's okay. God does. You have friends in high places. When you believe, God will bring the right people across your path. Don't be intimidated by the size of what you are facing.

Here's what I've learned: the bigger the problem, the bigger your destiny. The enemy would not be fighting you this hard unless he knew God had something amazing in your future. On the other side of that challenge is a new level of your destiny.

No disappointment. No setback. No injustice. No person. No hater. No jealousy can stand against our God. When you believe, all the forces of darkness cannot stop God from taking you where He wants you to go. Be a believer and not a doubter.

It says in the book of Hebrews, "When we come to God we must believe that He is." It doesn't really finish the Scripture. Believe that He is what? The passage leaves it open-ended. This is saying when you believe, God becomes whatever you need Him to be. He is strength when you're weak. He is healing when you're sick. He is favor when you need a good break. He is a way maker when you don't see a way. He is restoration when something has been stolen. He is vindication when you've been falsely accused. He is whatever you need Him to be.

You may know God by one name. You know Him as a Savior, and that's great. That's the most important way. But you need to find out what else He is. Do you know Him as a resurrection God, a God Who can bring back to life what you thought was dead? Do you know Him as an Ephesians 3:20 God, a God Who can do exceedingly, abundantly, above and beyond? Do you know Him as a healer, a restorer, a God Who gives beauty for ashes?

You may have endured hurts and disappointments, and people may have done you wrong, but you don't have to live defeated, depressed, in self-pity. God wants to heal the hurts, give you a new beginning, and bring you out better off than you were before.

But you've got to know Him as a God Who gives beauty for ashes. There is so much more to our God.

Don't keep Him in a little box. Discover what else He is.

This young couple who belong to Lakewood Church dreamed of buying their first home. For the last year and a half or so they've heard me talking about believing for Ephesians 3:20 and how God wants to show us His unprecedented favor. And they dared to believe. They let that seed take root. For the last ten years they've been working very hard, saving their funds, so they could hopefully purchase a home.

At one point everything came together. They found the house they liked. It was a good price. They had the money for the down payment and they were so excited. But when they went to close on the home, there was a problem. The young lady was finalizing details at the real estate agent's office when her husband called. He said he had just been let go from his job. He had worked for that company for over six years. He always worked hard and had a good attitude, but his supervisor never particularly liked him. Over the years his wife just kept encouraging him, "You're not working unto people. You're working unto God."

He did his best to stay on the high road, but it seemed like at the worst possible time he was let go. To make matters worse, this all happened on his birthday. He lost his job and the house of their dreams on the same day.

They were very disappointed. But the good news is this young couple didn't just know God as a Savior. They knew Him as a God of restoration. They knew Him as a God of justice, a God Who will make your wrongs right.

They could have easily gotten bitter and dropped out of church, but they understood this principle: if you believe, you will see the goodness of God.

Instead of sitting at home every day depressed, in self-pity, the young man was either looking for a new job or at our church working as a volunteer week after week, month after month, as faithful as can be.

In the natural it didn't look like anything was happening, but they weren't discouraged by the size of their problem. They knew that as long as they believed, the Lord their God would see to it that they were taken care of.

Five months after the husband was fired, he got a call from his old company. He hadn't talked to them since they let him go. It was an executive from the corporate headquarters. They had fired the old management team, and this new boss wanted him back. He not only restored his job but he restored all of his benefits, all of his retirement, all of his seniority.

That house they'd wanted to buy had been sold by this time, but they found a better house in a better neighborhood for a better price. Today, the young husband has his job back and they are living in their dream home. God is a faithful God.

Isaiah 3:10 says, "Say to the righteous, 'It shall be well with you.'" You may go through some difficulties. People may do you wrong. But because you're a believer it shall be well with you. You lost your job, yes, but another job is coming. It shall be well with you. The medical report doesn't look good, yes, but we have another report: it shall be well with you.

You may have been praying, believing for your situation to change for a long time but you don't see anything happening.

Just like with the Lakewood couple, God is working behind the scenes right now arranging things in your favor. The answer is already on the way. It's just a matter of time before it shows up. It shall be well with you.

I like to think having faith is like setting the temperature on a thermostat. You set the temperature to 72 degrees. Now it may be 96 degrees in the room, far off from where you set it. You could go to the thermostat and think, "This isn't working. It's not matching up." Instead, you know it's just a matter of time before the temperature in the room matches the temperature that you've set.

In the same way, we should set our thermostats on what God says about us. God says you will lend and not borrow. I'm setting my thermostat right there. That's what I'm choosing to believe. I may be far from that right now. I may be far in debt, but that's okay. I'm not worried. As long as I've set my thermostat, as long as I keep believing, keep honoring God, keep being my best, I know it's just a matter of time before the conditions in my life match up to the conditions in my thinking.

You may have a son who is at 140 degrees, out living wild. It doesn't matter. As long as your thermostat is set you're not worried. You're not frustrated. You don't have to live wondering if he will change. You know God is in complete control.

God goes to work when He sees you have a made-up mind. Your thermostat is set on His promises, on faith, on restoration, on healing, on victory. It may not happen overnight, but God is faithful. He will do what He promised.

You may need to readjust your thermostat. At one time you believed you would do something great. You believed you would start that business. You believed you'd beat that addiction. You believed you'd meet the right person and get married. But it didn't happen on your timetable. You grew discouraged and you gave up.

God is saying, "Reset the thermostat." Start believing once again. Believe you can live free from pain.

Believe you can move into that nicer home. Believe God is bringing the right people across your path. Keep the thermostat set. Have a made-up mind.

When it gets cold, or when it gets hot, stay in faith. Our attitude should be, "This is what God says about me. I am blessed. I will live and not die. My children will be mighty in the land. My latter days will be greater than my former days."

You may not see anything happening week after week, month after month, maybe even year after year. It doesn't matter. Your attitude is "My thermostat is set. I'm not moved by what I see, by what I feel, by what people tell me. I'm moved by what I know. And I know when I believe the incredible greatness of God's power is activated. I know when I believe strongholds are broken. Favor, healing, promotion, restoration, they are coming my way."

In the Scripture, Ezekiel was facing an impossible situation. There were dead bones in a valley. God had promised those bones would come back to life. Dead bones represent dreams and goals that we don't think will come to pass. God had the power to bring these dead bones to life, but God needed a person who believed so He could work through him.

God asked Ezekiel, "Do you believe that these dead bones can live?"

Isn't it interesting? God wanted to know what

Ezekiel believed. Ezekiel could have reasoned it out and said, "God, the bones are dead. I don't see how that's going to happen."

In the same way you could say: "The medical report doesn't look good, God. Business is slow. This is a big problem."

I can imagine God said, "Ezekiel, I'm not asking you all of that. All I want to know is: do you believe?"

All at once Ezekiel shook off the doubt and he said in effect, "Lord, I believe." The Spirit of God came on him. He started prophesying and somehow, some way, those dead bones came back to life.

God is asking us what He asked Ezekiel. "Do you believe you can live a blessed, prosperous, successful life? I've got the power. I'm just looking for someone who believes."

Do you believe God can turn that situation around? Do you believe you can overcome past mistakes? When you get in agreement with God and believe, that allows God to release the incredible greatness of His power.

When Lazarus was very sick his two sisters, Mary and Martha, sent word to Jesus and asked if He would come to their home in a different city and pray for Lazarus. But Jesus waited four days, which was too long. Lazarus had already died when Jesus finally showed up.

Martha was very upset. She said, "Jesus, if You would have been here sooner my brother would still be alive."

Have you ever felt God showed up too late for you? You prayed. You believed. But you still didn't get the promotion. You worked hard. You had a good attitude but the company still let you go. You stood on God's promises. You quoted the Scriptures, but your prayers were not answered.

That was the way Mary and Martha felt. They were discouraged, depressed, and probably a little bit bitter. Jesus looked at them and said, "Take me to the place where you have laid him." In other words, "Take me to the place where you stopped believing. Take me to the place where you decided it was over."

You have to go to that place in your life and ask yourself, "Is my God still on the Throne? Is my God still all-powerful? Is my God still El Shaddai; the God Who is more than enough?"

You've got to stir up your faith. God said, "Mary. Martha. It looks bad, but it's not over. If you will start believing once again, I will show you My power in a greater way."

Faith began to rise in their hearts. Martha said, "Jesus, if You would have been here my brother would still be alive. But I believe even now. You can raise him from the dead."

Sometimes you have to have "even now" faith where you say, "God, it looks impossible. It looks like it's over and done, but I know You are a supernatural God and I believe even now You can turn my finances around."

"Even now You can heal my body."

"Even now You can restore this relationship."

Mary and Martha shook off the doubt and they started believing once again. You know the story: Jesus raised Lazarus from the dead.

Back in those days the Sadducees, who were against Jesus, believed that the spirit left the body on the third day after a person died. It wasn't a coincidence that God waited for the fourth day to show up. Jesus waited on purpose so that when he raised Lazarus there wouldn't be any doubt. They would know that it was a great miracle.

Sometimes God will wait on purpose not only so you know that it's His power, but so your doubters, your naysayers, and your unbelieving relatives won't be able to deny that God has done something amazing in your life.

After Jesus raised Lazarus from the dead, He said to Mary and Martha, "Did I not tell you if you would only believe...?"

Mary and Martha at first were disappointed because Jesus didn't show up in time to heal Lazarus. They were disappointed that their prayers weren't answered in the way they wanted. But all along God knew what He was doing.

God wasn't planning a healing. He was planning something better. He was planning a resurrection. Just because you believed and it didn't work out your way, or on your timetable, doesn't mean that it's over. It means just the opposite.

God is planning something better. You believed and you didn't get the promotion. You believed and you didn't qualify for the new home. Keep believing. God has something better coming.

You believed but your child hasn't turned around. Keep believing. God will use your child in a great way.

You believed, but your year hasn't been that great so far. Keep believing. It's not over. God is still on the Throne. Even now God can still turn it around.

Keep the thermostat set. Right now, behind the scenes God is working in your life, arranging things in your favor. Don't be intimidated by the size of what you are facing. Stay in faith, and the Lord your God will make sure that it comes to pass.

Let this take root in your spirit. Because you are a believer, all will be well with you. All will be well with your family. All will be well with your finances. All will be well in your health. All will be well with your career. You need to get ready, because God's promises are about to come to pass in your life.

It may not have happened in the past on your timetable. That's because God is not planning a healing. He is planning a resurrection. It will be better, bigger, and greater than you've ever imagined.

Be a believer. Take the limits off God. Keep your faith stirred up. I believe and declare you are going to see God's goodness in amazing ways!

CHAPTER FOURTEEN

Have Uncommon Faith

One time Joshua was in the midst of a great battle. He and his men were trying to finish off this army, but the sun was going down. They were running out of daylight. Joshua knew that if he couldn't get this army totally defeated, then later on they would rise up and cause him problems. He could have easily got discouraged and thought, "It's not ever happening. Too bad for me." But Joshua had uncommon faith. He was bold. He said, "God, I know this is unusual. I know this out of the ordinary. But I'm asking You to stop the sun so I can have more daylight and totally complete this task."

Imagine the nerve of Joshua. He asked God to do something that had never been done before. God could have said, "Joshua, who do you think you are?

I am not going to stop the sun. That's kind of selfish. That might disrupt other people."

No, it's just the opposite. When you have this uncommon faith it brings a smile to God's face. I can see God turn to the angels and say, "Listen to what this man is saying. He's extreme. He's radical. He believes I can do anything. He's asking Me to stop the sun."

God said in effect, "Joshua, if you're bold enough to ask it, then I'm bold enough to do it." The Scripture says the sun stood still until Joshua completely finished off that army. There had never been a day like that before. The people stood there in utter amazement. What happened? God interrupted the entire universe just because one man had uncommon faith.

Uncommon faith is not average faith. It's not ordinary. It's above and beyond. It gives you a boldness and a confidence to believe for the extraordinary. Average faith says, "God, help me to survive this recession." Uncommon faith says, "God, I believe You will prosper me right in the midst of this recession." Average faith says, "Maybe one day I'll get out of this problem. I don't know. It's pretty bad." Uncommon faith says, "I know I'm not only coming out, I'm coming out better off than I was before." When you have uncommon faith you don't just believe to make your monthly house payment. You believe to totally pay off your house. You don't just ask God, "Help me to control my addiction." No, you ask God to totally set you free.

Uncommon faith is radical faith. It's extreme. You believe God can do anything. You don't make little plans. You don't say, "God, just let me go as far as my parents did. Let me do as much as they did. Then I'll be okay. Then I'll be successful."

Uncommon faith says, "God, give me a double portion. Let me do twice as much as those that went before me. Let me give twice as much. Let me have twice the influence, twice the wisdom, twice the friends, twice the creativity, and twice the income."

You may say, "Joel, that's kind of bold. Who do you think you are?" Here's who we are: we are children of the Most High God, full of uncommon faith.

Have you ever asked God for something out of the ordinary? When I began ministering right after my father went to be with the Lord, I was very concerned about keeping up our church attendance. I was doing my best every week, praying, believing, and studying. But I knew from years past that anytime it rained on Sunday mornings the crowds would be down. At our older facility the parking was spread out on thirty acres all around the building. If it ever rained it was almost impossible to come into the auditorium without being totally drenched.

This was all very new to me, being up in front of people. I'm naturally quiet and reserved. But for some reason, I had this uncommon faith, this unusual boldness. Every week I would pray that it would not rain during our Sunday morning services. I never told anyone but Victoria about my prayers. I know other people would think that was far out. "Joel, that's extreme. You can't pray to stop the rain. Who do you think you are?"

But for two years on the Sundays I was ministering, it might rain an hour before the service or two hours after the service, but it never once rained during those Sunday services. There were times when I would leave my house thirty minutes away and it would be raining very heavily, but by the time I was just a couple of miles from the church, it was like somebody had a big umbrella over the property. It was just as dry as could be.

On Wednesdays, I'd start watching the weather reports for the upcoming weekend. I learned so much about high pressure, low pressure, and dew points, I could fill in for the television weatherman. If I saw any sign of bad weather on the weekend I would go to work. "God, I'm asking You to hold this rain off." One time there was a major storm predicted for Sunday morning: A 90 percent chance of rain, thunder, and lightning. I could hardly sleep the night before. But when I woke up on that Sunday, it was just as clear and beautiful as can be. The front had been delayed.

Some may think, "Oh, that's just a lucky break. That's just a coincidence."

But I'm bold enough to believe that was the hand of God holding back the rain.

I've learned that when you have this uncommon faith you will see uncommon results. You may not need something as trivial as good weather. Maybe you need God to heal a child. Maybe you need a relationship restored or favor at work with a client. You may need a break in a legal situation. Are you releasing your faith for the extraordinary? For the uncommon?

This was what my father did. He was raised in extreme poverty. His parents were cotton farmers. They lost everything they had during the Great Depression. My father had no money, no education at the time, no future to speak of.

But at the age of seventeen, he gave his life to Christ. God put a dream in his heart that one day he would minister to people around the world. In the natural it looked totally impossible. He had no connections, no way to get out of that limited environment. All he had was this uncommon faith. He dared to ask God for the right breaks, and the right opportunities.

Years later, as we traveled to India together, the

young Indian ministers would recognize my father and hold up their Bibles. Then they'd say in their own language what they'd heard him write in his books and say on his tapes, videos, and television broadcasts: "This is my Bible. I am what it says I am."

One day, we were way back in the jungles of Thailand walking by this little hut, and we saw a family inside watching a video of my father ministering from Lakewood. Going down the Amazon River, back in the villages, we saw people reading my father's books in Spanish. How could it be that a young boy with no resources, no connections, could fulfill his dream and not only touch people here but people all over the world?

My father had this uncommon faith. He did not settle where many others would have settled. When all the odds were against him, instead of giving up, he believed that God would make a way. He was bold enough to ask for God's favor. He saw God take him places that he never even dreamed of.

What is holding you back? It's easy to make excuses:

"I come from the wrong family. I didn't get good breaks like you did."

"I've had this problem too long."

"The economy is too down."

"I've made too many mistakes."

No, God knows how to get you to your destination. I want to light a new fire under you. There is no obstacle too difficult for you to overcome. No dreams put in your heart by God are too big to accomplish. Ask yourself, "Is my faith radical? Is what I'm believing for, the vision for my life, is it big enough to make someone think, 'What's his problem? Who does he think he is?' Or, are you stuck in a rut and just accepting where you are as the way it will always be?"

If you are not stretching your faith, you're not tapping in to everything God has in store. For years, Elisha took care of the Prophet Elijah. He was his assistant. He would make sure he had food and water. He traveled with him from city to city. The Prophet Elijah was an older man, very well known, and well respected for the great miracles he performed and just for being a man of God.

When Elijah grew very old and was about to go to Heaven, he said to his assistant Elisha, "You've been faithful to me all this time. Now what do you want me to do for you before I leave?"

You might think Elisha would have asked for something simple. "Just give me a bonus. Give me a couple weeks off. Throw me a party."

Instead, Elisha was thinking in uncommon ways. He said, "Elijah, I would like to have a double portion of your spirit." He was saying, "I want to do twice the miracles that you've done. I want to have twice the influence, twice the wisdom, twice the friends, twice the income."

I'm sure Elijah thought, "You are bold. You are something else." He said, "Elisha, you have asked a hard thing; nevertheless..." That's the key word. He was saying, "It may be hard. You've asked for something big; *nevertheless*, it will happen. It is not too big for God."

If you study Elisha's life you'll find out that was exactly what happened. He did twice the miracles. He had a double portion of his anointing. I wonder what would happen if each one of us would be bold enough to say, "God, I'm asking You to let me do twice what my parents did. Let me have twice the influence, twice the wisdom, twice the favor, twice the income."

When my father went to be with the Lord, people used to come up to me and say, "Joel, do you think you can continue on what your dad and mom started?"

I never said this arrogantly, but I would always tell them, "I don't think that I can just continue it. I believe that I can go further."

That's the way God intended it, for every generation to increase. It's interesting; the former sanctuary that my mom and dad built had eight thousand seats. The current Lakewood Church auditorium has sixteen thousand seats, exactly double. I'm not bragging. I'm simply making the case that if you take the limits off God and release your faith in uncommon ways, then you will see God do uncommon things. Like with Elisha, God will increase you and take you further than previous generations. Like with Joshua, God will show you His favor and do the extraordinary. Like with my father, God will take you from the cotton fields to have an impact on the world, and you will experience the fullness of your destiny.

PART
IV

Keep the Right Perspective

CHAPTER FIFTEEN

Keep the Right Perspective

We all face challenges, but it's not the size of the problem that's important, it's our perception of that problem; it's how big or small we make it in our minds. When Moses sent twelve men to spy out the Promised Land, ten came back and said, "We'll never defeat them. There are giants in the land." But the two other spies, Joshua and Caleb, came back with a different report. They said, "Yes the people are big, but our God is bigger. We are well able to take the land. Let us go in at once."

Both groups saw the same giants and the same situation; the only difference was their perspective. One group focused on the size of their God, the other group focused on the size of their enemy. Out of the two million people camped next door to the Promised Land, only two made it in, Joshua and Caleb.

Could it be that your perspective is keeping you out of your promised land? If you see your challenges as impossible and you tell yourself, "I'll never get out of debt and I'll never overcome this sickness, and I'll never accomplish my dreams," then just like them, your wrong perspective can keep you from becoming all God's created you to be.

What you focus on, you magnify. If you stay focused on your problem or what you don't have and how it will never work out, all you're doing is making it bigger than it really is. When you magnify something you don't change the size of the object; you only change your perception of it.

That was why David said, "Magnify the Lord with me." He was saying if you want to make something bigger, then don't make your problems bigger, don't make the medical report bigger, don't make the opposition bigger. Learn instead to make God bigger.

When David faced Goliath, he never called him a giant. Everybody else did. They talked about his size, his strength, and his skill. But David called Goliath an uncircumcised Philistine. He never even gave him credit for being that big. Here's the key: David didn't deny it, but he didn't dwell on it. His attitude was: "If I'm magnifying anything I'm magnifying the source of my strength. I'm talking about God's greatness.

I'm not focusing on how big my problems are. I'm focusing on how big my God is."

His brothers and the other Israelites were afraid and intimidated, wondering what they were going to do. When David told them he wanted to fight Goliath they said, "You can't fight him—you're just a kid, you're too small, you don't have a chance."

But David had a different perspective. He knew if God be for him, who would dare be against him? He knew he was strong in the Lord. David knew he wasn't alone, that all the forces of Heaven were backing him up. They tried to warn him, "David, you better be careful, you're going to get out there and get hurt. Goliath is too big to hit."

David said, "No he's too big to miss."

He went out, stood before Goliath and said, "You come against me with a sword and a shield, but I come against you in the name of the Lord God of Israel!"

David was magnifying his God, talking about God's goodness. This teenage boy—half the giant's size with no chance in the natural—defeated this huge giant. How? He had the right perspective.

Philippians 1:28 says, "Do not be intimidated by your enemies." You may be like David, up against a big giant right now; a giant of debt, a giant of sickness, a giant legal problem. It's so big, it looks impossible in the natural. You could easily be over-whelmed and think, "I don't have a chance."

No, God is saying, "Don't be intimidated. Those for you are greater than those against you. Put your shoulders back and hold your head up high. You are not weak, defeated, or powerless; you are a child of the Most High God, anointed, equipped, well able. Don't you dare shrink back and think, 'It's just too big. It's been this way too long. My property is never going to sell. I'll never break this addiction, I'll never accomplish my dreams.'"

Do as David did—get a new perspective. You are full of can-do power. The greatest force in the universe is breathing in your direction. There is no challenge too tough for you, no enemy too big, no sickness too great, and no dream too far off.

The same power that raised Christ from the dead lives on inside of you. The enemy would not be fighting you so hard if he didn't know God had something great in store. I've found the size of your challenge is an indication of the size of your future. If you are facing a big giant challenge don't be discouraged; that means God has something amazing just up in front of you. He has a new level of your destiny.

Do you know what made David king? Goliath. God used the opposition to take him to the throne.

When you face great difficulties, it's because God wants to take you to your throne. He wants to take you to a higher level. Your challenge may have been meant for your harm, but God wants to use it to your advantage. That giant is not there to defeat you; it is there to promote you. You may be in tough times, but the right perspective to have is "I'm not staying here—I'm coming out. This too shall pass. I'm not buried; I'm planted. I may be down, but I'm coming up stronger, better, increased, promoted, and at a new level."

That is what it says in Exodus, "The more opposition, the more they increased." When you face adversity, don't get depressed and say, "God, why is this happening to me? I thought Joel said this would be a good year. I went to church last Sunday."

Your attitude should be: "I know this opposition is a sign increase is headed my way. It looks like a setback, but I know it's really a setup. It will not be a stumbling block to take me down. God will use it as a stepping-stone to take me up."

Like David, you need to have an attitude of victory. Sometimes we're talking to God about how big our problems are, when we should be talking to our problems about how big our God is.

I love the way David responded to Goliath when

the giant was laughing and making fun of him for being so small. Goliath said, "Am I a dog that you would come at me with a stick? Don't you have anything better than this little runt?"

David looked him in the eyes and said, "This day I will defeat you and feed your head to the birds of the air." He didn't say, "I hope so," "I believe so," or "I'm praying about it."

Your declaration should be: "I will have a blessed year, I will beat this addiction, I will come out of debt, I will live healthy and strong, I will fulfill my God-given destiny." You may be up against big opposition, but don't be intimidated by that medical report, don't be intimidated by that legal situation, and don't be intimidated by the size of your dream.

One of our Lakewood Church visitors told me she was in Houston for treatments, but she had such a positive attitude I found it hard to believe she was facing a serious illness. She told me "Everything is fine," and wouldn't even say the word *cancer.*

She would not give the disease credit for what it was. She wasn't denying it. She was choosing not to dwell on it. Her attitude was: "I'm not intimidated. This cancer is not bigger than my God. He made my body. He controls my destiny. No weapon formed against me will prosper. If it's not my time to go I'm not going." She had the right perspective. She didn't let the disease define her or dominate her life.

Her story reminded me of this little boy I'd heard about. There was a big bully from down the street who was always bothering him. The boy was trying to get his nerve up to stand up to the bully, but he was too afraid.

One day his father bought him a new telescope. He was out in the front yard playing with it, but he was looking through the wrong end. He was looking through the big side.

His father came out and said, "No son, you're doing it backward. Turn it around and it will make everything bigger like it was meant to do."

The little boy said, "I know that, Dad. But right now I'm looking at this bully. And when I look at him this way it makes him so small that I'm not afraid of him anymore."

You may need to turn the telescope around. You've magnified that problem long enough, you've thought about how impossible it is, and how it's never going to work out. But if you'll turn it around you'll see it from the right perspective; you'll realize it's nothing for God. All He has to do is breathe in your direction.

First Corinthians 15 says, "God has put all things under our feet." You need to see every obstacle, every sickness, every temptation, and every bad habit as being under your feet. It's no match for you. It's not permanent. It won't keep you from your destiny. It's already defeated, and it's just a matter of time before you walk it out.

That addiction won't dog you your whole life. It's under your feet. That depression in your family for so many years won't be passed to the next generation. It's under your feet. You're putting a stop to it.

That struggle, lack, barely getting by, is not permanent. It won't keep you from being blessed. It's under your feet. It's just a matter of time before you break through to a new level.

You need to shake off the lies that are telling you: "It's too big, I've had it too long, and it's never changing." This is a new day. God is saying, no enemy, no injustice, and no obstacle will defeat you. They will promote you, instead. Your challenge wasn't meant to be a stumbling block to take you down, but God is using it as a stepping-stone to take you higher. Keep the right perspective. It's under your feet.

David said in Psalm 59, "I will look down in triumph on all of my enemies." Notice he doesn't say "*some* of my enemies," but "*all* of my enemies." What am I going to do? "Look down in triumph." Why am I looking down? "Because they're under my feet."

You may be facing obstacles that don't feel like

they're under your feet; that sickness seems big, that financial problem looks impossible, or maybe you've had the addiction for years. But you can't go by what you see. You should go by what you know.

We walk by faith and not by sight. In the natural it may feel huge, but when you talk to that enemy as an act of faith, you need to do as David did and look down. It's under your feet.

When you talk to that sickness, that depression, that fear, look down. I've heard that if you want to say something to the enemy, write it on the bottom of your shoe, because he's under your feet.

Sometimes when there's a big boxing match, the two fighters will come out a day before at a press conference. They'll stand toe to toe, with their faces just two or three inches apart. They'll look at each other in the eye, staring, each trying to intimidate the other. They're saying, "I'm tougher, stronger, bigger, meaner. You're not going to defeat me."

When you face an enemy, something's trying to keep you from your destiny—a sickness, a bad habit, an unfair situation—unlike these two fighters, you don't stand toe to toe to look that enemy in the eye. That enemy is not at your level. It may have a big bark. It may seem larger, and tougher, like you'll never defeat it. But the truth is, it's no match for you.

For you to look it in the eye, you need to look

down under your feet. You are more than a conqueror. If God be for you who dare be against you? The enemy has limited power, but our God has all power. He said greater is He that's in you than he that comes against you.

Now quit telling yourself, "I'll never get out of debt, never lose this weight, I'll always struggle in this area." Change your perspective. You are not weak, defeated, or inferior. You are full of can-do power. The same spirit that raised Christ from the dead lives in you. You've got to start putting some things under your feet.

God said, "I've given you power to tread on all the power of the enemy." Notice that word *tread*. It has to do with a shoe. One translation says it means "to trample." If you'll start seeing those enemies as under your feet, as already defeated, then you'll rise up with a new boldness and your faith will activate God's power in a new way.

Isaiah said, "No weapon formed against you will prosper." It doesn't say that you won't have difficulties. That's not realistic. It says challenges will come, people will talk, you may get a negative medical report, or a family member may get off course. God said the problem may form, but you can stay in peace knowing that it won't prosper against you. That means it won't keep you from your destiny.

Because you belong to Him, and because you dwell in the secret place, God has put a hedge of protection around you, a hedge of mercy, a hedge of favor that the enemy cannot cross.

No person, no sickness, no trouble, no bad break, no disability, can stop God's plan for your life. All the forces of darkness cannot keep you from your destiny. When you're in difficulties and you're tempted to be upset, you need to remind yourself, "This problem may have formed, but I have a promise from almighty God that it's not going to prosper. They may be talking about me, trying to make me look bad. But I know God is my vindicator. He'll take care of them. My child may be running with the wrong crowd but it's not permanent, it's temporary. As for me and my house, we will serve the Lord. The medical report may not look good, but I know God made my body, He has me in the palm of His hand and nothing can snatch me away."

I read an article about scientists researching Alzheimer's disease. They studied the brains of those who had died with the disease and compared them to the brains of those who died without it. They found that many people had lesions on their brains that technically qualified them for having Alzheimer's, but the interesting thing was that when they were alive they showed no signs of Alzheimer's. Scientifically they had it, but the symptoms never showed up. Their minds were sharp. Their memories were excellent.

The common denominator was that these people were positive and hopeful, and they stayed productive. Isaiah said just because the problem formed doesn't mean it has to prosper. We may have things that come against us because of our genetics, things that were passed down, but the good news is God can override it. God has the final say.

That's what happened with Ramiro. He was born with no ears. The doctors told his parents he would never be able to hear, and never be able to speak. The problem had formed. In the natural it didn't look good, but we serve a supernatural God.

Ramiro had parents who believed his disability didn't have to prosper. They didn't sit around in self-pity thinking, "Poor old us." They knew they were armed with strength for the battle. They knew God put it under their feet. They just kept praying, believing, and speaking faith.

When Ramiro was a few months old, the doctors noticed that even though he didn't have ears, parts of his eardrums had formed. These incredibly gifted doctors performed a surgery to create ears for him and correct the problem. He got a little better, had more surgeries, and improved even more.

Today, Ramiro can not only hear and speak, he

can also sing. He leads worship for our young adults, and he appeared on *American Idol* singing "Amazing Grace" in front of millions of people.

Whatever you're facing, it's under your feet. It's not permanent, it's temporary. The power that is for you is greater than any power that will be against you. Keep the right perspective. Turn that telescope around. Don't focus on the size of the problem; focus on the size of your God. He's brought you through in the past, and He will bring you through in the future. The problem may have formed, but it will not prosper. I speak strength into you. I speak healing, determination, new vision, favor, wisdom, courage. I declare you will not be intimidated. You are strong, confident, and well able. This is a new day. The tide of the battle is beginning to turn. You will not be overcome. You will be the overcomer. You will not be the victim; you are the victor. God will not only bring you out, He will bring you out better off than you were before!

CHAPTER SIXTEEN

Stay in the Game

It's easy to have a good attitude and pursue your dreams as long as everything is going your way. That doesn't take a lot of faith. But what about the difficult times when a relationship doesn't work out, you get a bad health report, or a friend does you wrong?

It's easy to lose your passion when you are hurting. Many people are sitting on the sidelines of life because they're injured. They are nursing their wounds, and not moving forward because of what they've been through.

You may have a *reason* to feel sorry for yourself, but you don't have a *right*. God promised to give you beauty for those ashes. He said He would pay you back double for the wrongs, but you have to do your part. If you are to see the beauty, if you're to get double, you have to shake off your self-pity.

Shake off the discouragement and get back in the game. We all have wounds, but you can't let a loss, a health issue, or a divorce be your excuse to sit on the sidelines. Sometimes in life you have to play in pain.

This thought struck me while I was watching a football game in which one of the best players had a broken hand and bruised ribs. He was a big offensive lineman. He wasn't expected to play. The trainers wanted him to sit out, but he wasn't about to miss the game. He had a big cast on his arm and he was wearing a special vest to protect his ribs. He was so bandaged up he looked like a mummy.

A reporter asked him how he felt: "It's a little painful, but I'd rather be in the game in pain than sitting on the sidelines watching."

If you are to become all God created you to be, you can't let an injury, hurt, or disappointment cause you to sit on the sidelines, either. Be like that banged-up lineman. Bandage what's hurting. Forgive the person who did you wrong. Let go of what didn't work out and get back in the game.

I met a lady I hadn't seen in a long time in our church lobby. She's an older woman, very faithful, attends our services regularly. I said in passing, "I haven't seen you lately. Where have you been?"

She said, "Joel, I had to have emergency surgery. I've been in the hospital for three months."

"Wow! We're so glad to have you back," I said. "How are you doing?"

For as long as I live I will never forget her words.

She said, "I'm hurting, but I'm here."

That's the kind of people God rewards. Faithful people. People who are determined. People who get knocked down, but don't stay down. Instead, they get back up again. You can't let the hurt, the pain, or the bad break cause you to be bitter, or to lose your passion, or to start blaming God. Like this lady from our church, you need to stay in the game.

No matter what life deals your way, your attitude should be: "I'm hurting but I'm still here. A friend did me wrong but I'm still here. Business is slow but I'm still here. I didn't feel like coming but I'm still here."

You need to make up your mind to stay in the game. You can't just be faithful only as long as you feel perfectly well, as long as everybody treats you right, or as long as it's sunny and cool outside. You have to be like this lady with a made-up mind.

"I'm hurting, but I'm still coming."

"My boss did me wrong, but I'm still getting to work on time, being my best."

"My child won't speak to me. It's breaking my heart. I'm in pain but I'm still singing in the choir. I'm still ushering each week. I'm still being good to a friend in need. I've still got a smile. I'm still giving God praise."

Anybody can sit on the sidelines. Anybody can find an excuse to be sour, to drop out, or to give up on life. I'm asking you to stay in the game. When you're hurting and in pain, it's easy to become fixated on your hurt, your disappointments, or your bad breaks. All that will do is bring more discouragement, more self-pity, eventually even depression.

One of the best things you can do when you're hurting is go out and help somebody else who is hurting. Get your mind off your problems and pain by helping somebody else in need. When you help others in your time of need, you are sowing a seed God can use to change your situation.

This was what my mother did in 1981, when she was diagnosed with terminal liver cancer. She was given a few weeks to live. She didn't feel well. She had a good reason to be discouraged. She could have gone home, pulled the curtains, and been depressed.

She could have sat on the sidelines. Nobody would have faulted her. But my mother understood this principle. She stayed in the game. She would drive across town to pray for a sick friend. The truth is she needed prayer more than that friend, but my mother was sowing a seed. She would come to church every weekend and pray for other people in need. She was hurting, but she was still in the game.

God has a greater reward for people who are faithful in the tough times. Years ago my sister Lisa went through an unwanted divorce. She was in her early twenties. She was so devastated. It was an unfair situation. For weeks she was so depressed that she wouldn't leave the house. Most of the time, she wouldn't even come out of her room. In the morning, she couldn't wait for it to get dark. At nighttime, she couldn't wait for the morning. She wasn't living, just existing.

One day she called my father and she was crying. She said, "Daddy, I think I'm having a nervous breakdown." She was in so much pain. She was overwhelmed.

Our family tried to cheer her up. We tried to encourage her, but we couldn't get her out of that deep hole of depression. A minister friend, T. L. Osborn, called Lisa and said, "Nobody can bring you out of this except you. You know I love you, Lisa, but you've got to quit feeling sorry for yourself. Quit nursing your wounds. Quit thinking about your problem. Get out of the house and move forward with your life."

Lisa was defensive at first, almost offended. She was thinking, "You don't know the pain that I'm feeling. You don't know what I'm going through. This has ruined my life."

"Lisa, if you'll move forward," he said, "God will take your scars and turn them into stars for His glory."

When Lisa heard that, something ignited on the inside. It's like a stronghold was broken in her mind. Instead of sitting at home feeling sorry for herself, she went up to the church and started a class every week for people who were believing for their marriages to be restored. She reached out to other people who were hurting.

My sister was injured, but she got back in the game. Through her actions she was saying, "I'm hurting but I'm still here. I'm disappointed but I'm still here. They did me wrong but I'm still here."

Lisa could have remained bitter with a chip on her shoulder, blaming God, but she made the decision to get back in the game. Today, more than twenty years later, she's happily married, with a great husband and three beautiful children. She saw what God promised. He took the scars and turned them into stars. He gave her beauty for those ashes. But it all happened when she made the decision to get back in the game.

Isaiah put it this way, "Arise from the depression in which the circumstances have kept you. Rise to a new life." Notice, if you want a new life there's something you have to do. You can't sit back in self-pity.

You can't wait until all your wounds heal and you feel 100 percent. You've got to do as Lisa did and arise from that discouragement.

Shake off what didn't work out. Quit mourning over what you've lost. Quit dwelling on who hurt you and how unfair it was, and rise to a new life. When God sees you in the game, pain and all, bandages and all—when you show up with the attitude: "I'm hurting but I'm still here. I'm hurting but I know God is still on the Throne. I'm hurting but I'm expecting God to turn it around"—that's when the Creator of the universe goes to work. That's when God will pay you back for the wrongs that have happened to you.

You may be in a tough time. You may be sitting on the sidelines. If that's the case, God is saying, "Arise and get back in the game." If a friend betrayed you, don't go through life lonely. Go out and find some new friends. The right people are in your future. If you lost your job, don't sit around complaining. Go out and find another job. When one door closes God will always open another door.

If you're facing a health issue, fighting a sickness, don't give up on life and start planning your funeral. Arise from that discouragement. When God sees you do your part, He will do His part. He will give you a new life. He will restore your health, give you new opportunities, new relationships. He will give you a new perspective. You will see that even though it's painful for a time, it is not the end. Even though it was unfair, it is not over. There is still life after the sickness, life after the divorce, and life after the bad break. A full life is still in front of you.

The Scripture says Job experienced this. He went through all kinds of tough times. Everything that could go wrong did. He was tempted to sit on the sidelines of life. His wife told him, "Job, just give up. It's never going to get any better."

But in the midst of that pain Job said, "I know my Redeemer lives." He was saying in effect, "I'm hurting but I'm still in the game. I'm hurting but I know my God is still on the Throne."

A year later when Job came through that challenge, God not only brought him out; God paid him back double for what he lost. The Scripture says, "After this, Job lived 140 years and saw his grandchildren down to four generations."

Notice, after the trouble, after the loss, after the sickness, after the business went down, after the bottom fell out, his life still was not over. He didn't end on a sour, defeated note. He went on to live a blessed, happy 140 years, enjoying his grandchildren, accomplishing his dreams, fulfilling his destiny.

Your life is not over because you had a setback. God has an "after this" in your future. When you go through tough times, don't be surprised if the enemy doesn't whisper in your ear, "You'll never be as happy as you used to be. You've seen your best days. This setback is the end of you."

Let that go in one ear and out the other. God is saying to you what He said to Job: after the cancer, after the bad break, after the disappointment, there is still a full life. You have not danced your best dance. You have not laughed your best laugh. You have not dreamed your best dream.

If you stay in the game and do not grow bitter, God will bring you out just as he brought out Job. He will bring you out with double what you had before.

There was another pro football player whose younger brother was tragically killed in an accident the day before a big game. This player practically raised his siblings. They were extremely close. You can imagine the pain and shock he must have been in. The coach told him to go back home and spend as much time as he needed with his family. But he said, "No, Coach. I'm playing in the game tomorrow in memory of my brother. I know that's what he would want me to do."

It's interesting; this player had one of the greatest games of his career. He caught an incredible touchdown pass and made other great plays. Some people would see it as a coincidence, just the adrenaline of the moment. But I see it as the hand of God. I believe God was saying, "If you'll dare stay in the game, if you'll dare play with pain, then I'll breathe My favor on your life."

Nobody would fault you for being discouraged when you are nursing your wounds over a lost loved one, a serious illness, a child with special needs or a legal battle. That's what most people expect. But when you defy the odds, play in pain, and say, "Hey, I'm hurting but I'm still here," the most powerful force in the universe breathes in your direction.

You may be in a difficult time. You could easily be discouraged. But God is saying, "It's time to wipe away the tears. Wash your face. Put on a new attitude and get back in the game."

You may not be able to do what you used to. You may have some aches and some limitations. That's all right. God is not necessarily concerned about your performance. He is looking at the fact that you're in the game.

You could have a chip on your shoulder. You could be sitting on the sidelines. It takes an act of faith to ignore the voices giving you excuses to sit there. When you refuse to listen to them and get back in the game, God sees your effort. God knows what it took for you to come to church or to reach out to someone else in need.

Other people may not know the battles you had to fight to get back in the game. They don't understand the discouragement you had to overcome. They didn't see all the opportunities you had to get sour and throw in the towel. Just the fact that you showed up says to God, "You are still on the Throne."

You're saying to yourself, "I'm in it for the long haul." And you're saying to the enemy, "You're under my feet. There's nothing you can do to keep me from my destiny."

When Jesus was here on this earth, He felt every pain, every emotion, that we would ever feel. He knows what it's like to be lonely, to go through a loss, to be betrayed, or to be discouraged—so much so that He sweated great drops of blood. He's been where we are. The Scripture says, "He is touched with the feelings of our infirmities."

When you hurt, God feels the pain. You're His most prized possession. You're His child. When you arise in spite of the pain and get in the game, that's the seed God will use to take the scar and turn it into a star.

I met a man in the Lakewood Church lobby who was wearing a wristband from the hospital. I asked him if everything was okay. He explained that he'd had surgery earlier in that week, a major surgery. He was supposed to stay in the hospital through the weekend to recover. But he said, "Doctor, I've got to go to church on Sunday. I'm an usher. They'll be expecting me."

The doctor said, "No way, sir. I'm not even thinking about letting you out of the hospital. You're staying right here and recovering."

The man said, "Doctor, you don't understand. I have to be at church. I never miss a Sunday."

The doctor looked at him, said, "Let me ask you. Do you go to Lakewood?"

He said, "Yes, sir. I do."

The doctor said, "Lakewood people are the most dedicated, faithful, happiest people I've ever seen." Then he said, "I'm going to make a deal with you. I'm going to give you a three-hour pass to go to church on Sunday morning and then you get right back in here and get in that bed to recover."

The man showed up. He was hurting, but he was here. He told me before the service, "Joel, don't go long. I'll get in trouble!"

There's another younger man who attends Lakewood services. He always has a smile, seems as happy as can be. What I didn't realize is that he has been on dialysis for twelve years. I took my father to dialysis the last three months of his life. I know a little bit about that. It's not always easy. It can be a burden. This young man always wore long-sleeved shirts.

One Sunday he came up for prayer. I met him at the altar for the first time. I said, "Hey, I see you out there in the audience all the time. It's good to finally meet you."

He said, "Yeah, Joel. I never miss a service. I love coming." He rolled up his sleeve. His whole arm was as red as a tomato. It looked like somebody had taken an ice pick and poked at it for three hours straight. I'd never seen anything like that before.

I couldn't help but think about all the times I had seen him out in the audience with his arms up in the air in worship. It looked like he didn't have a problem in the world. Looked as happy as could be. What I didn't realize was under that sleeve he was injured. He was here but he was hurting. He was playing in pain.

It's one thing to go through a difficulty that everybody knows about. You're worried, discouraged. You've got your friends and family members praying. There's nothing wrong with that. We're all human. We all have emotions. We handle things in different ways.

But what really gets God's attention is when you're in a tough time, you're hurting, you're in pain, but like this young man, you're so stable, you're so consistent, you're so at peace, nobody knows anything about it. You show up to church each week with a smile. You go to work with a good attitude. You're kind, friendly, and compassionate. The whole time you're fighting a battle that nobody knows anything about. That gets God's attention in a great, great way.

About three months ago the young man who'd been on dialysis so long came back to the altar with another young man. He said, "Joel, my friend is donating one of his kidneys to me. I'm receiving a transplant on Tuesday."

The procedure went great. The new kidney responded perfectly. Today, he's not on dialysis anymore. He doesn't have to wear long-sleeved shirts anymore. He's healthy, free from that pain.

Twelve years after the dialysis, after the struggle, after the pain, there was still a bright future in front of him. Because he stayed in the game, like Job, he came into his "after this." God will do the same thing for you.

There's a young lady in the Scripture who went through a time of great pain because her husband was killed in a battle. Her name was Ruth. In a moment her life forever changed. Ruth could have easily given in to self-pity, or discouragement, feeling that life was just not fair.

But Ruth stayed in the game. She chose instead to look after her mother-in-law, Naomi, who was widowed and had lost her son. Naomi said, "Ruth, you're a young woman. I'm an old lady. You've got a full life in front of you. Don't worry about me. Go off and do your own thing."

Ruth said, "No, Naomi. I'm not leaving you by yourself, especially when you're hurting. I'm going with you and taking care of you." Even though Ruth was hurting, even though she was in pain, she reached out to somebody else who was hurting.

Month after month, Ruth just kept taking care of Naomi, getting the food, serving her dinner, being her friend. One day Ruth was out in the field gathering up wheat for the dinner. She met this man named Boaz. He was the owner of all the fields, the wealthiest man in that area. They fell in love and got married. God blessed them with a baby boy. They named him Obed.

Obed had a son named Jesse. Jesse had a son named David. David, of course, went on to be the king of Israel, one of the greatest men to ever live.

Ruth could have sat on the sidelines the rest of her life after that loss but she understood this principle: she played in pain. She was injured but she kept doing the right thing. God had an "after this" for Ruth. After the loss, after the pain, God said, "I'll give you a great-great-grandson that will change the world."

You may be in pain today. Maybe you've suffered a loss, been through a disappointment. My message is, "That is not the end. God still has a plan." Don't sit around nursing your wounds. Don't let bitterness and discouragement set the tone for your life. God is saying, "Arise. Wipe away the tears and get back in the game."

Have the attitude "I'm hurting but I'm still here. I'm disappointed but I've still got a smile. They did me wrong but I'm still giving God praise."

If you will stay in the game, God will always have an "after this" for you. After the loss, you'll meet the right person. After the layoff, you'll get a better job. After the sickness, you'll come out stronger. After the disappointment, you'll still live a blessed, full, happy life. Just like my mother. Just like the young man with the kidney. Just like Ruth, like Job.

I believe and declare, in spite of the pain, in spite of the adversity, because you're still in the game, God is going to make the rest of your life the best of your life.

CHAPTER SEVENTEEN

Your Second Wind Is on Its Way

We all grow tired sometimes, tired of trying to make a business grow, tired of dealing with a sickness, tired of raising a difficult child, tired of being lonely and waiting to meet the right person. We can even be doing what we love, whether it's living in the house of our dreams, raising great children, or working at a good job, but if we're not careful we can lose our passion and allow weariness to set in.

I watched a documentary about a long war involving our country. The United States troops had been overseas for many years engaged in conflict. A four-star general testified before Congress. A senator asked how the troops were doing. He said, "Sir, our troops are tired. We never expected the war to go on this long. Now they're dealing with battle fatigue."

The military was facing the same question we often face as individuals: what do you do when the battle has lasted longer than you thought it would? You've prayed. You've believed. You've done what you're supposed to, but you're still waiting to meet the right person. Or you're still looking for the right job. Or you're still praying that a child you care about will get back on track.

The word *weary* means, "to lose the sense of pleasure, to not feel the enjoyment that you once felt." When soldiers are first shipped off overseas they're excited. They can't wait to make a difference. Then when the battle goes on and on, fatigue can set in. The same can happen to any of us who've been fighting for something over a long period.

The problem is when you allow yourself to become weary you'll be tempted to quit: to quit growing, to quit standing for that wayward child, to quit believing that you'll become healthy and whole, or to quit pursuing your goals and dreams.

A woman visiting our church told me that she was in town for a checkup at the big cancer center in Houston, and she hadn't received the news she'd hoped for. She'd gone through six months of chemotherapy. She was hoping she was done, of course. She found out that the chemo did do some good, but they told her she needed another six months of treatments.

She was so disappointed. She said, "Joel, I'm tired. I don't think I can do this for six more months."

On the way to our victories we will always face the weariness test. We will be tempted to become discouraged and give up. The test never comes when we're fresh. It never comes when we first start out. It always comes when we're tired. That's when we're the most vulnerable.

The Apostle Paul said in Galatians 6:9, "Don't grow weary in doing what's right, for in due season you shall reap if you faint not." Two words are the key to this whole passage; "faint not." In other words, if you don't give up, if you shake off the weariness, if you put on a new attitude knowing that God is still in control, if you dig your heels in and say, "I've come too far to stop now," if you "faint not," you will see the promise come to pass.

Instead of complaining about how long the battle is taking, we should say, "This too shall pass. I know it's not permanent. It's only temporary. I'm not camping here. I'm moving forward."

Weariness kept the people of Israel out of the Promised Land. They were close to their victory, next door to the Promised Land. God had already said He would give them the land. All they had to do was go in and fight for it. But they allowed weariness to set in. They had gone through the wilderness, overcoming obstacles, defeating all kinds of enemies. Then they grew tired. Moses tried to get them to go in, but weariness leads to discouragement.

When you're discouraged you see the problem instead of the possibility. You talk about the way it is instead of the way it can become. The people of Israel started complaining: "Moses, our enemy is too big. We don't have a chance. We'll never defeat them."

They made a permanent decision based on a temporary feeling. If you allow yourself to become weary and you lose your passion, you, too, will be tempted to make decisions based on how you feel rather than based on what you know.

When you feel that weariness come on, you need to pray to build strength. "God, You said You have armed me with strength for every battle. You said I can do all things through Christ who infuses inner strength into me. You said I am more than a conqueror, a victor and not a victim." If you talk to yourself the right way, you will feel the second wind kick in.

But too often we do as the people of Israel did and think, "I can't take this anymore. I'm so tired. I'm so rundown. It's just too hard." Yet, the more you talk about how tired you are the more tired you become. You're just adding fuel to the fire. Don't talk about the way you are. Talk about the way you want to be.

You need to have words of faith and victory coming out of your mouth. In other words, "This may be hard, but I know I'm well able. I'm equipped. I'm empowered. I am strong in the Lord."

We all grow tired. We all become weary. In fact, if you never feel like giving up, then your dreams are too small. If you never feel like quitting, then you need to set some larger goals. When that pressure comes to be discouraged and to think you can't take it anymore, that is completely normal. Every person feels that way at times.

Isaiah gives us the solution. He said, "Those who wait on the Lord will find new strength. They will soar high on wings like eagles. They will run and not grow weary. They will walk and not faint."

God knew there would be times when we would feel battle fatigue. That's why He said, "There is a way to get your second wind. There is a way to have your strength renewed. What is it? Wait on the Lord."

One translation says, "Hope in the Lord." That doesn't mean to sit around and be passive, complacent. It means to wait with expectancy, not complaining, not discouraged, not talking about all the reasons why it won't work out.

If you want your strength renewed, the right way to wait is by saying, "Father, thank You that You are fighting my battles. Thank You that the answer is on the way. Thank You that You are bigger than these obstacles. Thank You that You are bringing my dreams to pass."

When you give God praise, you talk about His greatness; you go through the day expecting Him to turn it around. God promises He will renew your strength. The Scripture says, "You will run and not get weary." This is a reference to catching your second wind. That's God breathing strength, energy, passion, vision, and vitality back into your spirit. You won't just come out the way you were. You will come out on wings like eagles. You will come out stronger, higher, better off than you were before.

You may be up against major obstacles. When you look out into your future it can be very overwhelming. You can't see how you will make it. I know a woman who was in the same situation. She raised her children and got them off to college. She was looking forward to this new season in her life in which she would have some free time. But because of unusual circumstances she has had to raise her grandson, who is just a toddler. Of course she loves her grandbaby, but she said, "Joel, I don't think I can do this again. Another fifteen years? I don't think I have the strength to make it."

I told her she can't focus fifteen years down the road. If she looks that far out she will be overwhelmed.

You have to take it one day at a time. You don't have the strength you need for tomorrow. When you get to tomorrow you'll have the strength for that day.

But you can't think about struggling for years and years. Instead, focus on one day at a time. God asks only: "Will you do it today? Will you take hold of my strength today?"

Will you wait on the Lord today? Will you not give up and faint today? If you will pass the test and do it today, then when you get to tomorrow the strength you need for that day will be there. As long as you worry—"How am I going to make it next week, or next month, or twenty years from now?"—that worry will drain your strength, drain your energy, drain your passion, and drain your victory.

All worry does is weigh us down and keep us from enjoying life. Instead of worrying about your future, get up every morning and say to yourself, "I can do this one more day. I may not know how I can do it the next twenty years, but I do know this; I can do it for twenty-four more hours. I can stay in faith one more day. I can keep a good attitude one more day. I can have a smile on my face twenty-four more hours."

Take it a day at a time.

I like to exercise to stay fit. Sometimes when I am out running, especially when it's hot and humid, I get tired. Those thoughts start coming, saying, "You need to stop. You're uncomfortable. It's hard, and look at how far you've got to go."

The real battle takes place in our minds. If I dwell on those thoughts and start thinking about how I feel and how many hills there are and how far I've got to go, I'll talk myself out of it and stop. Instead, I quit looking at the next two miles and just start telling myself, "I can do this one more step. One more step. One more step."

When I focus not on how far I have to go but instead on the next step, before long I look up and I'm almost there. I've pressed past the pain of being uncomfortable. I've found a rhythm, and all of a sudden my second wind kicks in, and instead of barely making it I'm mounting up on those wings like eagles. I'm finishing strong.

Thoughts will come to you: "It's never changing. You're never getting well. You're never reaching your goals." But don't listen to them. God said in Job that He has set an end to the difficulty. God has already established an end date for the trouble. He has set an end to the struggle, an end to the sickness, an end to the addiction, an end to the loneliness.

Remind yourself of that when you're in a difficult season and you feel the weariness creeping in, telling you, "It's not worth it. You're too uncomfortable. You've got too far to go." Instead, remember, "I'm not always going to be lonely. God has set an end to this loneliness. He is bringing somebody great into my life.

"I won't always struggle in my finances. God has set an end to this lack. He has promotion and increase coming my way. I won't always be fighting these addictions. These bad habits won't dog me my whole life. God has set an end to it. He has freedom and victory in my future.

"I won't always have to deal with these medical issues. There will not always be this pain. Jehovah Rapha, the Lord my healer, has set an end to this sickness."

Remember, the end has already been set. I'm asking you to stand strong. Don't grow weary. Keep believing. Keep expecting. Keep being your best. If you stay on track and do what's right, you will see the end come to pass. That's what the Scripture means: "If you faint not you will receive the reward."

I know you are not a fainter. You are strong! You are a warrior, a victor and not a victim. When life gets tough, remind yourself that God said you have been armed with strength for every battle. Think about that: God calls strength a weapon. In the natural you could be armed with a pistol, a hand grenade, or even a bazooka. Those are powerful weapons, but they are nothing compared to the arms God has given you.

You are full of can-do power. Don't go around

feeling weak and defeated and like you can't take it anymore. If it was too much for you God wouldn't have allowed it.

Instead of complaining, tell yourself, "I can handle this. This child may be difficult but I can handle it. Business may be slow but I can handle it. The medical report wasn't good but I can handle it. The boss is getting on my nerves but I can handle it. It's hot outside but I can handle it!"

Put your shoulders back, look those obstacles in the eye, and say: "You're no match for me."

"Cancer, you're no match for me."

"Cranky coworker, you're no match for me."

"Depression, you're no match for me."

"Addictions, you're no match for me."

"Struggle and lack, you're no match for me."

"I know your end has already been set, and it's just a matter of time before God turns it around. It's just a matter of time before He brings that dream to pass."

A friend of mine is in the military, and he had just found out he would be deployed overseas for one year. He and his wife had never been apart for an extended time. They had two small children. His wife was very worried and wondered how she was going to make it.

I told her what I'm telling you: Your challenge may be difficult, but you can handle it. God has given you the grace for this season. If you weren't up to this,

God wouldn't have brought it across your path. In tough times remind yourself there is always a reward for doing right. God never fails to compensate you. He pays very well. The season may be difficult right now, but if you keep doing the right thing, get ready, the reward is coming.

When you stand strong and have a good attitude, even though you really feel like complaining...

When you serve and give and treat people right, even when they're not saying "thank you"...

When nobody gives you credit...

When you pass these weariness tests, the Scripture says a payday is coming your way.

You may be camped next to the Promised Land like the people of Israel, on the verge of stepping to a new level of God's favor, but the problem is you're tired. The battle has taken longer than you expected. You stand at a crossroads. You can either let that weariness weigh you down, causing you to give up and settle where you are, or you can dig your heels in and say, "I've come too far to stop now. I'll keep pressing forward. I'll keep pursuing my goals. I'll keep being good to people. I'll keep hoping, praying, stretching, growing."

When you have that kind of attitude, you will feel your second wind kick in. I've learned this: you face the greatest pressure when you are close to your victory. When the intensity has been turned up, that's a sign you're about to step to a new level of God's favor.

It's like a lady having a baby. When she faces the greatest pain, she is close to giving birth. It's the same principle in life. When it's the most uncomfortable, when it seems the most unfair, when you're most tempted to give up, that's a sure sign you're about to give birth to the new thing God wants to do.

I can sense in my spirit the season is changing. The depression is coming to an end and joy is about to break forth. Your lack and struggle is coming to an end and a new season of increase, promotion, and more than enough is coming your way. If you've had constant medical problems and not felt up to par, that is coming to an end. A season of health, wholeness, and vitality is coming your way.

Now don't act like the people of Israel who became discouraged, too weary, and just wanted to settle where they were. Instead, press past the pain and discomfort. Press past the feelings telling you to settle. Press past the weariness. Get your fire back.

You have not seen your best days. Your greatest victories are still out in front of you. Those adversities and struggles will not go to waste; God is using them to prepare you for the amazing future He has in store.

When I ran track in high school, our coach would give us unbelievable workouts. One time we had to run eighteen half-mile races. We would run a half a mile, take a two-minute break, and then run the next one. We had to do that eighteen times in a row. We thought, "This man is trying to kill us. There is something wrong with him."

But several months later, we were all running at new levels and breaking our old records, and we realized he wasn't trying to kill us. He was simply increasing our endurance. He was stretching us so we could reach our full potential. In the same way God sometimes will allow us to face difficulties to increase our endurance, to stretch us so we can reach our full potential. We may think, "This is too hard. This boss is too unfair. This math teacher is too difficult. How can I raise these children?"

It may be very difficult. It may have been meant for your harm, but stand strong and declare, "I can handle this. It's not too much for me. I've been armed with strength for this battle." Then when you make it to the other side, you will not only receive your reward, you also will have an inner strength, a confidence, and a resolve you never had before.

You will face situations that might have been too much ten years ago. They might have caused you to be upset and fall apart. But because you've passed these tests, something has been deposited inside your spirit. What used to be a big deal is not a big deal at all.

What's happening? You're growing. You're increasing. You're stepping up to new levels.

I believe right now the Creator of the universe is breathing a second wind into you. Just receive it by faith. Strength is coming into your body. Strength is coming into your mind. You will run and not grow weary. You will walk and not faint. You will not drag through life defeated or depressed. You will soar through life on wings like eagles!

CHAPTER EIGHTEEN

The God Who Closes Doors

We all know that God opens doors. We've seen Him give us favor, good breaks, promotion. That's the hand of God opening the door. But the same God Who opens doors will close doors.

Maybe you prayed, but you didn't get a promotion you wanted. You applied, but your loan application didn't go through. A relationship you'd enjoyed didn't work out. So often we can become discouraged and feel like God has let us down.

But God can see the big picture for your life. God knows where every road is leading. He knows the dead ends. He can see the shortcuts. He knows some roads are a big circle.

We would go for years and end up right back where we started, never making any progress. We can't see what God can see. A big part of faith is trusting God when you don't understand why things happen the way they do. God may close a door because you're believing too small. If He opened the door, it would limit what He wants to do in your life. Another door may close because it's not the right time, or there are other people involved and they're not ready yet. If God opened that door at the wrong time it wouldn't work out.

The bottom line is this: God has your best interests at heart. When a door closes, you don't know what God is saving you from. If your prayers aren't answered the way you want, instead of being discouraged or feeling like God let you down, why don't you have a bigger perspective? The reason the door closed is because God has something better in store.

If God wanted you to have that promotion you didn't get, He would have given it to you. Shake off the disappointment and move forward. Know that there is something better coming. Or if God wanted the person who left you to stay, that person would still be with you. Shake it off. The right people are in your future.

It's no accident that some doors are closed to you. You may not understand why right now. You may feel that the opportunity of a lifetime just passed you by. But one day you will look back and thank God for the closed door, because if God hadn't closed the door you wouldn't have met the right person. Or if God hadn't closed another door, you would have been stuck at one level and not seen the amazing favor He has in your future.

I used to get excited about my open doors, but I really felt down about my closed doors. Now I thank God for my closed doors just as much as I do my open doors. I want you to come to this place where you have the same trust in God, and you are so confident that He is directing your steps, you say, like David: "God, my life is in Your hands."

If you believe that then when a door closes and you don't get your way, you won't be upset. Your attitude will be: "I know this door didn't close by accident. God closed it on purpose, and what God closes I don't want to open. I don't want my way. I want His way. He knows what's best. He can see what I can't see. God, not my will but Yours be done."

That's a very freeing way to live. When you really believe God is in complete control, it takes all the pressure off.

A few years ago this man flew to Houston for a big job interview. He was so excited about it. It was a top position at one of the largest companies in the world. It looked like a golden opportunity, a huge boost to his career. He was ready to give up his position of nearly thirty years and move his family.

I know this because he came to the service at Lakewood Church and asked us to pray over his big interview. We prayed God would give him favor and cause him to stand out. In a few days he called and he was on cloud nine. Everything went great. It looked very promising.

Several weeks went by, and they invited him back for a second interview. He did the same thing. He came by the church. We prayed: favor, promotion, on and on. After talking with him for several hours that company called him back in and said, "We really like you. You're incredibly talented. We just don't feel you're the right fit for our organization."

It was like they let the air out of his balloon. He came to the service like he had lost his last friend. He looked twenty years older. He was so discouraged. He said, "Joel, I don't understand it. I prayed. I believed. How could God let this happen?"

I told him what I'm telling you: The same God Who opens doors will close doors. You have to trust Him. You may not understand the disappointment now, but one day you will understand it. One day you will thank God that you didn't get that position.

A couple of years later, this same businessman

showed up for a Lakewood service and he was smiling from ear to ear. The Houston company that had turned him down was in bankruptcy. Thousands of people were being laid off. It was a big scandal and all over the news. The company eventually shut down.

Here's how good God is: When he applied for the Houston job, the businessman was less than two years from retirement at the job he wanted to leave. If he had been hired by the Houston company, he would not only have been out of a job, but he also would have lost nearly thirty years of retirement benefits.

God knows what He is doing. Don't be discouraged by your closed doors. If God wants a door to open you can be certain it will open. All the forces of darkness cannot stop it.

What I want you to see is when you pray, you believe, you stand in faith; if the door doesn't open, take it as a sign from God. It's not His best. Sometimes, like this man, you may be disappointed, but God loves you too much to open that door. God is not letting you down. He is doing you a favor. He is keeping you from all kinds of heartache and pain.

If you really trust God you have to be content with the answer God gives you. So often we say we're trusting, but the truth is that we're happy only if God does it our way, on our timetable. You have to put the dream on the altar and say, "God, if this is what You want for me. If this is Your best for my life. I know You are in complete control. There is no power greater than Yours. God, I trust You. If it happens, I will be happy and thank you for it. If it doesn't work out, I won't be discouraged. I won't quit believing. I know that means You have something better in store."

This takes off all the pressure. You won't be frustrated if it doesn't work out. You won't live in self-pity if it doesn't happen your way. You know the steps and the stops of a good person are ordered by the Lord.

This was difficult for me to accept for a while, because some opportunities looked so great. In my mind I thought, "God, it's perfect. There will never be anything better." The problem is that our thinking is limited. God's plan for our lives is so much bigger than our own plans that if God didn't close certain doors they would keep you from the fullness of your destiny.

A couple of years after my dad went to be with the Lord and I took over at Lakewood, the church really started growing. We needed property to build a new sanctuary. My father said that he would never move the church. So we looked for property as close to our location as we could possibly find. We found this one-hundred-acre tract of land right off the freeway, about two miles from our existing location. It was perfect. We talked to the owner. He said it had been on the market for more than twenty years. He'd never had an offer, not one person had been interested.

We said, "Thank You, Lord. You've saved this property for us."

After about six months of doing our research and our soil tests we went to close on the property. We had an eight o'clock meeting. We walked in fifteen minutes early, and I'll never forget what happened. The secretary came out and said, "I'm so sorry, but the owner sold the property last night to another party."

I was so disappointed. I went home very discouraged. I told Victoria what had happened. She said, "Listen, Joel. God closed that door for a reason. We're not going to be discouraged. We'll keep a good attitude. God has something better in store."

In my mind I couldn't believe it, but in my heart, I knew what she was saying was exactly right. I thought, "God is still on the Throne. His plan cannot be stopped by a bad break, a disappointment, or by a person. God has the final say."

I made a decision that day. Instead of sitting around in self-pity saying, "God, why didn't it work out?" I chose to believe that God was still in control. A few months later, a friend called me. He said, "Joel, the Houston Rockets basketball team is moving out of the Compaq Center. That would be a great facility for Lakewood."

When he said that, something came alive on the inside. I knew right then and there that was the reason God closed the other door. It was too small. It would have limited what God wanted to do. Things began to fall into place, and now Lakewood Church has an amazing home in the former Compaq Center. But back then I couldn't fathom having a church in a basketball arena. It wasn't even on my radar. This was exceedingly, abundantly, above and beyond. I would have been happy with the other property. I would have celebrated God's goodness if He would have done it that way. But God's dream for your life is so much bigger than your own dream.

There will be times when a door closes and you can't understand why. In a relationship, you may feel that you'd found the perfect person, but it doesn't work out. Or maybe it will be the perfect house, but your offer will be turned down. It may not make sense when it happens, but one day it will. One day you'll have your Compaq Center moment. You'll look back and say:

"God, thank You that the other property was sold out from under me."

"God, thank You that the loan didn't go through."

"God, thank You that the other person walked out on me."

Here's the question: Will you stay in faith while

you wait to see what God is up to? Will you not grow discouraged and start complaining? "Nothing good ever happens to me. I can't believe I didn't get the promotion. I've been at the company longer than anybody else." Or, "I treated this girl like a queen and she just wants to be friends. She says I'm just like her brother. God, I don't want to be a brother. I want to be a husband!"

Trust God with your life. He knows what He is doing. I pray every day, "God, open the right doors and close the wrong doors. God, bring the right people across my path. Weed out those who shouldn't be there."

I've learned the closed doors are just as important as the open doors. You know what brought Lakewood Church to the former stadium location? A closed door. Don't be discouraged by your closed doors.

You may be like me. You may want a piece of property right now. But God has a building already built for you. He has more than you can ask or think—an exceedingly, abundantly, above-and-beyond future.

God loves you so much that He hasn't answered certain prayers. He hasn't allowed certain people into your life whom you really wanted, because they would have limited your growth. Learn to trust Him. Thank Him for your open doors. Celebrate His goodness. But thank Him just as much for your closed doors knowing that He is still directing your steps.

A hurting young lady came down for prayer at Lakewood Church a few years back. She was so discouraged because her boyfriend had broken up with her. She didn't think she could live without him. She believed he was the man of her dreams. Every Sunday we would pray that that relationship would be restored. This went on month after month. She was as faithful as can be. And I could tell, though, she was only going to be happy if God did it her way.

I tried to encourage her: "Stay open. God knows what's best. He can see the big picture."

She didn't want to hear any of that. She only wanted this young man back, but it didn't work out the way she hoped. He married someone else. She was so disappointed. She felt God had let her down. She said, "Joel, all those prayers we prayed. I quoted the Scripture. I was good to others. I did everything I was supposed to do."

She was so discouraged, she dropped out of church.

The Scripture says, "God's ways are not our ways. They are better than our ways." Maybe like that girl, you have prayers that weren't answered the way you wanted, or something didn't turn out the way you had hoped. Let these words sink down into your spirit: God's way is better than your way. His plan is bigger than your plan. His dream for your life is more rewarding, more fulfilling, better than you've ever dreamed.

Stay open and let God do it His way. Put the request on the altar. It's okay to be honest and say, "God, this is what I want. God, You know how badly I want it. You know how much it means to me. But God, if it's not Your best I don't want it. God, I trust You."

I didn't see that young lady for the longest time. She ended up moving to another city. About five or six years later, she came to church with this handsome man by her side. Come to find out they were married. They had a beautiful daughter. She was as happy as can be.

At one point her husband stepped away and she whispered in my ear, "Joel, you remember the young man we used to always pray about? He's already been married and divorced two times. He's constantly in and out of trouble. He can't hold down a good job."

She made the statement, "I thank God every day that He didn't answer my prayer."

When you want something so badly that you convince yourself you can't live without it, you try to make it happen. You may pray night and day for it, but God is so merciful that if it's not His best, He is not going to answer that prayer. He loves you too much to open that door. Why don't you trust Him?

He wants you to fulfill your destiny more than you do. He is in complete control.

When you come to a closed door, consider it a test of your faith. Will you become bitter, live in self-pity, and give up on your dreams, or will you move forward knowing that God is still in control?

If you pass the test, God will release what He has in your future. And many times it will be exactly what you're praying for. God will bring back the person you wanted. Or He may bring an opportunity you thought was lost, or a dream you'd thought impossible. God just wants to see if you trust Him enough to be happy even if it doesn't happen your way.

That's what happened with Abraham. God instructed him to put his son Isaac, the person who meant the most to him, on the altar as a sacrifice. Just when Abraham was going to harm him, God said, "No, Abraham. Don't do it. I just wanted to see if you trusted me enough to give me your own son."

Abraham passed the test. What happened? God gave him back what he really wanted, the person who meant so much to him. When you face a disappointment, or a closed door, or when your plans don't work out, if you keep a good attitude and stay in faith, you will pass the test. If you do that, it allows God to give back to you what you really want the most.

Proverbs 20:24 says, "Since the Lord is directing

our steps, why do we try to figure out everything that happens along the way?" You could find freedom if you would just quit trying to figure out everything.

"God, why did I go through that breakup? I'm a good person."

"God, why didn't I get that job I applied for? It's perfect for me."

If you're trying to figure out everything that doesn't go your way, you'll become confused and frustrated. Let it go and move forward. God can see things you can't see. It may not make sense right now, but one day when God's whole plan unfolds you will see what God was up to. A part of trusting is saying, "God, I don't understand it. It doesn't seem fair. But God, I believe that my steps and my stops are ordered by You. I know just as You can close doors, You will open them. So I'm keeping a good attitude. I'm moving forward in faith knowing that You have my best interests at heart."

There was a woman who complained constantly. After one particularly bad day, she said, "God, why did You let so many bad things happen to me? My alarm didn't go off, and I was late to work. At lunch they made my sandwich wrong, and I had to send it back. Driving home, my cell phone dropped the call right in the middle of a conversation. To top it off, God, when I got home I wanted to put my feet in the foot massager just to relax, but it wouldn't turn on. God, nothing went right today."

God said, "All right. Let Me go down the list. Your alarm didn't go off because there was a drunk driver on the freeway. I delayed you on purpose so you wouldn't be harmed. The sandwich you had to send back was made by a cook who was sick and I didn't want you to catch his flu, so I had someone else make you the new one. I cut off your phone call because the person you were talking to has been spreading rumors, and I didn't want you to hear too much. And that foot massager? I shut it down because there was a short in its wiring. If I'd let you turn it on, the power would have gone out in your entire house, and I didn't think you would want to sit around in the dark all evening."

God knows exactly what He is doing! Everything about your life is calculated. You may not understand when something doesn't go your way, but that's because you're not God. He has a reason for every door that closes to you. Since the Lord is directing your steps, don't try to figure out everything that happens. Trust Him instead.

A minister friend of mine once had this big outdoor event planned in another country. He and his staff spent more than two years preparing for it. They had government officials, business leaders, pastors, and several organizations involved. It was a huge undertaking, costing thousands and thousands of dollars.

Just a few days before the event, they were nearly done with preparations. They had the staging out. The sound system was up. Their advertisements were playing on the radio and television. Then they received word from the local government that because of a swine flu outbreak, all public meetings had been cancelled.

My friend was so disappointed. Two years of hard work came to nothing. It seemed like the biggest waste of time, energy, and money. He and his team got on the plane and came back home. That weekend, just when their event would have been underway, the military staged a coup and overthrew the government. It was total chaos.

People panicked. No law. No order. Shooting in the street. All kinds of mayhem. If his event had not been cancelled, he would have been right in the middle of it. No telling what would have happened. He said, "I know this sounds odd, but I thank God for the swine flu. We may have lost some time, energy, and money, but we could have lost our lives."

You may wonder why something you'd planned didn't work out, just as my friend did. But like him, one day you will thank God for the door that closed. You'll be grateful that it didn't work out.

First Corinthians 13:12 says, "Now we see in part

like looking through a glass dimly but one day we will see clearly face to face." Right now you may not see all clearly. You're only looking at it in part. But one day it will come into focus, and you'll look back and say, "Wow, God! You are amazing! You had it all figured out. You closed the door on purpose so Your perfect will would be done."

That's what happened to this one bright young man who was a straight A student in high school. He loves to study. Academically, he's in the top five percent of the nation. His dream was to become an engineer. It's always what he wanted to do. After he earned an undergraduate degree, he applied to do graduate studies at about a dozen or so of the best engineering schools in the nation, but he was turned down again and again.

It didn't make sense. Some of his friends with lower grades and scores were accepted, but he wasn't. He could not understand it.

While he was waiting to hear back from a few other grad schools, he went on a mission trip with a group of doctors from his church. He was there to just run errands and to help out. They were in a very poor nation. When he saw the doctors taking care of the people, treating their diseases, something new was birthed on the inside. He thought, "I don't want to be an engineer. This is what I want to do with my life. I want to become a doctor and help to take care of people."

After he returned home, he applied to medical school and he was immediately accepted. In fact, he had several schools to choose from. What was interesting is that the first engineering school he had applied to finally sent him a letter of acceptance. If he had received that letter months earlier, the young man never would have gone on the mission trip, and he might never have felt called to become a doctor. God closed the doors to the engineering school on purpose, to push him into his divine destiny.

You may be discouraged because your plans have not worked out, but those closed doors were not an accident. That was God directing your steps. The reason God closed them is because He has something better in store. Will you trust Him? It may not make sense now, but one day it will. Remember, you're not really trusting Him if you are happy only when things go your way. Put your desires on the altar. "God, this is what I want, but let Your will, not mine, be done."

If you adopt this perspective and thank God for your closed doors just as much as for your open doors, then like Abraham you'll pass the test. I believe and declare you will see the exceeding, abundant, above-and-beyond future that God has in store.

CHAPTER NINETEEN

God Is in Control of the Storm

Most of the time we believe God is in control when everything is going our way. We're getting good breaks. Business is up. The family is happy. The kids are making good grades. We know God is directing our steps. Life is good.

But having faith doesn't exempt us from difficulties. The storms of life come to every person. We get a bad medical report. A friend betrays us. Business takes a downturn. In the difficult times it's easy to think, "God, where are You? How could You let this happen to me?"

But the same God Who is in control in the good times is just as in control in the tough times. God will not allow a storm unless He has a divine purpose for it. He never said He would prevent every difficulty, but God did promise He would use every difficulty.

Here's the key: God will direct the winds of the storm to blow you where He wants you to go. We see storms as being negative. "Oh, this is so bad. Can't believe this is happening to me." But God uses the storm to move you from point A to point B. The winds may be strong, the circumstances may look bad, but if you will stay in faith, not get bitter, not start complaining, those winds will blow you to a new level of your destiny.

It may have been meant for your harm, but God knows how to shift the winds. Instead of blowing you backward He can cause them to blow you forward where you will come out better, stronger—and that storm also will move you to a place of greater blessing and greater influence.

A lot of people say they have faith, but in the tough times they fall apart. They feel like God has disappointed them. They won't be happy until the storm is over. But you have to remind yourself God is in control of that storm. Nothing happens without God's permission. If that storm was keeping you from your destiny, God would have never allowed it. If that person who left you, or that financial difficulty, or that legal situation was stopping God's plan for your life, He would have never permitted it.

The reason He did allow it was to move you one step closer to your divine destiny. Instead of using your faith to try to pray away every difficulty, you should use your faith to believe that when the winds stop blowing you will be exactly where God wants you to be.

The Apostle Paul did just that. God promised that Paul would stand before Caesar. Paul was doing the right thing, fulfilling his purpose, when he was arrested. They put him on a boat that was headed toward Rome. Paul told the captain and the crew, "This is not a good time to sail. There's bad weather up ahead."

Paul had inside information, but they wouldn't listen to him. Their ship was in the middle of the ocean when a huge storm arose. For fourteen days they didn't see the sun or the stars. It was dark. The sea was turbulent. The wind was howling.

The storm was so bad they started throwing equipment overboard to keep the ship from sinking. They were sure they would be killed. Imagine what must have been going through Paul's mind. Here he was doing the right thing, but he still ended up in the middle of this huge storm.

Sometimes you face difficulties not because you're doing something wrong, but because you're doing something right. It's just another step on the way to your divine destiny. With most storms, we can see the end. At some point we know it's ending soon. We just have to dig in our heels and endure it. But there are some storms, like the one Paul faced, that never seem like they'll end. You may have problems like that. It seems like they will never be resolved. You may think that in the natural you'll never get well, or never get out of debt.

Paul was facing that sort of never-ending storm. The crew finally said to him, "You were right. We should have listened to you."

Paul didn't say, "I told you so. Now look what you've done. You've doomed us all."

Instead, he said, in effect, "Don't worry about it. The God I serve has given me a promise. He said that I will stand before Caesar. He would not have allowed this storm if it would keep me from my destiny."

When you have a promise deep down in your heart, everything in the world can come against you. The dream may look far away, but like Paul, you know this setback is not permanent. It's only tempo-rary. It will not keep you from becoming who God has created you to be.

The wind became so strong, the waves so big, that the crew on Paul's boat could not control the ship anymore. Instead of fighting it, instead of trying to steer it where they wanted it to go, it says in Acts 27 that they took down the sails and let the wind blow the ship wherever the storm wanted it to go.

Like with that crew, there comes a point when you've done everything you can. You've prayed. You've believed. You stood in faith. Now you've got to do as they did. Quit fighting it. Quit trying to make it happen your way. Quit trying to force it to work out and just relinquish control. Let the storm take you where God wants you to go. God will never take you someplace where He won't sustain you.

It's a powerful attitude to relinquish control—when you quit worrying about it, quit losing sleep, and quit dreading it—and say, "God, I trust You. I know You control these winds. They can either blow me backward, forward, sideways, up, or down. But one thing I'm confident in: where You take me is where I'm supposed to be."

When my father was seventy-seven years old he had to go on dialysis. He was still ministering most weekends, but his health started to go downhill. He ended up in the hospital. The whole church was praying, believing that he was going to come out of it like he had done so many times before.

Unfortunately, this time he didn't make it. It could have looked like that storm got the best of him. But God was still in control. That storm didn't defeat him. It promoted him. Those winds blew him into his eternal home, into the arms of his Heavenly Father.

For our family, though, it seemed like everything was out of control. This was one of those storms we could not see the end of. We didn't know how it would work out. The critics were saying Lakewood would never make it without my dad. My own thoughts were telling me, "It will never work out. Lakewood has seen its best days."

God could have changed it. God had healed my mother of terminal cancer years before. He is God. He could have healed my father as well. We all face situations that don't turn out the way we had hoped. We prayed. We believed. Still, our loved one didn't make it. Our prayers weren't answered the way we wanted, on our timetable.

It's easy to be negative, to grow bitter, and to give up on our dreams. My father and I were best friends. I worked with him for many years. We traveled the world together. All of a sudden he was gone. I had to do what I'm asking you to do. I said, "God, I know this storm is not a surprise to You. I can't bring my dad back. I can't make it happen my way. So God, I'm turning loose the sails and I'm letting Your wind blow me to where You want me to go."

I relinquished control and came back to that place of peace.

I refused to go around worrying, "How will it work out? What will happen next?" Instead, I said, "God, I trust You. I know You are in control of these winds."

That storm blew me from behind the scenes at Lakewood to the position I'm in now as leader of our church. I never dreamed I could speak in front of people, but that is where the storm took me. This is what the Scripture means when it says, "What was meant for your harm God will use to your advantage."

The stormy winds may be blowing in your life today, the waves raging. Maybe you can't see the end. Why don't you take a step of faith and say, "Okay, God. I'm letting You do it Your way. I know You have my best interests at heart. This storm cannot take me where You will not permit it to go. So God, I trust You."

When you do that, those winds will blow you to a new level of your destiny. It may not happen overnight, but God is a faithful God. His plan for your life will not be stopped by a storm, by a bad break, by the loss of a loved one, or by an injustice. God said no weapon formed against you will prosper. He said when the enemy comes in like a flood He will raise up a barrier.

You may be in a storm. There may be pressure all around you. You could easily be worried, but know this: the battle is not yours. The battle is the Lord's. God is saying, "If you'll trust Me, I will shift those winds, and instead of blowing you backward they will thrust you forward."

Today, Lakewood Church is experiencing its greatest days of ministry. The critics said we would never make it, but today Lakewood is stronger than ever. God used the winds of the storm that were meant to destroy us. He shifted their direction, and those winds have taken us places we never could have gone on our own.

The same winds that try to hold you back will be the winds God uses to thrust you forward. I read about this executive who worked for a large home improvement company. He had been with the company for more than thirty years and was in senior management. They had retail stores all over the country. Then the company did a corporate restructuring, and its leaders decided that they didn't need him anymore. Here he had practically built the company from the ground up. Just when he thought he could relax and enjoy the fruit of his hard work, he had to start all over.

He felt betrayed, but he understood this principle: God can direct the winds of the storm. Instead of becoming bitter and sitting around all angry, he forgave those who hurt him.

He let go of the job that didn't work out. He began to dream of new opportunities. He found some friends and they started another company. This new company took off, and it has become one of the largest, most successful home improvement stores in all the nation. In fact, his new company put his old company out of business.

God knows how to shift the winds that were meant to destroy you and instead use them to increase you. Quit mourning over what you lost. Let go of whatever didn't work out. Forgive those who hurt you. When you dare say, "God, I trust You to make my wrongs right," then those winds trying to hold you back will shift direction and push you forward.

God is in complete control. If God wanted you to have that job from which you were laid off, you would still have it. Let it go. He has something better. If God wanted that person who left you to stay, then that person would have stayed. Let it go.

If your prayers are not answered the way you wanted and on your timetable, don't be bitter. Don't be discouraged. Let it go. God has something better, something greater, something bigger in your future.

The three Hebrew teenagers Shadrach, Meshach, and Abednego were facing a huge storm. They were about to be thrown into a fiery furnace because they wouldn't bow down before the king's golden idol. I'm sure they prayed, "God, please keep us out of this fire. This is dangerous. We could be killed. God, we're asking You to not let this happen."

They wanted God to do it their way, but God chose to do it another way. Sometimes God will deliver you from the fire. Other times God will make you fireproof and take you through the fire. There are two kinds of faith. There is a delivering faith and there is a sustaining faith.

Delivering faith is when God keeps you from the fire. God keeps you out of the adversity. But most of the time we need sustaining faith. Sustaining faith is when God takes you through the storm, through the difficulty, and the wind is blowing. You are filled with doubt, anxiety, fear, and bitterness. You have all these opportunities to get discouraged. But when you know that God is in control of the storm you won't be worried. Even if you go through the difficulty, you know God will take care of you. He will make you fireproof.

These three teenagers had their hands and feet bound with cords, and they were thrown into the fiery furnace. But the only thing the fire burned off were the cords that were holding them back. They went in tied up, but they walked out totally free. The God we serve knows how to burn up the limitations that are holding us back while not harming anything we need.

It would have been a great victory to simply survive the fire. We would all celebrate that. But really, it was a greater victory for God to take them through the fire and make them fireproof.

The same God Who kept them safe in the fiery furnace has put a hedge of protection around you. Whether you realize it or not, you are fireproof. Don't complain about the storms. Don't be discouraged and think, "Oh, this is too big. This health issue, this financial difficulty, this legal battle, it will be the end of me."

No, all it will do is burn up the limitations that are holding you back. You are coming out stronger, increased, promoted, and without smelling like smoke, just like those teens.

Why? Almighty God is in control of the furnace. He is in control of the winds. God is even in control of our enemies.

When Moses told Pharaoh, "God said, 'Let the people go,'" Pharaoh said *no*—not once, not twice, not three times. He said *no* again and again and again. What's interesting is the Scripture says, "God caused Pharaoh to say *no*." It wasn't even Pharaoh's choice. God caused him to refuse. Why? So God could show His power in a greater way.

Sometimes God will not remove the obstacle. He won't deliver you from the storm, not because He is mean, and not because He is trying to make your life miserable. He wants to show His favor in your life in a greater way. You may be in a storm, but remember: God is in control. Stay in peace.

Do like Daniel in the Scriptures. His enemies had him thrown into the lion's den, with hungry lions. The king came back the next morning to check on him, fully expecting to find him torn apart. You know what he found? Daniel, sound asleep, right next to hungry lions.

Daniel wasn't worried. He wasn't taking tranquilizers and he wasn't hiding in the corner. Daniel was in peace. He knew he was lion proof. He knew the storm could not take him where God could not keep him.

Maybe you feel like you're in the lion's den, or maybe a fiery furnace. You could easily live all stressed out, and worried. God is saying, "Come back to that place of peace." He has you in the palm of His hand.

As long as you're being your best, honoring Him, the fierce winds may come, but he will shift the winds in your direction. Instead of defeating you, they will promote you. What is now your test will become your testimony.

This lady I know received a bad medical report. The doctors found what they thought was cancer. We prayed and believed that the report would come back negative, but a few weeks later they found out indeed it was cancer.

She's been coming to Lakewood Church a long time. She knows she is not a victim. She is a victor. She understands that God is in control of the storm. She didn't get bitter. Her attitude was, "God, I've prayed. I've believed. I've done my part. Now God, I'm going to trust You. I believe these winds will blow me to where You want me to go."

For one year she took chemotherapy. Now, she has been cancer free for more than six years. She is one of Lakewood's Prayer Partners. She prays for others and she goes back to that hospital and volunteers, encouraging others facing cancer.

It's great for God to deliver us from the fire. That's always our prayer, but even if it doesn't happen that way, God will still take care of you. Stay in faith. That just means you will have a greater testimony. You will see God's favor in a new way. I love the fact that this woman who survived cancer is now helping people overcome in that same area.

Your test will become your testimony where you can tell people, "Hey, look. God did it for me. He can do it for you."

The Apostle Paul's ship hit a big sandbar and broke apart. He and the others on board swam over to a small island called Malta. That was not where

Paul had planned on going. He could have thought, "God, You said I would stand before Caesar. What happened? Your plan didn't work out."

But that storm didn't stop God's plan. It was a part of God's plan. On that small island the father of the tribal chief was extremely sick. Paul prayed for him and he was healed. They brought others one by one to Paul. He prayed and God healed. Paul shared his faith, and the whole island came to know the Lord.

What happened? God used the winds of that storm to blow Paul to people in need. Had it not been for the storm the chief's father could have died. The people of Malta never would have heard the Good News.

The storms you experience may be meant for your harm, but God knows how to direct the winds. He will not only protect you but also take you to a place where you can be a blessing to others in need. On the way out of your storm, don't be surprised if you have interruptions, inconveniences, and other setbacks you hadn't planned on. God ordained them so you can be a blessing.

Don't just look for your miracle. Become somebody's miracle. When you reach out to others in need—when you lift the fallen, when you encourage those who are down, when you befriend the lonely—your own breakthrough will come. The

Scripture says, "Pray one for another so that you may be healed." One of the tests you have to pass is being good to others in the midst of your storm.

I've heard the saying, "When everything comes against you, remember that airplanes take off against the wind, not with the wind." Those winds were never meant to push you down. They were meant to lift you to a higher level of your destiny.

When an eagle faces a storm he doesn't try to fight his way through the wind, through the rain, frustrated, struggling, putting forth all this effort. He simply stretches out his wings, and he lets the strong winds lift him higher and higher. Finally he rises above the storm, where it's as calm and peaceful as can be.

Maybe you are worried about a medical report, a child, or a challenge at work, and you can't sleep at night because of anxiety and fear. When the winds are blowing and things come against you, it's easy to get frustrated and start fighting and trying to change what you were never meant to change.

Be an eagle instead. Put your trust in God. "I've done everything I can. Now I'm going to quit struggling. I'm not trying to make it happen my way. God, I'm trusting You."

When you come back to that place of peace knowing that God is in control of the storm, then those winds meant to push you down will end up lifting you higher and higher.

You may be in a difficulty right now. God didn't deliver you from the fire like He did the Hebrew teenagers. But let me encourage you. God has made you fireproof. You will come out of that fire promoted, increased, and better, without the smell of smoke.

What is your test now will soon become your testimony. Shake off the discouragement. Shake off the self-pity and get ready for God to do something new. Those winds blowing against you are about to shift direction. They will thrust you forward into the fullness of your destiny.

PART
V

Don't Settle for
Good Enough

CHAPTER TWENTY

Don't Settle for Good Enough

In Genesis 38, there is a story about a woman who is pregnant with twins. When she gave birth one of the baby's arms came out first. The midwife tied a small cord around it, planning to gently pull him, but before she could do that, the baby pulled his arm back and his brother broke through and was born first.

One stretched and one settled.

In a similar way, inside each of us there are two people. One says, "I will become everything God has created me to be. I can do all things through Christ. I'm surrounded by God's favor."

The other says, "I'll never get out of debt. The economy is too bad. I'll never lose the weight. My metabolism is off. I'll never break that addiction. I'll just learn to live with it."

One wants to stretch. The other wants to settle. You can choose which person you will be. Too many people make the choice to settle.

"My marriage is not what it should be, but at least we're still together. It's good enough." Or, "I don't really like this job, but at least I'm employed. It's good enough." Or "I would love to make As in school but I'm not that smart. These Cs are good enough."

No, don't make the mistake of settling for "good enough." Good enough is not your destiny. You are a child of the Most High God. You have seeds of greatness on the inside. If you are to see the fullness of what God has in store, you have to have the right attitude: "I'm not letting good enough be good enough. I know I was created for greatness. I was created to excel, to live a healthy life, to overcome obstacles, to fulfill my destiny. I am not settling. I'm stretching. I'm letting go of the things that didn't work out and reaching forward to the new things God has in store."

Maybe you have lost your fire. At one time you may have known you would break an addiction, beat a sickness, or find someone to marry, but you've gone through disappointments. Your life has not worked out the way you thought it would. Now you've accepted the fact that your vision for your life will probably not happen. You've become comfortable with good enough. But God is saying to you what

He said to the people of Israel: "You have dwelt long enough on this mountain."

It's time to move forward. God has new levels in front of you, new opportunities, new relationships, promotions, and breakthroughs. But you need to stir up what God put on the inside, stir up the dreams and the promises you've pushed down.

"It's not going to happen, Joel. I'm too old. I don't have the connections. I don't know the right people."

God has it all figured out. If you start believing again, start dreaming again, start pursuing what God put in your heart, God will make a way where you can't see a way. He will connect you to the right people. He will open doors no man can shut. What God spoke over your life, what He promised you in the night, what He whispered in your spirit, those hidden dreams, He will bring to pass.

The good news is just because you gave up a dream doesn't mean God gave up. You may have changed your mind, but God didn't change His mind. He still has a victorious plan in front of you. Why don't you get in agreement with Him?

I read a story about a young man who dreamed of playing professional football. In high school he was a star player and won all kinds of awards. He came from a very small town where everybody knew him. All the children looked up to him, and wanted to be like him; a local hero. But most of the coaches thought he was too small to play in college. All the major universities turned him down. He ended up at a junior college and took a job at a pizza restaurant. He quit playing football.

One night he was delivering a pizza and a ten-year-old boy answered the door. When this boy saw the young man his eyes grew so big. The boy was star-struck. He couldn't believe this was the same person he'd watched play at the local high school, the same athlete who had thrilled the crowd so many times. After a second or two, the boy's father walked up and the young man gave the father the pizza. The little boy was very confused. He looked up at his father. He looked at the young man and said very innocently, "What are you doing delivering pizzas?"

Those words from a ten-year-old boy lit a new fire on the inside for the young man. After work that night he went to the gym and started training. That summer he trained harder than he had ever trained before. He gained seventy pounds, and became bigger, stronger, quicker, and faster.

That fall, he tried out at a major university that had accepted him as a student. He'd always wanted to play there. He made the team and kept working until he also became their star player. After college, he was drafted in the first round to play professional football. Today, he is a star in the NFL living out his dream. But he said, "It would have never happened if that ten-year-old boy hadn't asked me, 'What are you doing selling pizzas?'"

My questions for you are: Have you settled somewhere way beneath what you know God has put in you? Have you given up on a dream, or let go of a promise, because it didn't happen the first time?

Maybe you had a setback. Maybe somebody told you, "You're not talented enough. You're not big enough." But I ask you respectfully, "What are you doing there? You have so much in you. You are full of talent, ideas, creativity, and potential."

When God breathed His life into you, He put a part of Himself in you. You have the DNA of Almighty God. You were never created to be average, to barely get by, to always struggle, or to just have to take the leftovers. You were created as the head and not the tail.

You are equipped. Empowered. Fully loaded. Lacking nothing. Don't you dare settle for second best. Don't get stuck in a rut thinking that you've reached your limits. Draw the line in the sand and say, "That's it. I've let good enough be good enough long enough. Today is a new day. My dream may not have happened the first time I tried for it, or even the fifth time or the thirtieth time, but I'm not settling. I'm stretching my faith, looking for opportunities, taking steps to improve. I'm going to become everything God has created me to be."

When you do the natural, God will do the supernatural. When you do what you can, God will come and do what you cannot. Don't take the easy way out. Stand strong and fight the good fight of faith.

In the Scripture, Abraham is listed as one of the heroes of faith. God made one of the first covenants with him. But what's interesting is that God spoke to Abraham's father many years before and told him to go where he later told Abraham to go.

It says in Genesis 11 that Abraham's father left Ur and headed out toward Canaan. He had his goal. He was going to the Promised Land just like God told Abraham. But it says, "He stopped along the way and settled in Haran."

Why did he stop? There were too many difficulties. It was hard traveling with all of his flocks and herds. He had his family and their possessions. It wasn't comfortable. He finally decided, "I can't go any farther. I know this isn't the Promised Land, but it's good enough. At least we can survive out here. At least we can make it."

How many times do we do the same thing? We

start off right. We've got a big dream. We're fulfilling our destinies. But along the way we face opposition. Adversity arises. Too many times we say, "What's the use? I'm never breaking this addiction. My marriage is never getting better. I'll never accomplish my dreams. I'm just settling here. It's good enough."

But I want to light a new fire in you today. You are not weak, defeated, or lacking. You have been armed with strength for every battle. That obstacle is no match for you. You have the most powerful force in the universe breathing in your direction.

Don't be a weakling. Be a warrior. Your marriage is worth fighting for. Your health is worth fighting for. Your dreams and your children are worth fighting for. Dig in and say, "I am in it to win it. I know God didn't bring me this far to leave me here. I'm not settling halfway, three-fourths of the way, or nine-tenths of the way. I will make it all the way in to my Promised Land."

If you're to be victorious you must have a made-up mind. Be determined. You can't give up when life becomes difficult. You can't complain because it's taking a long time. You can't be discouraged because you went through a setback. Everything God promised you is worth fighting for, so you need to be in it for the long haul.

You may need to pull up your stakes. You camped

halfway like Abraham's father. You have become comfortable and decided that your dreams will never come to pass, your health will never improve, or you'll never get out of debt. I'm asking you to pack up your tent, gather up your belongings, and start moving forward.

You may have hit a temporary delay, but that's okay. That won't stop you from fulfilling your destiny. Today can be your new beginning. God is breathing new life into your spirit. He has greater victories in front of you. Get a vision for it.

"This sounds good Joel, but I'll never meet the right person, I'll never earn the promotion at work, I'll never break this addiction." Every time you dwell on those negative, discouraging thoughts you are stopping short of your Promised Land.

The first place we lose the battle is in our thinking. If you don't think you can be successful, then you never will be. If you don't think you can overcome the past, or meet the right person, or accomplish your dreams, you'll be stuck right where you are. You have to change your thinking. The Creator of the universe is arranging things in your favor. He said no good thing would He withhold because you walk uprightly. He will not withhold the right person, the wisdom, the breaks, or the turnaround.

I read about this university professor who was giving his students their most important test of the year. Before he gave them the test, he told his students he was proud of them because they had worked so hard. He made them a special offer. He said, "Anyone who would like an automatic C on this test, just raise your hand and I'll give you a C. You won't even have to take the test."

One hand slowly went up, and then another and another, until about half of the students opted out of taking the test. They walked out of the room so relieved, and so happy.

The professor next passed out the test forms to the rest of the students. He placed a form facedown on each desk, then asked the students not to turn their forms over until he told them to begin. For the next few minutes he gave them encouragement, saying they would do great things in life and how they should always strive to do their best.

Then he told them to turn over the test forms and begin. But when they looked at the test, there were only two sentences: "Congratulations. You just made an A."

Too many times, like those students, we settle for a C when God has an A for us. If you say you will never recover from an illness, that's taking a C. You need to change your thinking: "God is restoring health unto me. I will live and not die. I'm getting stronger, healthier, better."

That's going for the A.

Or, "This guy I'm dating, I know he's not good for me. He doesn't treat me right, but I may not ever meet anybody else." That's not a C. That's a D!

God has an A, but you'll never see it if you keep taking the Cs. Yes, the Cs are easier. You don't have to stretch. You don't have to leave your comfort zone. But you'll never be truly fulfilled if you keep settling for Cs. The good news is God already has As in your future. He has the right person, a happy marriage, a successful career, health, wholeness, freedom, and victory.

Don't take the easy way out. The As are worth fighting for. I can't think of much that would be sadder than to come to the end of life and have to wonder, "What could I have become if I didn't settle for good enough? What could I have been if I didn't take so many Cs but instead I pressed forward, striving to be my very best?"

You may have taken some Cs in the past. We all have. But make a decision with me that from now on you're only going for the As.

Here's a key: if you're not seeing the things in your life that God promised in your spirit, then keep moving forward. It's only temporary. Like the young man delivering pizzas, you may be doing something that's below your potential, working at a job in which you're not using your gifts. Don't slack off when you're there. Keep being your best, but see that as only temporary.

You are just passing through. Don't put your stakes down. Don't settle there. If the medical report doesn't agree with what God says about you, don't accept it as the way it will always be. Your attitude should be: "This is just a season I'm passing through. I'm coming into health, wholeness, and victory."

Maybe God has blessed you with good things like a great family, a wonderful job, and good health. You've seen His favor. But you know there are greater levels in front of you. It's easy to think, "I'm happy. I have no complaints. God has been good to me."

But I've learned that good is the enemy of great. Don't let that be an excuse to keep you from God's best. Stir up your greatness. Stretch into a new level.

This is where the people of Israel missed it. God brought them out of slavery. They were headed toward the Promised Land, a land flowing with milk and honey. The spies came back and said, "Moses, we have never seen such a magnificent land so beautiful, luscious, green." The fruits and vegetables were like nothing they had experienced. It took two people to carry the bushels of grapes because they were so big.

That was the vision God had in front of them. That was the A.

In the wilderness they saw God's goodness. They saw God part the Red Sea, bring water out of a rock, and rain down manna from heaven. But do you know that was all only temporary provision? That was only the C. The mistake they made was that when they came to the Promised Land, there were people living on it. All the people of Israel had to do was fight for the land. God had promised them the victory, but they were not willing to fight. They thought, "It's not worth it. It's too much trouble. Besides, those people are bigger than us, anyway."

I believe one reason they settled for the C so easily is because they had seen God's favor in the wilderness. They thought, "It's not so bad out here. God takes care of us. He feeds us. He clothes us. It's good enough." They were too easily satisfied. They didn't realize everything God had done up to that point was only temporary provision. It was to sustain them until they reached their land of abundance.

You can probably say, as I can, that you've seen God be good to you. God has blessed you with health, a family, and a job. He has opened doors that should not have opened. He has shown you favor and protected you. Can I tell you that these were only temporary provisions?

You have not made it into your Promised Land. God is taking you somewhere greater than you've ever imagined. The Scripture says, "No eye has seen, no ear has heard, no mind has imagined the amazing things God has in store for those who love the Lord."

Don't make the mistake made by the people of Israel when they built houses where they should have pitched tents. Don't let your temporary provision become permanent. Yes, God has been good to you, but you haven't seen anything yet. What God has in your future will supersede what you've seen in the past.

Thank God for His goodness. Be grateful for the Red Sea's parting. Thank Him for the protection, the provision, and the favor. But if it's not what God put in your spirit, be bold enough to pick up your stakes and say, "God, this is all great. You've been awesome in my life and I thank You for it. But God, I believe this is only temporary provision. Where You're taking me is to a land of abundance, a place like I've never experienced before."

That's not being selfish. That's releasing your faith for the fullness of your destiny. After all, God said, "I will give you houses that you didn't build."

Let those words sink down into your spirit. "I will give you houses that you didn't have to build. You will reap from vineyards that you did not plant." One version says, "May the God of your fathers make you a thousand times more than you are."

I don't know about you, but I can't settle here. I've got to pull up my stakes. God has a thousand times more: more joy, more peace, more influence, more wisdom, more ideas, more creativity, and more good breaks. Take the limits off God.

When Joshua was leading the people of Israel, God said, "Joshua, you have not passed this way before." God is saying the same thing to us. Something out of the ordinary is coming your way; new levels of favor, unprecedented opportunities, or divine connections. God has As in your future.

People are already lined up to be good to you. You don't have to find them. They'll come find you. When you honor God, His blessings will chase you down. You won't be able to outrun the good things of God.

My challenge to you is this: Don't settle where you are in your health, your relationships, your career, or your walk with the Lord. Keep stretching. Keep growing. Keep believing. Keep dreaming. Don't let good enough be good enough. Be determined to become everything God created you to be.

You may have dwelled on that same mountain long enough. It's time to pull up your stakes. Pack up your belongings. Start moving forward. Enlarge your vision. Make room in your thinking for the new thing God wants to do. Don't let your temporary provision become permanent.

If you'll learn this principle of stretching and not settling, then you will see the fullness of what God has in store. I believe you will overcome obstacles and accomplish dreams. Not like Abraham's father but like Joshua, you're going to make it all the way to your Promised Land.

CHAPTER TWENTY-ONE

You Are Uncontainable

When God created us He put seeds of increase on the inside. We were never made to reach one level and stop. We were created to grow, to move forward, and to increase. We should be constantly breaking the barriers of the past, taking new ground for our families and advancing God's Kingdom.

But throughout life there will always be forces trying to keep us where we are. They can't stop the progress we've made, but they'll do their best to contain us, to keep us in a box and to limit our influence.

A few years ago the swine flu was a big threat in Houston. Many experts believed it started in Mexico. Officials there shut down Mexico City. No one could come or go. It looked like a ghost town: no traffic, no people, and no business. What were they doing? They were trying to contain it. They knew it might be contagious and if a few people were infected the illness could spread all over, and that's what happened.

Eventually, it couldn't be contained. That's the way the forces of darkness work against us. They're constantly trying to push us down, limit our influence, and keep us from taking any new ground.

But can I give you some good news today? You are uncontainable. The forces in you are greater than the forces trying to contain you. If you're to become everything God has created you to be, you can't get stuck in a rut and think you've reached your limits. Keep stretching your faith, looking for new opportunities, new ideas, and new ways to expand your influence.

When I was twelve years old, I played football. A friend of mine was the running back on an opposing team. He was very fast, quick, and almost impossible to stop. The week we were playing his team, our coach came up with a special defense to try and contain him. That was the phrase our coach used all week: "Contain him."

I must have heard that phrase a thousand times. The coach had us focus one group on the outside, one group on the inside. We worked and worked trying to figure out how to stop him. When the game rolled around, it was like we had not even practiced.

My friend was so much quicker than us. The coach could have put the whole team on him. He still would have run by us all. Even when we were able to grab him, it was like he was covered with oil. We couldn't hang on. He would twist and turn and always get away. What was the problem? He was uncontainable.

That's the way I want you to see yourself. You have the Spirit of the Living God on the inside. His anointing on your life is just like oil. When something tries to stop you or hold you down, it doesn't have a chance. In your imagination you just twist and turn and see that something slide off. You are uncontainable.

You may have grown complacent and settled where you are, believing those lies that you've gone as far as you can go. Maybe you feel you've made too many mistakes, or you come from the wrong family, or that you have a handicap.

I'm here to infect you with a virus. It's a good virus: a God virus. It says, "You were made for more, to influence more, to accomplish more, to love more, to give more, and to have more."

I've got to warn you: I'm highly contagious and I'm infecting you with faith. I'm infecting you with vision. I'm infecting you with joy.

God is saying you have not touched the surface of what He has in store for you. He will take you places you've never dreamed of. He will bring opportunities that give you amazing influence. You have not seen your best days. They are still out in front of you.

You need to dig your heels in and say, "I will not be contained by negative people, by the way I was raised, by mistakes I've made, by injustice, disappointment, or even some handicap. I have my mind made up. Where I am is not where I'm staying. I'm rising higher. I'm a barrier breaker. I'm taking new ground for God's Kingdom."

It's time to rise up and become leaders and have influence and respect and credibility, not just in our own circles, but also in the marketplace. That means in the general public, in the schools, in the government, and in arts, sports, and entertainment. We're not supposed to hide our gifts and go around feeling like we're second-class and we don't have that much to offer.

Put your shoulders back. Hold your head up high. You are a child of the Most High God. He breathed His life into you. You have something incredible to offer. In the coming days God will increase your influence.

I love the story in Acts 4, in which Peter and John prayed for people and they became well. Great miracles had taken place. They had a big service. All kinds of good things happened. But the city leaders didn't know what to do with Peter and John. They weren't for them. They didn't fit into their box. Instead of being happy about it, the authorities ordered it to stop. They said: "We cannot deny that a notable miracle has taken place. But here's our plan: that it spread no further."

They were saying in effect, "We're pushing them down to lessen their influence and contain them." But Peter and John understood this principle. They knew: "We cannot be contained. God put this dream in our hearts, and as long as we stay in faith, nothing can shut it down."

Their message was not restricted. It spread like wildfire, and we're still talking about it today. In the same way, you cannot be contained. People may try to push you down. Somebody may try to discourage you and close some doors. But if you'll just keep pressing forward and shake off that discouragement, God will open doors that no man can shut. God will raise you up even though somebody else is trying to push you down.

Nelson Mandela was put in prison because he opposed the government of apartheid. The leaders thought they finally were rid of him. They wouldn't have to deal with his opposition anymore.

Mr. Mandela could have thought, "I did my best, gave it my all. I guess it wasn't meant to be." Instead,

Nelson Mandela knew he couldn't be contained by people, by injustice, by racism, by hatred, or even by prison walls.

Twenty-seven years later, he walked out a free man. Eventually, he became president of that same country and won the Nobel Peace Prize.

What God has destined for your life will come to fulfillment. You may think you have too many obstacles. You've had too many closed doors. It's been too long. You can't see how it could ever happen. Get your fire back. Get your dream back. It may seem impossible, but God says, "That setback cannot contain you. That injustice, that disappointment, that bad break, cannot hold you down." If you will rid yourself of that limited mentality and press forward in faith, God will take you where you're supposed to be.

That's what happened to the Apostle Paul. He was put in prison for spreading the Good News. Paul could have become depressed, discouraged, and given up. Instead, his attitude was, "I may not be able to go out and minister, but I do have a pen. I do have a piece of paper. I can write."

Paul wrote much of the New Testament from a prison cell. His captors thought they were containing him, but their plan backfired. Paul had more influence with his writings than he ever had in person.

I want you to receive this in your spirit: God is going to increase your influence. The Scripture says God will cause His face to shine down on us.

That's His favor. You need to start expecting this favor as never before. God wants you to be a barrier breaker. He wants you to take new ground for the Kingdom.

We think: "Well, I'm not that talented. I don't have much to offer." Too often we've thought, "Let us just take the leftovers. We can't afford anything. If you can just give us a discount. If you can just please help us."

No influence. No abundant mentality. In fact, this is exactly how my father started out. My dad grew up extremely poor. He developed a barely-get-by mentality. He never thought he would have enough, and he certainly never thought he would have any influence. It took him years and years to get rid of a poverty mind-set, a second-class mentality.

One day he realized he didn't have to be contained by how he was raised; he was created to live an abundant life. He developed this new mind-set. Early in his career, my father went to a store to buy a suit. When the salesperson found out he was a minister he said to my father, "Let me go talk to my manager. Maybe we can give you a minister's discount." Years earlier my father would have been jumping up and down, rejoicing, "God, You're meeting my needs." My dad loved to get a good deal. We're certainly not against that. But he had come through so much poverty and lack and defeat that didn't set well with him.

My father said, "I appreciate you wanting to help me, but I don't need a minister's discount. I'm not looking for a handout. I am not a beggar. I am not second-class. I am a child of the Most High God. I am blessed. I am prosperous and I am well able to pay the full price."

That salesman looked at my father and said, "I have never met a minister like you!"

My father was a barrier breaker. He believed he could rise higher. He was not contained by how he was raised and what was modeled growing up. He saw God do amazing things in his life. But many people see themselves as second class, poor and defeated. They are content to just scrape by with no influence, no respect, and no credibility.

Thank God, this is a new day. There's a new generation rising up with people who say, "I know who I am: a child of Almighty God. I don't have to be contained by how I was raised, by what I've seen in the past. I know I am a barrier breaker. I am a person of influence. So I'm moving forward and taking new ground, not just for my family but also to advance God's Kingdom."

It all begins in your thinking. Don't be contained in your mind. Who said you can't rise any higher? Who told you that you would never be successful, that you'll never own a nice house, that you'll never be in management, or that you'll never have any more influence? Those are lies.

Let me tell you what I know about you. Some of you will write books that will touch millions of people. Some of you will develop medicines that will affect our world. Some of you will see your movies at the top of the box-office charts. Some of you will have a ministry that will shake nations. Some of you will develop software that will revolutionize businesses. Some of you will start companies that will be global forces in the economy. Some of you will be the next leaders of communities, cities, states, or even nations.

Don't you dare sit back and say, "Well, that couldn't be me, Joel. I don't have the education. I'm not that smart. I don't have the contacts."

You need to see yourself differently. You are a barrier breaker. You are uncontainable. You have so much talent in you, so much potential. There are seeds of greatness on the inside. If you will break free from your limited mind-set and enlarge your vision, you will see God take you places that you've never even dreamed of.

That's what God did for our Lakewood Church. I

tried to go the traditional route and buy some property and build a sanctuary on it. But God's dream for our lives is always so much bigger than our own. God gave us a premier building in the fourth largest city in America.

We broke barriers. God helped us pave the way, to go further. Now other people can come behind us and do the same thing. That's the way God wants it to be. Every generation should increase.

Our former church campus was on a very small side street in a rural section of town. There were great people over there, but the area had become run-down. Through the years people used to say to my parents, "What are you doing still over here in this part of town?"

Some even ridiculed them and treated them as second-class. But isn't it interesting how God has a way of always giving you the last laugh? Today, we're not on a side street. We're on the second busiest freeway in the nation, sitting on a prime piece of property. God didn't just give us a building. He increased our influence. It's happening all over and in many different ways.

When I was growing up, you could hear Christian music only in our church services. Maybe every once in a while another radio station would play it, but not often. This is a new day; a couple of months ago I was watching a ball game, and a national commercial came on for a cell phone company. The music in the background was, "You are good all the time. You are good." It's the song that Lakewood's worship leader Israel Houghton wrote, and we sing it all the time.

We can't be contained. We are dangerous. We're on the loose. My children were watching *American Idol* a while back. At the end of the program all of the contestants came back on and they started singing a song that our friend Darlene Zschech wrote, "Shout to the Lord, all the earth, let us sing." This time, her worship song was heard not simply during a church program but on the number one program on television.

I want you to get this down in your spirit. God is increasing your influence. He is causing your gifts and talents to come out in greater ways. His face is shining down on you right now. Rid yourself of every limited thought about being untalented, or lacking what it takes, or being second-class.

You have exactly what you need. You have gifts, talents, ideas, inventions, books, and movies. They are just waiting to come out. When they do, it will be like an explosion. You'd better get ready. God is about to thrust you into a new level of your destiny. You cannot be contained.

It's been said that the most famous sports facility in the world is Yankee Stadium. A while back, as the team owners were finishing building their new ballpark, someone from their organization called us. They invited us to bring one of our "Nights of Hope" to New York City and become the first nonbaseball event held in the new Yankee Stadium.

When my staff told me I thought they were joking. I said, "Why do they want to invite me?" They could invite the Rolling Stones, or Madonna. But instead they invited this minister from Texas. What was God doing? He was increasing our influence. God was opening doors that no man can shut. We were able to take new ground for the Kingdom.

But so often we think, "Oh, nothing like that would happen for me. You don't know my circumstances, Joel. You don't know what I've been through."

God is not limited by your circumstances. God is not contained by your education, by your environment, or by how you were raised. All God has to do is breathe in your direction. All He has to do is blow the wind of His favor your way. That's what happened to a friend of mine, Dr. Todd Price. He grew up poor in a small town in Kentucky. Some might have thought he'd never be able to contribute much to the world.

But as a young boy he saw a program on television about starving children desperately in need of food. The show said that for $15 a month you could sponsor and feed a child. Nobody asked young Todd Price to do it. His parents didn't encourage him, but he was very moved by that program. At twelve years old he went out and started mowing lawns, and he used that money to sponsor a child. That was more than forty years ago.

Today, Dr. Price has a successful medical practice, and so far he has given more than $250 million in medicine to needy people around the world. His donations went from $15 to a quarter of a billion dollars.

Dr. Price is a barrier breaker. He didn't let the limitations of the past or how he was raised keep him from rising higher. In the natural, it didn't look like he could ever go to medical school, or ever make much of his life. But he didn't allow those strongholds to take root.

Deep down he knew he was uncontainable. He knew the Creator of the Universe was breathing in his direction. Today, Dr. Price is making a mark that cannot be erased.

I saw a report on television once about a young girl with severe autism. Her name was Carly. For years, she did not speak a word or communicate her feelings in any way. It looked as if she was mentally disabled.

All through the day she would just flail her arms and have uncontrollable fits. When Carly was seven years old, the authorities tried to talk her parents into putting her in a special home. They said, "She's never going to get any better. She doesn't even comprehend the love that you're showing, much less what you're constantly saying to her."

Carly's parents wouldn't hear of it. They just kept loving her, training her, and speaking faith into her. When she was eleven years old, Carly sat down at the computer one day and typed these words: "I have autism, but this is not who I am. Take the time to know me before you judge me. I am smart, cute, funny and I love to have fun."

At that point her parents realized Carly was in there. She had just never found a way to communicate. Later she typed, "Dad, thank you for believing in me. I know I'm not the easiest child in the world to love, but you are always there for me to pick me up when I fall."

Her father said seeing Carly's note was worth every frustration, every sleepless night. They even discovered that Carly has a sense of humor. When asked about her little brother she sat down and typed: "Matthew smells so bad even skunks run and hide."

Today, Carly still amazes us. She has written her first novel even though she still has severe autism. She's still confined to a body that doesn't function normally, but she cannot be contained.

I'm asking you to get rid of your excuses. Quit

thinking, "I'm not talented enough. I've made too many mistakes. I've got this handicap." Let these words sink deep down into your spirit: You are uncontainable. You're a barrier breaker.

God wants to use you just as you are. He wants to use you to influence others. Get a vision for it. You can set a new standard for your family. If Carly can do it, you can do it. Unlock what's on the inside. Your seeds of greatness are waiting to take root and flourish.

And know this: God is breathing in your direction. Your vision is increasing. Your faith is rising. Your dreams are coming back to life. You have not seen your best days. You may have had some victories in your past, but what God has in store in your future will supersede anything you could even imagine.

Take the limitations off God and off yourself. Quit looking at what you don't have and what you can't do and how big your obstacles are. Shake that off and have the attitude: "I am uncontainable. This sickness can't contain me. I'm a child of the Most High God. I will fulfill my destiny. These people trying to push me down can't contain me. If God will be for me, who dares be against me? Even prison bars, can't contain me. I may not be able to leave but I can do like the Apostle Paul. I've got a pen. I can write. My gifts will still come out to the full."

In the coming days, God will bring opportunities for you to increase your influence in amazing ways. Don't shrink back in fear. Don't be intimidated. You are well able. You are equipped. You are anointed.

Dare to take those steps of faith. Make up your mind: "Where I am is not where I'm staying. I'm not getting comfortable. I'm not stuck in a rut. I know I am uncontainable. So I'm pressing forward, stretching my faith, believing for bigger things, expecting God's favor in unprecedented ways."

I declare that you will go places you've never dreamed of. You will have influence in circles that you've never imagined. You will be a barrier breaker. You will set new limits. You will take new ground for your family. You will advance God's Kingdom. Your gifts and talents will come out in a greater way.

What you've seen God do in the past will pale in comparison to what God is about to do. Get ready for God's favor. Get ready for increase. Get ready for His blessings. You are uncontainable.

CHAPTER TWENTY-TWO

Develop Your Pearl

You may not have realized this, but pearls—one of the most beautiful and natural jewels—are made from irritations. Oysters feed off the bottom of the ocean, and occasionally something will become lodged on the inside of the shell and irritate the oyster. It responds by covering it with the same material used to create the shell. When fully coated, the "irritant" becomes a beautiful pearl.

Pearls are expensive. People pay thousands of dollars for pearls. Ladies wear them around their neck. But pearls are born of something uncomfortable. Oysters would prefer not to deal with irritants in their shells. If you could ask them, they would say, "We don't like being uncomfortable. Don't give us any more irritations. Make everything easy."

But God designed the irritation to become something beautiful, to make it more valuable. In the same way, every irritation in our lives is designed to become a pearl. The Scripture talks about how God is the Potter and we are the clay. God forms and molds us by allowing us to be in uncomfortable situations: We're not getting our way. We're not being treated right. It's not happening as fast as we would like.

This pressure brings to light impurities in our character, things like pride, selfishness, being critical, or easily offended. These are traits we need to get rid of. We may not like it, but God uses every situation, including every traffic jam and every difficult person, for a purpose. Every time we could get our feelings hurt we need to remind ourselves, "This is only a test. This is an opportunity to come up higher."

The irritation was never designed to frustrate you. It was designed to help you grow, to help you develop the pearl. I've learned you can't pray away every uncomfortable situation. You can't rebuke every trial. God allows difficulties to help us grow. He uses people who are hard to get along with like sandpaper to rub the rough edges off us. If we don't understand how God operates and the process He uses, then we'll go through life frustrated, wondering why God is not answering our prayers, and running from every difficulty.

You may say: "My supervisor gets on my nerves.

He is inconsiderate. He is grouchy. I don't have to put up with this. I'm leaving this job."

It may be that God put that supervisor in your life to help develop your pearl, so you could learn to love those who are not lovely, to be good to people who are not being good, to develop patience, kindness, and long-suffering. Do you know what long-suffering is? It's when you have to suffer a long time putting up with something you don't like.

I often tease that I learned long-suffering growing up with my brother Paul. If every irritation can become a pearl, he helped me to have a whole strand. Between him and my sister Lisa I could open up a jewelry store!

But if you don't let God do the work in you and you leave a job because the boss is hard to deal with, God will send two more people just like him to your next job! Understand that the irritation, just like the oyster, is not God trying to make our lives miserable. It's just that God knows there is a pearl in each of us waiting to be formed. The only way we can develop them is by passing these tests, by being kind to a coworker who is not kind to us, biting our tongues when we feel like telling somebody off, or by keeping a good attitude even when stuck in traffic.

Those are opportunities to develop our pearls. Our attitude should be: "If this is where God has me,

I must need it. I'm not fighting against it. I'm not trying to pray it away. I'm embracing the place where I am. I know God has given me the grace to be here. He has put me on the potter's wheel, so I'm keeping a good attitude because I know right beyond this irritation is a beautiful pearl."

To grow, you may have to suffer through irritations and be uncomfortable for a while as God refines you. But if you stay on the wheel—if you'll be willing to change and not try to pray away every traffic jam or difficult person—you will pass those tests and step into a new level of your destiny.

The Apostle Paul said in Romans 8:18, "These present sufferings are nothing compared to the glory that is coming." Paul was mistreated, lied about, and persecuted. He had to put up with all kinds of unfairness, but he didn't complain. He didn't try to run from every difficult situation. He said in effect, "These hard times, these irritations, are no big deal. They're helping to develop my pearl. I know God is using them to do a work in me."

The Scripture says if we're to share in Christ's glory, we must be willing to share in His sufferings. This suffering doesn't mean accidents, tragedy, cancer, injustice, or abuse. The suffering the Scripture refers to occurs when we have to say no to our flesh, when we remain calm after we don't get our way, and when we stay in faith even when life seems unfair. When we pass those tests, our flesh—the human or natural part of us—will not like it. We will be uncomfortable. We will want to do what we feel like doing. But if we stay on the high road and suffer through the discomfort, it allows God to refine us. Our character is being developed in this way. Our pearls are being polished. The Scripture talks about how vessels of clay and wood are used for ordinary purposes, but a vessel of gold is used for God's highest purpose. If we let God refine us so we treat people well and handle disappointments without complaining, then we won't be vessels used for ordinary purposes like clay, wood, and silver. Instead, we can go for the gold and be used for God's highest purposes.

We all start off at the same place. We're lumps of hard clay. We have impurities including pride, selfishness, impatience, anger, and resentment. God puts us on the potter's wheel and begins to spin us around. When He comes across one of those lumps, those impurities, He will put us in a situation to work it out. The key is to pass the test. Don't fight against everything you don't like. Learn to overlook an offense. Make allowances for somebody who is hard to get along with. Quit feeling hurt because someone offended you. Toughen up and pass those tests.

The Scripture talks about the "fire of affliction"

where you could either give up and get sour or you can say, "God, I'll show You what I'm made of. I'll forgive those who hurt me. I'll keep believing even though it looks impossible. I'll stay in faith even though it was unfair."

When you pass those tests, something is deposited on the inside that nothing can take away. There is a trust, a confidence, a knowing that can be developed only by going through the fire of affliction. I've learned that God is not as interested in changing my circumstances as He is in changing me.

Where you are is not nearly as important as who you are. While God is changing the "where," allow Him to change the "who." He wants to bring the pearl out of you.

Questions I ask myself quite often include, "How much have I grown in the last five years? Do I have a better attitude? Do I trust God more? Do I treat people better? Am I more patient? Do I forgive quicker?"

We should be growing, bearing more fruit. We shouldn't be in the same place this year as we were last year. If you are still getting upset over the same things that upset you five years ago, it's time to grow up.

If the same person who was getting on your nerves five years ago is still stealing your joy, you need to look inside and make some changes. God may not change them. He wants to use them to change you.

Life is flying by. We cannot waste time going around the same mountain year after year like the people of Israel headed toward the Promised Land. That was an eleven-day trip, but it took them forty years. You and I cannot afford to waste forty years learning lessons we could easily learn in a fraction of the time. Put your foot down and say, "That's it. This is a new day. I will not keep going around that same mountain, having a bad attitude every time I don't get my way, arguing with my spouse over the same petty issues, giving in to the same temptation time and time again."

Look inside yourself and decide to make the necessary changes. The sooner you start passing these tests, the better off you will be. There is a pearl in you. You may have a lot of rough edges. You may have a thousand areas you need to improve in, but know that as long as you are moving forward God is pleased with you.

As long as you are making progress, even if it's small, God is up in the heavens cheering you on. But if your attitude is no better now than it was five years ago, God is saying, "Let's get busy." He's got you on the potter's wheel. You can pray all day long, "God, deliver me from these rude people. God, take away all these inconveniences. God, change my spouse." It's not going to happen. God wants you to change.

You've got to pass that test. Every time you pass, it will get easier and easier and easier. The truth is, God may never remove the irritation, but you will have grown to such a point that it won't even bother you anymore. What's happening? Your character is being developed. Your pearl is being polished.

First Peter 4:12 says, "Trials are to test our quality." We may not like it, but trials are beneficial. They bring to light things we need to deal with. Most of the time you are tested in areas where you need to improve. For instance, if you struggle with being impatient, don't be surprised if you get behind every slow driver out there. You will catch every red light, find every freeway under construction, and have to wait for every passing train.

God has you there for one reason: not to frustrate you, but to refine you. You've got to recognize that trial, that irritation, is not a coincidence. It's a test of your quality. Are you getting upset and losing your cool like you've done in the past? Or are you saying, "I recognize this is an opportunity to grow. God wouldn't have me here if I didn't need it, so I'm staying in peace, keeping a good attitude, and passing this test."

When you do that, you will come up higher. Anytime you pass the test, you're headed for promotion. When Victoria and I first got married and we were about to go somewhere, I would ask her if she was ready to leave. She would say yes, so I would go sit in the car and wait and wait and wait. Five minutes, ten minutes, fifteen minutes. I'd get so frustrated. I'd go back in and say, "Victoria, I thought you said you were ready."

"I *am* ready," she'd say.

"Well, would you mind walking out to the car?" I'd ask.

This would happen time and time again. I would get so stressed. I was praying, "God, You've got to change her. God, make her into this. God, make her into that."

I had her on the potter's wheel. One day I realized I'm not the potter; God is. It's funny, God never changed her. He used her to change me. My prayers backfired. God has a sense of humor.

Now when she says she's ready, I know that means in general she's ready. It's kind of like the two-minute warning in football. The clock officially says two minutes, but you know it's going to take fifteen or twenty minutes. When she says she's ready now I'll go sit down, watch TV, get something to eat, take a walk. It's no big deal. She doesn't realize God has used her to help develop my pearl. She's a good irritation, though!

So often we pray for God to change the other person. "God, change my spouse, change my child. God,

You have got to change my boss." I've learned not to pray for God to change somebody else without first saying, "God, change me."

A lady who attends Lakewood Church always comes without her husband. She deals with a lot of issues at home. For years she came down front for prayer. She had this list of all the things she wanted God to fix. She didn't think she could be happy unless they all turned around. The main thing she wanted to change was her husband.

Then, I saw her one day at church and she was just beaming with joy. She was more beautiful and more at peace than I had ever seen her. I thought surely everything must have worked out. But she said, "No, Joel. My husband is just the same. He still has a lot of issues. He hasn't changed, but you know what? *I* have changed. I don't let that frustrate me anymore. I don't let him keep me from enjoying my life."

What happened? She let that irritation become a pearl. When you can be happy, not because of your circumstances, but in spite of your circumstances, then nothing can take your joy. You may be in a trial right now. That is a test of your quality.

I was in New York City a while back and I went to a little diner to eat breakfast. A gentleman sitting a couple of tables over came up and said when he'd walked into the restaurant that morning the person in front of him let the door slam in his face. This person clearly saw he was coming, but it appeared that he let go of the door on purpose.

Normally this gentleman might have told him off, but he said he'd watched my sermon on the potter's wheel recently.

He told me: "Just when I was about to let him have it, Joel, I heard your voice saying, 'Let it go and God will fight your battles.'"

He let it go and sat down to eat breakfast. When he did that, he felt a joy bubbling up on the inside like something he had never felt before. When I walked into the diner five minutes later, he said, he nearly passed out.

"I knew that was God saying He was pleased with me," he told me.

When you pass these tests you will feel God's sense of approval. You will feel a new joy on the inside. You will know the Creator of the universe is smiling down on you.

The Scripture says, "Our faith is tried in the fire of affliction just as fire tests and purifies gold." Maybe you are in that refiner's fire right now. You don't like the situation. It doesn't seem fair. But let me encourage you. If you will stay in faith and keep pushing forward, you will come out refined, purified, stronger, and better off than you were before.

There was once a couple who loved to shop for antiques. One day they were in this small country store when they found the most beautiful teacup they had ever seen. It was magnificent. As they admired it, the teacup began to talk.

"I haven't always looked like this," it said. "There was a time that nobody wanted me. I wasn't attractive. I was just a hard lump of clay. But then this potter came along and shaped and molded me."

The teacup told the couple that the process was painful so it said to the potter, " 'Hey! What are you doing? You're making me uncomfortable. That hurts. Leave me alone.' "

The potter simply smiled and replied, "Not yet.

Then the potter put the teacup on a wheel and began to spin it around and around.

"I got so dizzy," the teacup told the couple, "but after a while I had taken on a new shape. He formed me into this teacup you admire. I thought he was finished, but then he put me into a furnace. It was so hot I didn't think I could stand it. When he came and checked on me and looked through the furnace window, he had a sparkle in his eyes. I screamed out, 'Let me out of here! It's too hot!' But he smiled and said, 'Not yet.' He finally took me out and put me up on a shelf so I could cool off. I thought, 'Thank goodness it's over. Now I can go back to being my normal self.'

But then the potter painted me, changing me from the old gray color to this beautiful blue."

The teacup went on to tell the couple that the paint was sticky and uncomfortable. "I thought I was going to choke. I told the potter to stop, but he said, 'Not yet.' Then he put me into a second oven twice as hot as the first one. This time I knew it was over. I screamed, 'I'm not kidding! I can't take it! I'm going to die!'

"Again the potter said, 'Not yet.'

"Finally, he opened the oven door, and put me on a shelf. A few weeks later he came by and handed me a mirror, and when I looked at myself I couldn't believe how beautiful I had become. I couldn't believe how much I had changed. I didn't look anything like that old lump of clay I used to be. There was a time that nobody wanted me, but now I'm this beautiful teacup: valuable, expensive, and unique, all because of this potter. He made me into something amazing."

That's the way God works in all of our lives. He is changing us little by little, from glory to glory. But on the way to the glory there may be a little bit of suffering that we have to endure. There may be times we say, "God, get me off of this potter's wheel. I can't take it anymore. I can't deal with this child. I can't handle this grouchy boss."

But God will smile and say, "Not yet."

God sees your value. He knows what He is making you into. Sometimes when we look at ourselves we think, "I've got a lot of flaws. I've got a hot temper. I've got a problem with my mouth. I'm not that disciplined." We see the clay, but God sees the beautiful teacup. The good news is you're not a finished product. God is still working on you, and if you will work with God and let Him remove those impurities, He will make more out of your life than you've ever dreamed.

One day you will look back and, like that teacup, you will say, "I can't believe how far God has taken me."

The Scripture says, "After you have passed the test you will receive the victor's crown of life." My challenge for you is that you pass your test. There is a victor's crown waiting for you. Recognize that God has you on the wheel. Don't fight against it. Let God refine you.

Your sufferings are nothing compared to the glory that is coming. If you stay moldable, pliable, and willing to change, you won't be at this same place next year. God will take every irritation and turn it into a pearl. You won't be wood, clay, or silver. I believe and declare you will become a vessel of gold, a vessel of honor used for God's highest purposes.

CHAPTER TWENTY-THREE

Get over It

Too many people go through life thinking somebody owes them something. If they didn't have a perfect childhood, they're angry at their parents. If they were laid off after many years with a company, they're upset with their bosses. Or maybe they came down with an illness. Life threw them a curve. Now, they have a chip on their shoulder and bitterness on the inside. They ask: "If God was so good, how could He let this happen to me?"

But, God never promised life would be fair. He did promise that if you stay in faith, He would take what is meant for your harm and use it to your advantage. Nothing that happens to you is a surprise to God. The people who raised you might not have given you everything you needed. It might not have been fair. But that didn't catch God off guard.

Don't think you were cheated and use it as an excuse to be bitter. If you get over it, God will still get you to where you're supposed to be. The person who did you wrong in a relationship, the betrayal, or the divorce might have caused you pain, but if you get over it, quit reliving all the hurt, and move forward, then you'll come to the new beginning God has in store.

My message is very simple and I offer it with respect: get over whatever wrongs have been done to you.

Maybe you are single and all your friends are married. Get over it. Don't let bitter feelings take root. That attitude will only keep the right person from entering your life.

Maybe you wish you'd been born into a different family or in a different country. Get over it. God knows what He's doing. God wasn't having a bad day when He created you. You are not at a disadvantage. You have been fearfully and wonderfully made.

I've heard it said, "You can be pitiful or you can be powerful, but you cannot be both." Instead of sitting around thinking about all the reasons you have to feel sorry for yourself, take the hand you've been dealt and make the most of it. Nothing that you've been through has to keep you from becoming all God's created you to be.

My mother had polio as a child. She had to wear a brace on her leg. Now one of her legs is much smaller than the other. When she buys shoes, she has to buy two pairs of the same shoe because her feet are different sizes. That could have embarrassed her. She could have shrunk back and tried to hide it. But she never did.

My mother knows she was made in the image of Almighty God. Growing up, she never worried about wearing a dress. In fact, she still wears dresses today. At nearly eighty years old, she is still showing off her legs!

She never let her leg keep her from working out in the yard. Her experience with polio didn't stop her from praying for others in need of healing. Despite the "disadvantage," she's lived a full and blessed life.

Why? She got over it. She didn't make excuses. She didn't fall into the self-pity trap. Sometimes we may be tempted to think, "If I had a different life I'd be better off. *If I had his talent or her family or their house, things would be great.*" But don't compare your situation to anyone else's. You're not running their race.

It may seem like others have more advantages, or more going for them, but God has given you the grace you need to fulfill your destiny. You're not anointed to be them. You are anointed to be you.

Shake off any self-pity and any bitterness. Your attitude should be: "Nobody owes me anything. I am not at a disadvantage. I didn't get left out, short-changed, passed over, or cheated. I am equipped, empowered, and anointed. All the forces of darkness cannot keep me from my destiny."

Your time is too valuable, your assignment too important, to go through life thinking about what you didn't get, who hurt you, and what didn't work out. That is a trick of the enemy to get you distracted and wasting valuable energy on things that don't matter. He would love to keep you discouraged, in self-pity, blaming others, blaming yourself, and even blaming God.

I'm asking you to get over anything holding you back: A bad attitude. An offense. What somebody did to you. A mistake you made. Don't be pitiful when you can be powerful. The Creator of the universe breathed His life into you. Every day of your life already has been written in God's book. The good news is that your book ends in victory.

We all go through tough times, but we're not supposed to stay there. Keep turning the page and you'll come to another victory.

God knew there'd be unfair situations in your

life. That's why He's arranged a comeback for every setback, a vindication for every wrong, and a new beginning for every disappointment. Don't let one bad break, a divorce, or a rough childhood cause you to sour on life.

If your boss didn't give you the promotion, get over it. God has something better in store. If certain "friends" leave you out, and won't give you their approval, get over it. You don't need their approval. Don't play up to them or try to win them over. You have Almighty God's approval, that's all that matters.

Maybe your business didn't make it. You had a setback. Now you think, "What did I do wrong? I blew it. This is the end." No, get over it. Don't condemn yourself. You are not a failure. You took a step of faith, and a door closed. That means you're one step closer to an open door.

When you are knocked down, don't stay down. Get back up again. Nothing good will happen as long as you're down on yourself, down on life, focused on your mistakes and your disadvantages. That attitude will keep you from the amazing future God has in store.

You may be dealing with a sickness, and my heart goes out to you. I will stand in faith with you. But don't you dare sit around nursing your wounds, thinking, "Poor old me. I guess my life is over. I've got this disadvantage."

Instead, fight the good fight of faith. God did not bring you this far to leave you. When the going gets tough, the tough have to get going. Get over the disappointment. Get over the self-pity. Get over the doubt.

You have been armed with strength for this battle. No weapon formed against you will prosper. Nothing can snatch you out of God's hand. The enemy doesn't have the final say; God has the final say. And He says the number of your days He will fulfill. So, keep turning that page, praying, believing, being your best, being good to other people, and you will come into another chapter, a chapter of victory.

Think about the story of Job. He had a lot to get over. He lost his health, his family, and his business. If anybody had a right, at least in the natural, to have a chip on his shoulder, to be angry and bitter, it would have to be Job. He was a good man. He loved God. He was being his best. Yet his life was turned upside down.

The Scripture says, "Rain falls on the just and the unjust." I'd love to tell you that if you have faith and you love God, then you'd never have any difficulties. But that's not reality. I can tell you when the storms come, if you've got your house built upon the rock, if you've got an unshakable confidence in God, if you know the Lord as your shepherd, then the storms will come, but you will not be defeated.

When it's all said and done, you may go through the fire, through the flood, and through the famine, but you'll come out standing strong. Don't be discouraged by the storm. Don't fall into self-pity. "I don't know what I did wrong." You may not have done anything wrong. Maybe it's because you're doing something right. You may be taking new ground for the Kingdom. You're setting a new standard for your family. The enemy will not roll out the red carpet to allow you to fulfill your destiny. But know this: the forces for you are greater than the forces against you.

Job could have given up on life, blamed God, and thought, "Just my luck. I do my best and look what happens to me." Instead, right in the middle of his challenges, when he could have been bitter and sour, he looked up to the heavens and said, "Though he slay me, yet will I trust Him."

He was saying in effect, "No matter what comes my way, I'm not getting bitter, angry, offended, or carrying a chip on my shoulder. My situation may not be fair. But I know a secret. My God is still on the Throne. He will make my wrongs right. I may not like it, but I'm going to get over it and keep moving forward."

Nine months later, Job came out with twice what he had before. When you get over it, you position yourself for double. When you forgive someone who did you wrong, get ready for double. When you have a good attitude even though life has thrown you a curve, get ready for double. When you go through life being your best, even though it seems like you're at a disadvantage, get ready for double.

Your thoughts may tell you that you aren't as talented, as influential, or as advantaged as others, but you know better than to believe those lies. Instead of becoming depressed, you shake it off, knowing that you have been made in the image of Almighty God. You have royal blood flowing through your veins.

You don't let what people say or tough circumstances pull you down. No matter what comes your way, you get over it and keep moving forward. When you do that, you better get ready. God says to you what He said to Job, "Double is coming your way."

Double the joy. Double the peace. Double the favor.

Is there something you need to get over today? Do you need to get over a friend's betrayal? Do you need to get over a business deal that didn't work out? Do you need to get over a childhood that wasn't so great? Unless you get over, they will keep you from the fullness God has in store.

The key to earning the double is to not get bitter. Don't have a chip on your shoulder or feel you are owed something. Don't make excuses or live in a sour mood. Many people blame their pasts for their bitterness or lack of success. They blame the way they were raised, what they weren't given, or who wasn't around.

God is not surprised by what was lacking or hurtful in your past. Don't use those things as an excuse to go through life feeling shortchanged. Move forward. This is a new day. God knew who your parents would be. He knew what kind of environment you would be raised in. I'm not making light of hardships and hurts. Some people grew up in very unfair and difficult situations. They didn't get the love, the approval, or the support they should have had. But I don't believe in giving people the right to feel sorry for themselves.

That will keep you from the amazing future God has in store. It may not have been fair, but if you have the right attitude, then instead of being a setback it'll be a setup for God to do something great in your life.

I know people in their fifties who still talk about what Momma didn't give them. Have you ever thought that maybe Momma didn't have it to give? Maybe your father did the best he could with what he had. Sometimes we rely too much on people when we should be relying on God.

Psalm 27:10 says, "God adopts us as His very own

children." Your mother or father may not have given you what you needed, but if you start looking to God, He will make up for everything you lacked.

I've heard it said, "If you want someone to give you 100 percent, don't look around. Look up. God is the only One who can give you everything you need."

Some people were never taught to show love, to express approval. They had no role models for that. They pass down what they've experienced. If you look only to other people, you'll be disappointed. They will let you down. And if you're not careful, you'll become bitter and resentful toward them. You may think, "You owe me. Why won't you give it to me? What's wrong with you?" But maybe God is teaching you to rely not on people but on Him. Let people off the hook. Quit trying to make another person be everything to you. No one has 100 percent. No one can meet all your needs—it doesn't matter how good that person may be, how loving or how kind. At some point, that person will fall short.

Look up to your Heavenly Father instead and say, "God I know You will give me everything I need."

My father told me that when he was in his late forties, he started thinking about how rough his childhood had been. His family was very poor. At times, they barely had food to survive. He went around with old raggedy clothes, with holes in them. One day, it hit him as being so unfair. He became aggravated at his parents. He thought, "Why didn't they raise me better? Why wasn't my father around to give me the support, the encouragement, that I needed?"

When you open the door to self-pity, to blame, all kinds of negative thoughts will flood your mind. The enemy will be right there to add to it and tell you, "You're right. They did you wrong. You got cheated. You should have a chip on your shoulder. You need to go straighten them out."

My father was about to drive from Houston to Dallas to tell his parents they didn't do a good job raising him and they put him at a disadvantage, which just wasn't fair. Before he left, God spoke to him. Not out loud but down in his heart.

He had a conversation with God along these lines:

"Son, they did you wrong, didn't they?"

"Yeah, God, they did," Daddy said.

"They didn't give you what you needed, did they?"

"No, God, they didn't."

"It wasn't fair was it?"

"No, it wasn't fair."

"Son, how would you have done if you had been in their shoes? With no money? With no air-conditioning? No dishwasher? No washing machine?

Your mother was working twelve hours a day making ten cents an hour. Your father had a fourth-grade education and lost everything on the farm during the Great Depression. He had to stand in line for food," God said. "Son, do you think you may have made a few mistakes?"

When my father saw it from that perspective, he realized his parents had done an amazing job considering the circumstances they had. It's easy to dwell on what we didn't get and where our parents made mistakes, or how they should have done better. But most of the time, if we put ourselves in their shoes, we'll find they did the best they could with what they had.

Why don't you let those who hurt you off the hook? Quit expecting them to be perfect. Look to God to give you what people cannot give you. Otherwise you will get bitter, and when you're bitter it poisons every area of your life.

Hebrews 12 talks about a root of bitterness. I've learned that a bitter root will always produce bitter fruit. Bitter people don't have good relationships. They're too negative. When we're bitter it affects our attitudes. We see everything through a critical lens. Nothing is ever good enough. Bitter people can smile on the outside, but on the inside they're thinking, "I don't like you. Why did you show up here?"

Bitterness taints everything about them. It infects everything you do and follows you everywhere you go. There was a grandfather whose grandkids decided to play a trick on him during his regular afternoon nap. They took some potent awful-smelling cheese and rubbed it on his moustache while he was sound asleep on the couch. Within a couple of minutes, his nose began to twitch. He quickly woke up and said, "Boy, it stinks in this room."

He left the family room to escape the smell, but it was in the kitchen, too. He took a sniff here and a sniff there. "It stinks in this room, too," he said.

Frustrated, he went outside to get a breath of fresh air. He took a deep breath, shook his head, and said, "Man, the whole world stinks!"

If the whole world ever stinks for you, might I suggest you look inside? Maybe there are some adjustments you need to make. Bitterness will follow you everywhere you go. A man I know was bent out of shape because he felt his former employer mistreated him. Overall, this boss had been very good to him, loving and kind, but the man felt a few bad things had been done to him here and there. He could have overlooked it and focused on the good. But he made the mistake of letting the bitterness take root. More than twenty years later, the bitter fruit from those roots of resentment is obvious. He's negative. Always finding fault, he has a chip on his shoulder.

When we hold on to things we should let go, refusing to forgive, remembering the worst, we only poison our own lives. God is saying, "Get over it."

Life is flying by. You don't have time to waste another minute being negative, offended, or bitter. If someone did you wrong, get over it and God will make it up to you. If you had a bad break that left you at a disadvantage, get over it. God is still on the Throne.

My friend Nick Vujicic was born with no arms and no legs. He could be sitting around saying, "God, it's not fair. I have no reason to live. I have no future in front of me." No, Nick has taken the cards he was dealt and he's making the most of it. Today, he's a minister who travels the world challenging people not to let any disadvantage hold them back.

Are you making excuses for why you can't succeed or be happy? Do you feel you can't forgive someone who hurt you badly? You are responsible for your happiness. You need to forgive those who hurt you, not for their sakes but for your own. Forgive so you can be free.

"I've had some rough times. I've had a bad break in my business."

Get over it. You wouldn't be alive unless God had another victory in front of you. Nothing in life has happened to you. It's happened for you. Every disappointment. Every wrong. Even every closed door has helped make you into who you are. You are not defined by your past. You are prepared by your past. You may have encountered some great obstacles, but only because God has a great future in front of you. If you will get over what you think is a disadvantage, God will take what looks like a liability and turn it into an asset. It may not be something physical, but maybe with your childhood or past. Someone did you wrong, you made a mistake or something bad happened to you.

"If only I hadn't had that accident, then I could fulfill my dreams."

"If only I hadn't been through that divorce."

"If only I hadn't gotten laid off."

Those "if only" thoughts can keep you from fulfilling your destiny. Nick Vujicic could be saying, "If only I had arms and legs, then I could make something of my life."

My mother could say, "If only I had not had polio."

My father could have said, "If only I was raised in a better environment."

David could have said, "If only Goliath wasn't so big."

Gideon could have said, "If only I came from a better family."

Joseph could have said, "If only my brothers hadn't sold me into slavery."

Everyone has challenges, but you can't "if only" your way through life. What happened to you may seem like a disadvantage in your eyes, but it is not a disadvantage in God's eyes. It's not keeping you from your destiny. It will *thrust* you into your destiny. Now you have to do your part and get over anything that's holding you back. Get over what anyone said about you. No one else can determine your destiny. God does that.

Get over those things that haven't worked out as you'd hoped. Get over the mistakes you've made. Get over the disappointments. Something may have surprised you and set you back, but it's not a surprise to God. He's already arranged the comeback.

Your attitude should be "Nobody owes me anything. I am not going through life with a chip on my shoulder. I'm letting go of those things that didn't work out. I'm forgiving those who did me wrong. I'm pulling up the roots of bitterness, and I'm moving forward into the amazing future God has in store.

If you learn this simple principle to get over it, then I believe and declare no disappointment, no bad break, no injustice, will keep you from your destiny.

God will take what's meant for your harm and use it to your advantage.

Like Job, you will not only come out of the difficult times, you will also come out better, stronger, and increased, with twice the joy, twice the peace, and twice the victory.

CHAPTER TWENTY-FOUR

Put Actions behind Your Faith

The Scripture tells us there was a paralyzed man who spent his days in bed. One day he heard that Jesus was in a nearby town teaching in a private home. He asked four of his friends to carry him to that home. When they arrived it was so crowded they couldn't get in.

They'd gone to great lengths to get there. I'm sure the four men were tired. Their shoulders were sore. Their backs were hurting. They'd hurried to get there, so when they couldn't get in they were let down and disappointed. They could have easily given up and thought, "Too bad. It's not going to happen."

But the paralyzed man was not about to give up. He said to his friends, "Take me up on the roof. Tear a hole in it and then lower me down so I can have a front row seat."

They hoisted him up on the roof. Jesus was in the middle of his sermon and dust began to fall from the ceiling. People looked up, thinking, "What in the world is happening?" All of a sudden a tile came off, then another and another. Finally they lowered this paralyzed man into the room, all curled up on his bed, right in front of Jesus.

The Scripture says in Mark 2:5, "When Jesus saw their faith." That's my question for you. Do you have a faith that God can see? Are you doing something out of the ordinary to show God you believe Him? It's not enough to just ask. It's not enough to just believe. Like the paralyzed man, you've got to do something to demonstrate your faith.

Jesus looked at the paralyzed man and said, "Rise, take up your bed, and walk." Immediately the man rose from his bed, picked up his mat and went home, perfectly well.

This all started when he did something so that God could see his faith. Don't you know there were other people in the room who didn't get well? Other people had the same opportunity. The difference was this man put actions behind his belief. God is looking for people who have faith that He can see. Not a faith that He can just hear, not a faith that just believes, but a faith that is visible, a faith that is demonstrated.

One day after a Lakewood service, I talked to a gentleman who had smoked cigarettes since he was in high school. He looked to be in his midforties. He'd been smoking three packs a day for the last ten years. He smoked the same amount without giving it a thought every day. He wanted to quit. He had prayed. He had believed. He had friends and relatives trying to help him. They encouraged him to give up smoking, but nothing worked.

Then one day he heard this principle: you have to put actions behind your faith. So he started taking simple actions every day to break his nicotine habit. Whenever he'd open a new pack he would immediately throw away three cigarettes. This was his way of saying, "God, I'm trying. I'm not just asking for Your help; I'm not just believing that I'm free of this addiction; I'm not just hoping that one day I'll stop. I'm taking it one step further and showing You I mean business by putting action behind my faith."

The action you take does not have to be something big. It could be just a small step to show God your faith. After a couple months of throwing out three cigarettes from each pack he wasn't missing them anymore, so he doubled up and every day began throwing out six from each pack. Eventually he got to where he could eliminate a whole pack a day, so he kept cutting back more and more.

Several years after he first took action to break his addiction, he realized the cravings were gone. He no longer smokes at all.

"Joel I haven't felt this good in thirty years," he told me.

Here's my point: He could have prayed twenty-four hours a day for God to take away his addiction. He could have believed it would just happen one day and last for the rest of his life. But the power came when he took it one step further and showed God he meant business by putting action behind his faith.

Are you doing something to show God you're serious about your dreams coming to pass? God is not moved by our needs. He's concerned about our needs, but God is moved by our faith. When God sees you doing what you can to get well, when He sees you getting to work a little earlier because you want that promotion, when He sees you bypass the cookie jar because you've been believing you'll lose weight— that is when extraordinary things will happen.

Like the man who took small steps to kick his nicotine addiction, you'll find that you have a power to do what you couldn't do before. You'll see favor and opportunity that will thrust you to a new level when you take action to show your faith.

When my sister Lisa was about three years old, she wanted to go to the office with my father. She heard my dad saying he was going to the church. When she asked to go with him, he said, "No, Lisa, I'll take you some other time, but not today. I have meetings and I'm going to be busy. Maybe tomorrow or next week."

But Lisa wouldn't take no for an answer. She didn't want to go some other time; she wanted to go that day. She was so determined she ignored my father, ran back to her room, and got dressed as if she were going with him. You would have thought she hadn't heard a word my father said. His negative response simply didn't register in her mind.

After dressing, Lisa heard the back door open. She realized our father was about to leave. She took off to grab her shoes, going full speed. My father turned around and saw his little three-year-old daughter suddenly dressed and struggling to put her last shoe on. His heart melted.

He couldn't say no.

"Come on, Lisa, you can go with me," he said.

What made the difference? He saw her faith. When he saw how badly she wanted to go, when he saw how determined she was, when he saw her going all out to prepare herself, he was so touched he changed his mind and allowed her to go with him. Lisa's actions spoke louder than her words. She could have begged him all day. She could have sat in a corner pouting. Neither of those approaches would have worked. Our father wasn't moved by begging or by pouting. He was moved when he saw little Lisa's faith.

God is the same way. Can He see your faith? It's one thing to ask for God's help, it's one thing to believe He loves you—but if you want to get God's attention, take it one step further and put actions behind your faith.

A man I know felt called into the ministry. He took a step of faith by renting the small auditorium of a high school for his first service. He invited his friends and neighbors to come, and he spread the word through the town's newspaper.

He was so excited. The first big meeting started at seven o' clock. He couldn't wait to see how many people were going to come. But at 6:30 there was no one. Six forty-five, and still no one. The clock struck 7:00 p.m., and the auditorium was empty. Not a soul in the seats. My friend was alone onstage. The only other person was a technician in the sound booth. He was so disheartened. He felt like going home and calling it quits. But just as he was about to give up something rose up on the inside, a holy determination.

"I'm not going home a failure. I've prepared my message," he thought. "I've taken this step of faith so I'm giving it my all."

He went up on the platform, and without one person in the auditorium seats he preached as if the place was packed. He went on for over an hour doing his very best.

At the end he even gave an altar call and invited people to receive Christ. It looked as if he was just going through the motions. Later, he told me he'd felt like a fool and a total failure.

But as he finished his altar call invitation, a side door opened and this older gentleman, who was part of the cleaning crew, walked down to the front, shook the young minister's hand, and said, "I want to accept Christ."

The man told him later, "It wasn't your message that got to me—it was the fact that you preached your heart out without a person in the room."

A few seconds after the janitor came down, the sound technician joined them, saying, "I want to make a commitment to Christ."

The young minister went home that night not feeling like a failure at all. Instead, he knew the hand of God was on his life. That was a turning point. Door after door opened to him after that. Today, he has a church with thousands of people in the congregation.

He travels the world ministering. When God can see your faith, extraordinary things are going to happen.

The Scripture tells us that a group of lepers once saw Jesus passing by. They came over and said, "Jesus, please make us well." Jesus could have healed them right there easily enough. But he asked them to do something to express their faith. He said, "Go show yourselves to the priests."

And as they went, they were cleansed of their disease. Jesus asked them to do something that they were not allowed to do by law. They were not supposed to be near other people. They had a contagious disease and were considered unclean.

I'm sure they debated whether to follow His instructions. "Should we do what He asked us to do? My skin doesn't look any different. I'm not well. Why should I go?"

But they put actions behind their faith. The Scripture says, "As they went they were cleansed." In other words, if they had not had the courage to demonstrate their faith, then they would not have seen God's goodness. As they started down the road, I can imagine every few blocks they said, "Look I'm getting a little better." Another mile: "Can you see it? I think my skin is clearing up."

They just kept moving forward, demonstrating

their faith, and by the time they reached the priests they were perfectly normal.

A lot of times we want change without taking action. "God open all the doors, then I'll step out. Give me the power to break this addiction, then I'll cut back. Give me the big crowds, and then I'll launch my ministry. Let my husband straighten up, and then I'll start treating him better."

Yet God says, "As you go, as you show me your faith, then I'll give you what you need."

Lakewood Church was still in its first small auditorium back in 1972. It held 270 people, and it was very crowded during most services. We needed a bigger building. My father had some plans drawn for a building that would seat one thousand people. It was estimated to cost about $200,000.

One Sunday he took a special offering for the church's building fund and the donations were right at $20,000. Month after month went by as my father waited for the rest of the funds to come in. The donations trickled in a few hundred dollars here and there. At that rate, Lakewood would have needed another five or ten years to raise all the money needed for a new church.

One day an old friend of my dad's came by.

"John, what are you still doing in this little

building?" he asked. "You've got to have more room so you can grow."

My father said, "I know that. But I don't have the money."

"How much do you have?"

"I only have $20,000," my father replied. "That's just enough for the foundation."

The man looked at my father and said very sternly, "John, pour the foundation and watch what God will do."

He was saying, "Put some actions behind your faith." My father got his courage up, and they poured the foundation. Before long the money came in for the steel, and then for the exterior. It wasn't any time before the whole building was up and totally paid for.

What happened? Just like those lepers, my father took a step and saw God's goodness. As he demonstrated his faith, he saw God show up in amazing ways.

You may have a dream that's on hold. Like my father, you have waited and waited for everything to fall into place, thinking once it does then you'll stretch, and then you'll make a move. And yes, it's good to have a plan, it's good to stay in God's timing, but you cannot wait around your whole life. At some point you've got to say, "I'm taking a step of faith to put actions behind what I'm believing. I'm going to show God I'm serious about fulfilling my destiny."

When I was growing up my father traveled overseas for ministry work, often for weeks at a time. My mother stayed home to take care of all five of us by herself. When my father was away on these long trips, invariably a couple of us kids would either get sick or have some kind of accident that made it even harder on our mother. One time I cut my leg playing in a Little League baseball game and I had to get stitches.

It seemed like these little emergencies always occurred when my father was away. My mother began to dread him leaving. If he had a trip planned, we'd seem to catch cold or run a fever before he started packing. My mother would think, "Here it goes again."

My father got fed up. He said, "God, I'm going away to do Your work, to help people, and here my own family is falling apart again." My father was bold. So he decided he would make sure God could see his faith. Instead of just praying over us he asked all of us kids to come outside. The oldest, Paul, was about thirteen and the youngest, April, was about three at the time.

He lined us up from the oldest to the youngest, and we had to grab the shoulders of the person in front of us, like a choo-choo train. My mother and father stood at the front.

Our dad led us around the perimeter of our property saying, "Father, I want to thank You that no weapon formed against my family will prosper, and You said Your angels will watch over them and no sickness would come near our dwelling."

He had us repeat his words, "No sickness, no disease, and no accidents."

We were in the backyard, and I was hoping he wasn't leading us out to the front yard. The neighbors already thought we were crazy. We were about to prove them right. Sure enough, my father marched us right out to the front. I was so embarrassed I had my head down. I saw friends going by staring, neighbors looking out the windows, cars slowing down.

Do you know from that day forward when my father went on those long trips we never got sick again while he was gone? We never had any more of those accidents when Mom had us on her own. Years later, when we were trying to acquire the former Compaq Center to be our church, Victoria and I would go to it at night when nobody could see us and walk around it.

We circled the arena saying, "Father, thank You that this building is ours. Thank You that You're fighting our battles for us. Thank You that You're making a way where there is no way."

Can God see your faith? Are you doing anything to demonstrate your trust? It's not enough to just pray. It's not enough to just believe. The Scripture says, "Faith by itself, if it is not accompanied by action, is dead." I know good people who have faith and love God, but they're not living an abundant life. They have faith, but it's not doing what it should be doing. It's not helping them overcome obstacles. It's not helping them accomplish dreams.

Why is that? Their faith is dead. They're not putting any actions behind it, so it's not activating God's favor. It's not activating God's goodness.

Your action doesn't have to be something big. When you go to work each day and give it a hundred percent, that's demonstrating your faith. Sometimes just getting up in the morning and putting a smile on your face is putting action behind your faith. Just the fact that you go to church is an action of faith that God can see.

You could be resting, working, running errands, but when you take time to honor God, He knows it. Right now, reading this, you are putting action behind your faith. That tells me your faith is not dead. Your faith is alive. Your faith is activating God's power. Your faith is allowing God to fight your battles. Your faith is opening the door for the extraordinary.

I heard about this lady diagnosed with ovarian cancer. She was trying to stay positive and hopeful, but she was so afraid. She had two children. The doctors had given her only a 15 percent chance of surviving. She prayed and believed, and she had friends and family supporting her.

One day somebody gave her a little gray rock with the words "Expect a miracle" written on it. We've seen little trinkets with Scriptures on them and such. But when she was given that simple rock, something on the inside came alive.

Her faith was ignited. She knew: "It's going to happen to me. I'm going to be well." From then on, everywhere she went, she kept that rock with her. All during the day she would keep it in her pocket. At night when she went to bed, she put the rock right by her pillow. It was a reminder to thank God that He was working and to thank Him that He was restoring her health.

The little rock in itself was nothing special, but it was her way of putting actions behind her faith. When God looked down and saw her always carrying that rock, He recognized a faith that he could not just hear, but a faith that He also could see.

The woman went through chemotherapy and several surgeries. After months of fighting the good fight, it came time for her doctors to perform biopsies to determine whether the treatments had worked. The doctors examined one hundred different places where they thought it could have spread. They told her not to get her hopes up. There was little or no chance that they would all come back cancer free.

She went to the exams with her rock right by her side. When she woke up after the procedures, she saw a beautiful older lady dressed in a bright white dress. She thought she was a nurse. The lady said very gently, "Are you the one expecting a miracle?"

This cancer patient was kind of groggy, but through the haze she wondered how this strange lady could know that she was hoping for a miracle. She answered, "Yes, I am."

The lady in the white dress handed her a small plaque that read, "Miracles happen every day." When the patient read it, she felt a warmness go all through her body. The next thing she remembered was waking up and seeing her husband leaning over her with a big smile.

He said, "Honey, the results are in. There was no cancer in any of the one hundred biopsies."

She never found out who that lady in white was, but she still has the plaque on her wall. "Miracles happen every day." Let me challenge you to have a faith that God can see. Put actions behind what you believe. It's not enough to just pray, not enough to just believe. Take it one step further and demonstrate your faith.

You may not see how your dream could ever work out, but like those lepers, as you take steps of faith you'll see God begin to open new doors. You'll have the strength to do what you could not do. You'll see His favor in unusual ways.

CHAPTER TWENTY-FIVE

God Will Finish What He Started

The moment God put a dream in your heart, the moment the promise took root, God not only started it, but He set a completion date. God is called the Author and the Finisher of our Faith. God wouldn't have given you the dream, the promise wouldn't have come alive, if He didn't already have a plan to bring it to pass.

It doesn't matter how long it's been or how impossible it looks. Your mind may tell you it's too late. You've missed too many opportunities. It's never going to happen. "No," God is saying, "it's not over. I have the final say. I've already set the completion date." If you will stay in faith and not talk yourself out of it, it's just a matter of time before it comes to pass.

Maybe at one time, you believed you could do something great. You had a big dream. You believed you could start that business. Believed that you'd get healthy again. Believed that you'd fall in love and get married. But it's been so long. You tried and it didn't work out. The loan didn't go through. The medical report wasn't good. Now, the "never" lies are playing in your mind. "I'll never get well." "I'll never get married." "I'll never accomplish my dreams."

No, you have to have a new perspective. The Creator of the universe has already set that completion date. Just because it hasn't happened yet doesn't mean it's not going to happen. God has already lined up the right people, the right breaks, the right answers. Everything you need is already in your future. Now, you've got to shake off the doubt, shake off the discouragement. Whether it's been a year, five years, or fifty years, what God promised you He still has every intention of bringing it to pass.

In the Scripture, an angel appeared to a man named Simeon and said, "You will not die until you see the birth of Christ." You can imagine how far out that promise seemed.

Years went by, and Simeon didn't see any sign of the Messiah. Five years. Ten years. I'm sure the negative thoughts came: "You heard God wrong. It's been too long. It's never going to happen."

We have the same type of thoughts today: "Do you really think you're going to get well? You saw the medical report. Do you really think you could accomplish those dreams? You don't have the funds, the connections."

Let those thoughts go in one ear and out the other. I can see Simeon thinking all through the day, "God, I know You're a God of completion. You said I wouldn't go to my grave without seeing this promise come to pass. So, Lord, I want to thank You that it's on the way."

Simeon awakened every morning believing, expecting, and knowing that it would happen. Twenty years later, he saw Christ born. The promise came to fulfillment.

God is saying to you what He said to Simeon: "You can't die yet—there are too many promises that have not come to pass in your life." God is going to finish what He started. No one can stop Him from fulfilling His promises. Bad breaks can't stop it. Sickness can't stop it. Death can't even stop it.

You need to get ready. God will complete your incompletions. You will not go to your grave without seeing your dreams come to pass—even the secret petitions of your heart. It may seem impossible, but remember, our God is all-powerful. He spoke the worlds into existence, and He has you in the palm of His hand.

God did not create you to be average, to drag through life unfulfilled or unrewarded. He created you to do something amazing. He's put seeds of greatness on the inside. He's whispered things to you in the middle of the night that may seem too big, far out, impossible. But God is saying, "That was My voice. That's My dream for your life. It's bigger, it's more rewarding."

It may look impossible, but if you'll stay in faith, everything God promised you will come to fulfillment. I met a 106-year-old man in our lobby after the service a while back, and he was so happy. He looked at least thirty years younger. I asked him how long he planned on living. He said he was going to be around awhile, because he has seven children, and one of his sons had gotten off course.

"I can't die yet because God promised 'as for me and my house, we will serve the Lord,'" he said. "I can't go to heaven until I see God bring every promise to pass."

Life will try to push you down, steal your dreams, and talk you into settling for mediocrity. But I want you to have this new attitude and believe that whatever God started in your life, He will finish. Here's the real question: Will you keep believing even though it looks impossible? Will you stay in faith, even though every voice tells you that it's not happening?

My friends Jeff Hackelman and his wife, Eileen,

pastor Family Faith Church in Huntsville, Texas. Jeff told me that when he was in high school he drove down to the Gulf of Mexico near Galveston, Texas, to go fishing one day. Jeff had done this many times before, but this day, he and his friend decided to fish an area he was not familiar with, one near some off-shore gas wells.

As Jeff was launching the boat, he asked the man at the dock how to return to the dock from the area near the gas wells. The man said, "We're directly north of them. If you're anywhere around the gas wells, just go due north and you'll make it back to this dock."

Jeff and his friend traveled an hour in their little boat before reaching their destination near the off-shore rigs. They were having so much fun and catching so many fish. What they didn't realize was that a heavy fog had set in. It happened so quickly they were caught by surprise.

Suddenly, they could see only twenty to thirty feet in each direction. The sun started to go down, and Jeff became concerned about finding his way back in the fog and darkness. He told his friend, "Pull up the anchor. We need to go."

In the fog, Jeff had lost his sense of direction. He couldn't see any shoreline. The stars weren't visible yet. All of his logic said, "We need to go this way."

His friend, who'd grown up fishing with his father, said, "No, Jeff, it's not that direction. It's this way."

Then Jeff remembered he had a compass on board, so he checked it. It showed that they were both wrong. Against all of his instincts, Jeff cranked up the motor and started traveling due north. Everything in his mind told him, "You're making a big mistake. You're going the wrong way. You better turn around."

His mind flashed back to what the man at the dock said. "Go due north and you'll make it back." He kept the engine speed down, creeping along because he couldn't see in the fog and fading light. They traveled fifteen minutes, thirty minutes, forty-five minutes, then an hour had passed.

Now it was totally dark. Jeff's inner voice told him, "If you were headed in the right direction, you should be seeing the shoreline by now." How many times as we're believing for what God promised us do we hear these same type of voices. "If you were going to get well, you'd feel better by now. If you were going to get married, you would have met somebody by now. If you were going to be successful, you would have been promoted by now."

There will always be voices trying to convince you that you are headed in the wrong direction, that it's never going to happen, or that it's too late to fulfill

God's promise. Others may try to convince you that they know better, just as Jeff's friend did.

At one point, the friend became panicky, yelling at Jeff. "Turn the boat around. You're taking us out to sea. We're going to run out of gas. We could get killed."

Despite all of their confusion and concerns, Jeff kept traveling in the direction his compass said was due north. Another thirty minutes. Another forty-five. Another hour passed.

Then, just as they were running out of fuel, they caught a glimpse of land off in the distance. Greatly relieved, they crept toward it and followed the shoreline until they found their dock and made it back safely.

Sometimes in life, the fog will set in. You won't know if you are headed in the right direction. You know God's put a promise in your heart. But every voice is telling you that you're too old, you missed too many opportunities, and it's not going to happen. In those foggy times, you have to dig in your heels and say, "God, I believe what You promised me despite how I feel, despite what people are telling me, despite how it looks. God, I will believe that what You said is true. I believe You are on the Throne. I know You are a faithful God. What you promised You will bring to pass."

The Scripture says that God put a dream to have a baby in Rachel's heart. Year after year went by and she couldn't conceive. At the same time, her sister, Leah, had a child. Rachel was happy for her, and congratulated her, but all the while Rachel kept praying and believing that one day she could have a baby.

Rachel remained without a child while Leah went on to have one baby after another. Rachel was happy for her sister, but still wished for her own child.

It's good to be happy for others, it's good to rejoice with them, but God doesn't want you to just celebrate the lives of others. God wants to bring your dreams to pass. God wants to give you the desires of your heart. He wants you to be celebrated. Rachel did her best to keep praying and believing. But after years of frustration, seeing her sister have baby after baby, Rachel grew discouraged and said, in effect, "This is my lot in life. It's never going to happen."

One of the things I love about God is this: just because we give up on a dream doesn't mean He gives up on it. The Scripture says, "God remembered Rachel." It doesn't say that Rachel remembered God.

This is how much God wants you to fulfill your destiny. It says, "God remembered Rachel, answered her prayer, and gave her a baby." God is so loving. He's so merciful. Even when we become too discouraged to believe, God does not forget what He promised you.

You may feel like Rachel. Maybe your life hasn't turned out the way you had hoped. You prayed. You believed. You worked hard. You put forth the effort, but it didn't work out.

You may have decided: "I'll never be happy again. I'll never be married. I'll never accomplish my dreams." But understand that God not only remembers you, He remembers the promise He put in you. He knows what He has destined you to do. You may have already said, "Forget it, it will never happen." The good news is, you don't have the final say. God has the final say, and He says, "What I started in your life, I will finish." You may have given up on your dream, but God didn't.

When my brother, Paul, was twelve years old, he went to Africa with my father. They were in a tiny nation, once known as Northern Rhodesia, standing on a hot tarmac, waiting for their small plane to refuel. There on the airport runway, God planted a dream in Paul's heart that one day he would go back to Africa and do medical missions. The Creator of the universe birthed that in him that day. Paul went on to become a doctor, and he spent seventeen years as the chief of surgery at a hospital in Little Rock, Arkansas. Deep down, he still wanted to do medical missions, but he was so busy. He had so much responsibility to his patients. He couldn't do it.

Then, in 1999, while driving home from my father's memorial service, Paul heard God speak to his heart, telling him to give up his medical practice, come back home, and help us pastor the church. In the natural, that didn't make sense. Paul had so many years of medical education and training as a surgeon. How could he walk away from his thriving practice in Little Rock?

For ten years, Paul helped us in the ministry and never thought anymore about medicine. He thought his days as a surgeon were over. But God doesn't forget what he promised you as a child. God remembers the dreams, the goals, and the things that you always wanted to do.

One day, a group of doctors from our church asked Paul to go on a medical mission to Africa with them. He joined their group, thinking he'd just watch from the sidelines and support them. But when he arrived in Africa, the other doctors assigned my brother to an operating room and said, "We need you to do these surgeries." He hadn't performed surgery in more than ten years. I just thank God I wasn't the first patient that day!

The medical mission trip to Africa lasted two weeks. Late on his last night there, Paul woke up and went outside. He looked up at the star-filled African sky and the thought hit him: he was doing what God had put in his heart when he was twelve years old.

What God starts, He will finish. You may not

understand how it can happen. It may look like you're too old, you missed too many opportunities, and it's no longer possible. But God has it all figured out. He knows how to connect the dots.

Here's the key: God is not okay with you fulfilling half of your destiny. He's not okay with you fulfilling part of it. God will make sure you complete what He put you here to do.

Today, my brother spends five months a year over in the remote villages of Africa operating on the poor and needy. One of the places he returns to often is Zambia—formerly called Northern Rhodesia—the exact place where God planted the dream in his heart some forty-five years ago. God knows how to finish what He started.

I thought of this while reading a story about Bill Havens, a rower who had been favored to win at least one gold medal in the 1924 Summer Olympic Games in Paris, France. But his wife became pregnant, and her due date was at the exact time as the Summer Olympics.

Back in those days, they didn't have high-speed air travel like we do today. Havens would have had to travel by boat to France. He would have missed the birth of his first son. He informed his coach that he could not compete in the Olympic games.

He missed the Olympics, but he was there when

his son, Frank, was born. As the years passed, the father and son grew close. Young Frank shared his father's love of rowing, especially canoeing in whitewater. They spent many hours on the water together, and soon the son's skills surpassed his dad's. He kept practicing, and training, getting better and better.

In 1952, Frank Havens qualified for the Summer Olympics in Helsinki, Finland. He went over and competed. One day, Bill Havens received a telegram. It said, "Dear Dad, thanks for waiting around for me to be born. I'm coming home 28 years later with your Olympic gold medal."

Frank won the gold medal. Then he returned home and presented it to his father. After so many years of thinking it would never happen, Bill Havens had the gold medal that he always dreamed about. But this medal meant far more to him, because it came from the son he loved so much.

That's the way our God is. We may think, "It's too late. It could never happen. I've missed too many opportunities." But God still has a way to bring your dreams to pass.

Here's how the Scripture puts it: "Be confident of this: he that began a good work in you will bring it to completion." God is saying to you that He will complete your incompletions. He remembers the dreams He placed in your heart. He has lined up the right people, and the right opportunities. It's not too late. You haven't missed too many opportunities. You haven't made too many mistakes. Get your fire back. Get your passion back. Things have shifted in your favor. God is going to finish what He started.

Now do your part and break out of anything holding you back. Pray God-sized prayers. Don't settle for good enough. *Yes* is in your future. Move forward in faith, and your seeds of greatness will take root. You will go beyond your barriers and become everything God created you to be, and you will have everything He intended for you to have.

WE CARE ABOUT YOU

I believe there is a void in every person that only a relationship with God can fill. I'm not talking about finding religion or joining a particular church. I'm talking about developing a relationship with your Heavenly Father through His Son, Jesus Christ. I believe that knowing Him is the source of true peace and fulfillment in life.

I encourage you to pray, "Jesus, I believe You died for me and rose from the dead, so now I want to live for you. I am turning away from my sins and placing my trust in You. I acknowledge You as my Savior and Lord, and I'm asking You to guide my life from now on."

With that simple prayer, you can get a fresh, clean start, and establish a close relationship with God. Read the Bible every day, talk to God through prayer, and attend a good Bible-based church where you can find friends who will lift you up rather than pull you down. Keep God in first place in your life and follow

His principles. He will take you places you've not yet imagined!

For free information on how you can grow stronger in your spiritual life, we encourage you to contact us. Victoria and I love you and we will be praying for you. We'd love to hear from you!

To contact us, write to:

Joel and Victoria Osteen
P.O. Box 4600
Houston, TX 77210-4600

Or you can reach us online at www.joelosteen.com.

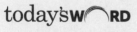